NOT GUILTY

MEN: THE CASE
FOR THE DEFENCE

NOT GUILTY

MEN: THE CASE FOR THE DEFENCE

David Thomas

WEIDENFELD & NICOLSON : LONDON

First published in Great Britain in 1993 by
Weidenfeld & Nicolson, Orion House,
5 Upper St Martin's Lane, London WC2H 9EA

A catalogue record for this book is available from
the British Library

ISBN 0 297 81216 5

Phototypeset in Great Britain by
Deltatype Ltd, Ellesmere Port, Cheshire

Printed in Great Britain by
Clays Ltd, St Ives plc

Contents

Acknowledgements

This is a book about men, but it would not have been possible without the efforts of two women, Allegra Huston and Lesley Baxter. Their encouragement, advice, good humour, and the rigour with which they challenged any arguments that were slack or loosely expressed, were as inspiring as our conversations were enjoyable.

That we were working together at all was due to two men, Lord Weidenfeld, who commissioned this book in the first place, and Anthony Cheetham, who inherited and supported it. My thanks go to them, too.

En route, I received an immense amount of help from people who spared me their time and the benefit of their own work and experience, including (in approximate chronological order) Dr Brian Novack, Cloy Morton, Carey Kennedy, Douglas Thompson, Dr Irene Kassorla, the staff of Gold's Gym, Sue Peart and Jean Carr at the *Sunday Express Magazine*, Steve Smethurst, Neil Lyndon, Sally Ann Lasson, the production team at BBC2's *Fifth Column*, Paul Whyte, Charles Kreiner and all the men of the Sydney Men's Festival, Lindsay Foyle and Lyndall Crisp at *The Bulletin*, Mark David, Steve Panazzo, Stephanie-Anne Lloyd at Transformations, Dr Steve Jones, Dr Robin Skynner, Myriam Medzian, Claire Rayner, Melvyn Bragg, Maureen Rice at *Options*, Mike Sharman, Marsha Dubrow, Peter York, Dr Malcolm George, Trevor Berry and Bruce Liddington at Families Need Fathers, Lucy Jaffe of Relate, Anne-Marie Hutchinson, Andrew Gerry, Renate Olins and the staff at London Marriage Guidance, Susan Faludi, Andrew Harvey at *The Times*, Dr Liam Hudson, Bernadine Jacot, Stephanie Jeavons, Jenni Manners, DCI Crozier of the Metropolitan Police, DI Aston of the West Midlands Police, Misha Hervieu, Joel Mahabir, Mr Hugh Millington at Charing Cross Hospital, Robert Hart at the Everyman Centre, Cathy Lever at Move, the staff of the American Humane Association, the librarians at the American Embassy in London, and all the many men to whom I spoke about their experiences of domestic violence and/or divorce, who must remain anonymous. Finally, my thanks go to all the various commissioning editors at newspapers, magazines, radio stations and TV channels dotted around Britain who have, over the years, allowed me to write the articles and scripts that were the first rehearsals for the ideas that appear in these pages.

One of the themes that run through this book is the vital importance of a secure family background. No man could have asked for a more supportive family than my own. Conversations with my mother started me thinking about sexual politics when I was a teenager ... and I haven't stopped since. My father was not only my inspiration when I was a boy, but also an eagle-eyed editor of the earliest drafts of this book. And my wife, Clare, was, as she has been since I first started out as a journalist, a constant source of support, encouragement and love.

Finally, an observation from another writer: just before I settled down to write this book, I was talking to P. J. O'Rourke, the American satirist whose work I had the great pleasure of publishing in *Punch*. I told him that I was trying to write about the situation in which men found themselves today. 'Tell me,' I said, 'what is the solution to our problems?'

The great man paused for a moment and then replied, 'I think that the answer is to be found in a bottle of Dewar's.'

'Is there an answer which does not involve getting smashed on Scotch?' I asked.

'No,' he said, 'we're surrounded by women. We'll just have to drink our way out.'

So if the book that follows becomes too depressing at any point, or feels too much like hard work, just remember ... there's always an alternative.

Not Guilty

Here's a simple question. As everyone knows, men earn more money than women. Men run all the world's governments and fill the vast majority of seats on the boards of its major corporations. Men are generals, bishops, judges, newspaper editors and movie studio heads. Moreover, men – if we are to believe the campaigns waged by women on both sides of the Atlantic – oppress women to the point of open warfare. They beat them, rape them and attempt to control their powers of reproduction. They stereotype them sexually and enslave them to ideals of beauty that lead thousands of women to undergo surgery or starve themselves half to death. And every time women look as though they are making any progress, men knock them back down again.

That's what we've been told. So what I want to know is this: if men are so much better off than women, how come so many more of them kill themselves?

In 1991, 886 women committed suicide in Great Britain. In the same year, 3,007 men committed suicide in Great Britain. Seventy-seven per cent of all suicides were male. For every dead woman, there were nearly four dead men. And there are more numbers to come.

Since the early 1980s, the rate of female suicides has nearly halved. Since the early 1980s, the rate of male suicide has gone up by approximately 5 per cent.

Similar patterns apply to America and Australia. Wherever you look, male suicides are rising, while female suicides decline. We should be glad that women no longer feel driven to end their own lives as often as they once did. Were I a feminist I would consider that to be a concrete sign of achievement. But let me ask two more questions.

1. Why doesn't anyone pay attention when men are killing themselves?

2. If women comprised almost four-fifths of all suicide victims, don't you think we'd have heard about it by now?

Western society is obsessed with women to the point of mass neurosis. One of the sources that I used when researching this book was the library at the US Embassy in London. It is an invaluable source of information, a repository of books and magazines that are otherwise difficult to find in Britain. One morning I was searching through the *1991 Index to The New York Times*, which lists every article published in America's most famous newspaper. The *Index* is published in four, quarterly sections and as I flicked through one of them I happened to notice that the list of articles under the heading 'Women' was far higher than that under the heading 'Men'. Intrigued, I started to count them up. Between July and September 1991, the *New York Times* published twenty articles about men, including fashion pages, and 135 articles about women. I wondered whether this was an anomaly. With the zeal of the natural obsessive, I resolved to go through the entire index and count up the articles published on men and women for the year as a whole. The final tally was: Men, 104 articles; Women, 679 articles.

Many of these were simply news stories. And some were listed under both headings. But even so, not only were women written about nearly seven times as often as men, but they were also the subject of far more editorial 'think' pieces. Over those twelve months, readers of the *New York Times* were regaled with opinions about the liberation of women in Africa and the slaughter of tens of millions of unwanted girls in Southeast Asia. They pondered the meaning of *Thelma and Louise* and considered, contrariwise, the reasons why women went to see movies that degraded them. Acres of newsprint were devoted to contemplating sexual harassment, date-rape and the significance of the latest books to come rolling off the feminist presses.

Men were mentioned, of course. They were the Africans who couldn't cope with women's liberation and the Americans who felt threatened by *Thelma and Louise*. They were the Chinese who were killing women, and the Hollywood directors who were making violent movies. And then, of course, they were the office bullies and fraternity house rapists. They were William Kennedy Smith, Mike Tyson and Judge Clarence Thomas. They were, in short, the bad guys.

Had I checked the indices of the London *Times* or *Guardian*, the results would probably have been comparable. The London telephone directory illustrates the point, too. Under 'Men' there are two entries: Men At Work, a building firm from Croydon, and Men Only, a hairdressing salon in SE13. The section for 'Women' begins with Women Against Rape, followed by Women Against Sexual Harassment, and ends 114 numbers later with the Women's Transport Service.

Looking through the directory, I was reminded of a conversation I had had with Dr Liam Hudson, a psychologist, a former member of the Institute for Advanced Study, Princeton, and the Visiting Scientist at the Tavistock Clinic. I asked him, as I did a number of my interviewees, 'What are men?' Dr Hudson smiled and said, 'What's left over when you've finished talking about women.'

Along with his wife, Bernadine Jacot, Dr Hudson had written a book called *The Way Men Think*. The subject matter of the book is exactly summed up by its title. It is a book about men. And yet, said Dr Hudson, when it came out it was reviewed as if it was really all about women. 'People seem to be in the grip of some necessity to talk about women,' he said. 'They don't know how to stop themselves. We weren't wholly surprised when it came from feminists in their twenties, thirties and forties. But some of the people who did it to us were men in their seventies, who were in no way part of that movement.'

Men certainly feel under attack. During the two years I spent working on this book, I kept on being told that men were not interested in the question of what it means to be male today, and that they were completely untouched by all the arguments over the ways in which men were allegedly mistreating women. But then, again and again, I had conversations that demonstrated that this was not the case: increasingly, men felt as if they stood accused. They felt as if they had been put in the wrong. And they didn't like it.

On a flight from Los Angeles to New York in August 1992, a casual conversation with the guy in the next seat moved from the standard, 'Well, what do you do for a living?' to a two-hour heart to heart when he, an investment banker, discovered what I was writing about. Out it all came: his longing to have a family and his wife's refusal to contemplate children, even though she was not working; the resentment he felt when he read stories about domestic violence that painted men as the sole aggressors; the pressure he was under to provide for his wife, which meant that he spent long hours working at a job he no longer enjoyed.

This was more than the grumble of a man in an unhappy marriage (despite it all, I believe he still loved his wife very much). This was a dissatisfaction comparable to the one which fuelled the original women's movement – a feeling that he, as a person, was becoming buried under the expectations imposed on him as a result of his gender. The demands of conventional masculinity were destroying him as an individual human being.

In November 1991, I had to go to Sydney, Australia, to make a speech at an annual gathering of Aussie cartoonists. (I was then the editor of *Punch* and thus, quite unjustly, considered an authority on the art of cartooning). My supposedly masculist reputation appeared to have gone before me. During a radio interview to promote the event, the DJ turned to me with a broad grin and said, 'So, David, I hear you love men.'

'Well, no,' I replied, 'that's not quite how I'd put it.' I switched onto radio patter mode: 'After all, I'm a married man and a father of two, ha-ha. Of course, so was Oscar Wilde, but that's another story, ha-ha-ha. But, no, seriously, I am interested in some of the issues facing men today', and I gave a brief outline of what these might be.

That evening I was due to have a drink with a couple of cartoonists, Mark and Steve, both men in their early thirties. Now Australians are famously bullshit-free and deeply suspicious of la-di-da psychological nonsense, particularly when it's coming from a Pommie. And cartoonists are, almost by definition, a fairly cynical bunch. So when, as Steve went for the beers, Mark turned to me and said, 'I heard you on the radio this morning,' I prepared myself for the worst.

Instead, he gave me the thumbs-up and said, 'I just wanted you to know that I agreed with every bloody word you said.'

At this point, Steve returned, plus drinks, and the conversation turned to more significant matters, such as the recent rugby World Cup final between England and Australia. A little later, it was Mark's round. He disappeared barwards and Steve said, 'Heard you on ABC this morning. I'll tell you what, mate – you've got my support.'

These two men were not, by any means, unreconstructed Ockers, the chauvinist pigs of Australian folklore. They were as right-on as most contemporary comedians. They knew the party line and would unquestionably think of themselves as being non-sexist, liberal men. In fact, so reluctant were they to betray their true feelings in public, that each waited until the other was out of earshot before making the devastating suggestion that he might have opinions of his own that deviated from the acceptable norm. In public they were silent; underneath, they were desperate for change.

Of course, it can be a dangerous business for a man to tell his side of the story. As I was having my conversation in Sydney, Mr David Fletcher, a forty-year-old British Aerospace engineer from Preston, Lancashire, was writing a letter to his local paper. In it he observed, 'I have never encountered a more pampered and selfish set of people than today's so-called modern young housewife. I am left with a feeling of shame when I stand back taking in the sight of so many young men, many in their working clothes, pushing trolleys round supermarkets and hurrying about the market.'

This was not the most brilliant of arguments. Some might even see it as the final war cry of a sexist mastodon, doomed to extinction in the modern world. But it wasn't really all that different from the many letters, articles and reports which purport to show what an idle, good-for-nothing slob the British (or American, Australian, French, Italian and, for all I know, Balinese) husband is. One such letter, indeed, was published in the *Independent* on 8 November 1991, almost exactly coincidental with Mr Fletcher's little outburst.

Written by one Diana Holba, of Aston, Hertfordshire, it followed an article in which a writer called Anne Spackman had recounted the tale of how her two-year-old son had swallowed a £1 coin, and what had happened when she and the nanny took him to the local casualty ward. Ms Holba remarked, 'Where was Anne Spackman's husband during the swallowed £1 drama? Why did she, and not he, have to hang around hospital waiting rooms? Why couldn't he do the Tesco run and leave nanny at home with the children? At home or at work, children still call the tune, but isn't it time the husband learned a chord or two?'

This letter attracted no media attention whatsoever. Mr Fletcher, on the other hand, found himself on the end of a hurricane of abuse. To quote an awestruck *Daily Mail*: 'His furious wife Linda and daughter Laura, fifteen, stopped speaking to him. Women at work shunned him. He received hundreds of angry letters and phone calls . . . Mrs Fletcher was incandescent with rage. "I paint, fix hinges, do a little plumbing, put on plugs, decorate, act as nurse to the children, attend their parents' evenings and do the laundry. How dare he moan about being sent to do the week's shopping?" '

At first, Mr Fletcher was defiant. He told the *Mail*, 'Modern women are whingeing about nothing. My grandmother worked in the cotton mills all day from the age of fourteen and, at the same time, brought up children and kept her house spotless.' Nor was he any less scathing about modern men: 'They are just wimps who have got men into this mess.'

This unapologetic stance did not last long. Overwhelmed by the rage that his letter had unleashed and unnerved by being ostracised by his family, friends and workmates, Mr Fletcher spoke to the *Mail* again a few days later. He produced a series of self-loathing apologies whose grovelling tone, complete with admissions of guilt and promises of new thinking, reads like a confession at a Chinese Communist show trial.

I'll say sorry as many times as necessary to get myself out of the hole I dug myself into. I never believed my observations would upset women so much. That letter was the biggest mistake of my life.

I sat down before Linda and apologised. I asked her to please start talking to me again and, thankfully, she has. I am forgiven. I've also stirred up a hornet's nest among the women at work. But when I go back tomorrow I'll apologise to them, too. I hope they forgive me.

I don't suppose I appreciated the vast amount of work my wife, and other women do. It is said a woman's work never ends. Now I agree. It has been spelled out for me in capital letters – down the phone and in domestic silence. My big mistake was that in trying to make a point with humour and emphasis, I went over the top and paid dearly for it. I had the choice – to see the light or be a social leper with at least half the population. I rethought my views and decided, for sanity's sake, on the first.

Just to show what a great sport she was, Mrs Fletcher added, 'I have accepted his apology. Life is getting back to normal. I don't know what possessed him to write that letter, but there will be no more.'

The most bizarre aspect of the whole affair was that no one, for one moment, would even consider that Mr Fletcher might have had a point. Or even if he actually was in the wrong, that he had a right to voice his opinions. Just imagine the situation in reverse. A woman writes a letter to a local paper observing that all men are sexist pigs. Her husband, who believes that he is not a sexist pig, sends her to Coventry. So do the equally outraged men at work. Eventually she confesses her sins and confirms her repentance to a writer from the *Daily Mail*. Her husband smugly remarks, 'There'll be no more letters from my Linda.'

It's inconceivable, isn't it? Because if a woman did write that letter, the response would be one of anguished self-examination on the part of the men concerned. No man would dare respond as Mrs Fletcher did. That would be sexist. Instead, he would be quoted accepting responsibility for his faults and promising to do better next time.

The reason for our double standard is that men, being so much better off than women, are expected to remain silent. Women, being so much worse off, are thought to have every right to complain. If I have learned anything at all, however, during the writing and researching of this book, it is that unhappiness and oppression are far more evenly distributed than we have been led to believe.

It is the desperation that hits me the most. I think of the men I know who have been stripped of their wives, their houses and their children, and the beaten, baffled looks on their faces. I think of a soldier from Texas I once read about, with his brains blasted all over his kitchen because he couldn't stand the lie of being a macho master-sergeant all day, and a battered husband at night, belittled and humiliated in front of his own kids. I think of the salesman I interviewed in a transvestite club in Manchester, who was dressed in a tatty skirt, with his leg hairs showing through his stockings and the make-up on his face beginning to melt, because he couldn't dress as he wanted and still be truly a man.

Then I remember all the books and articles I've seen which claim that men are conspiring to take away the concessions and equalities for which women have been fighting for twenty years or more. Some of the writers maintain that those of us who are beginning to write about men's lives are misogynists. Or we're wimps. Sometimes we're both.

In response, I can only say that I belong to no conspiracy, and this book has got nothing at all to do with misogyny. I have two daughters, whom I love beyond all measure. I want them to grow up to be cherished, respected and admired. I want them to be able to work in any job they choose and raise a family with men they love. The last thing I want to do is add to the sum of hatred in the world. There's enough of that already. There are too many gender politicians with their self-righteous theories packed away in their cases. I for one have had it with -isms and ideologies. This century's been crippled by them: Nazism, Communism, Maoism, Thatcherism, Reaganism, feminism ... Their adherents all think that they, and they alone, know the answers. And every time a new one comes along, another set of victims is prepared.

The fact is, people are in pain. And right now, the ones who wear trousers and stand up to piss don't seem to count for much when it comes to being healed.

We are faced, as a society, with a series of devastating social problems that hinge upon the relationship between men and women: rape, child abuse, domestic violence, the material and emotional chaos wrought by the breakdown of the traditional family unit. But none of these problems, including those which involve male assaults upon women, will be solved unless we look at the situation as a whole and consider the point of view of both sexes equally. Too often in recent years, gender-based issues have been presented purely in terms of woman as helpless victim, man as evil protagonist. Not only is man seen to be oppressive, but he is also held to possess a set of inherent moral and psychological weaknesses amounting to inferiority.

It is almost impossible for a man publicly to discuss any of the positive qualities of men or masculinity without being accused of sexism, on the grounds that he is, by implication, demeaning women. He must, on the other hand, accept full responsibility for a wide range of failings which are held to result, automatically, from his gender. This grossly distorts our analysis of social issues, denies men a voice in areas which are of concern to us and is having a catastrophic effect on the self-image of an entire generation of young men. And, incidentally, it has a powerful negative effect on the struggle for women's equality into the bargain.

Are we to believe that men are simply born bad? Or is there something that happens to men that makes them more likely to act in destructive ways than might otherwise be the case? Are women, fundamentally, any better than men?

The casting of the two genders into the roles of male oppressors and female oppressed ignores the possibility that the balance of power may be far more complex and flexible than that. The undoubted strength and privilege that some men have in the public world should not blind one to the fact that their private selves may be very much less privileged. For example, just think of George Bush. Here is a man whose career reads like a litany of patriarchal power. He's been the American ambassador to China. He's run the CIA. He's been Vice-President and President of the United States. But ask yourself this: would you really want to be George Bush? Does his life seem like an epitome of human fulfilment? Sure, he's had all the public power that any human could ever desire. But the private human being has withered away behind that shell of pomp and circumstance. I'm prepared to bet that even George Bush doesn't know who he is any more.

If the White House seems too distant, consider your father. He may be alive, he may be dead. He may have been a decent man who did his best, or he may have been a monster. But did he look to you like an all-powerful patriarch? Did he seem to be someone who was getting any great personal benefit from all this male power that we hear so much about? What was in it for him?

Although men are prime ministers, presidents and chairmen, they constitute the bulk of alcoholics and prisoners as well. They display a far greater propensity than women for sexual perversion, fetishism and dysfunction. They form the vast majority of the homeless beggars who line our city streets: in America, 86.5 per cent of all people arrested for vagrancy are male.

Men live, on average, lives that are about 7 per cent shorter than those of women. They are more likely than women to suffer heart attacks, lung cancer, cirrhosis of the liver and strokes. Indeed, they are more prone to a whole range of physical and mental illnesses, some of which – haemophilia, for example – are only manifested in the male.

Trouble is, people are so busy looking at the men on top of the heap that no one notices them when they fall. Most Western governments are becoming increasingly aware – quite rightly – of the special medical needs of women. But similar provision is scarcely ever made for men. Laudable efforts are made to screen women for breast, uterine and cervical cancers. Yet there is a dismal ignorance and lack of attention displayed towards cancers that are exclusively male, to wit those affecting the testes and the prostate gland.

In 1989, according to official figures, 12,742 British men died from cancers of their genito-urinary organs. That same year, 10,200 women died from equivalent cancers. Of the men, 7,861 died from prostate cancer. Of the women, 3,264 died from cervical or uterine cancers. In other words, more than twice as many men died from prostate cancer as the number of women who died from cervical and uterine cancer combined. Yet there is no national screening programme for prostate cancer.

Mr Ewan Milroy, consultant urologist at the Middlesex Hospital, has been quoted as saying: 'Relatives and doctors in this country haven't made much fuss about these figures because in my thirty to forty years' experience there simply hasn't been any public demand for attention to be given to men's problems . . . Most urologists would agree [that men's problems are ignored] and I think we all resent it. It is very difficult to get money for research into prostate cancer whereas it is relatively easy for research into carcinomas of breast or cervix, simply because they are much more fashionable.'

No one is saying that we shouldn't care about women's cancers. But why can't we care about men's ones as well?

This wilful ignorance of men's issues arises from three apparently contradictory sources. In the first place, orthodox feminism has convinced the vast majority of academics, writers, broadcasters and legislators that the relationship between men and women is inherently oppressive, and in only one direction. So it follows that any problems faced by the oppressor should be regarded as being worthy not of sympathy, but of derision. This attitude is equalled by the stupidity of traditional male machismo, which, fuelled by fear and braggadocio in about equal proportions, leads men to refuse to admit to any of their problems lest they be accused of weakness or – worst of all – effeminacy.

Middle-aged men, in particular, are famously reluctant to give in to any form of frailty. In the recent past, at least three men of my acquaintance have refused to see a doctor when suffering from serious medical complaints. Only when they actually collapsed would they agree to be admitted into hospital. Once there, each was discovered to be suffering from a potentially life-threatening condition (two heart attacks and one case of stomach cancer). Yet so conditioned were they by countless generations' worth of upbringing in which boys were told that it was unmanly to give in to pain or illness that they risked their own lives rather than threaten their fragile masculinity.

Such apparent indifference to physical suffering is matched by a wilful blindness to psychological disturbance. The very fact that so many men drink themselves to the point of oblivion, thereby causing irreversible long-term damage to their health, indicates that all is not well. Yet they remain obstinately convinced that they have no need of special treatment.

One example of this phenomenon (the obstinacy, that is, not the alcoholism) was a man I met at a business dinner. He was a highly successful barrister in his mid-fifties. Over the course of a long meal with our respective spouses, we discussed the subject of the fledgling men's movement. He couldn't see the point of it all and said that for men of his generation it was impossible to conceive of what men's issues might be. A little later on he told a story about his childhood. His mother, he said, used to take an ice-cream scoop and flick it at his genitalia whenever he was naked – when he had just got out of the bath, for example.

I asked him whether he liked this. Of course not, he said. He found it acutely embarrassing. He hated it. But, he added, as if to correct any misgivings we might have, it was just a family game.

Was it a game his sisters played? No, he was the only player.

A little later on he was talking about his father. He had left home for twenty years and when he returned, his father was extremely ill in hospital. One day, sitting by his father's bed, the barrister leaned over, took him in his arms and kissed him. 'I'm sorry, Dad,' he said, 'but I just had to do that.'

When he looked again, he saw that his father's face was wet with tears. He was stunned. Here was a hard man, the rock of the family, and he was crying. Then the father spoke: 'I've always prayed that one day you would do that.'

When the man finished his two stories, I pointed out that he had just given a perfect illustration of the need for a men's movement. His childhood had contained casual brutality of the sort meted out to boys in the hope of toughening them up. So 'tough' had he become that he was unable to show his feelings to his own father until the man was on the point of death. He had, in other words, been crippled by his upbringing.

The truth is that we all of us carry wounds that we spend most of our lives trying to cover up. We dare not reveal them for fear that if we do we will be considered unmanly, even by those who appear to hold manliness in contempt. The self-hatred that arises from the deception we all practise leaves us defenceless before accusations that we are, in some way, bad people who must be blamed for what is wrong with the world and who cannot expect to be treated with kindness or consideration.

The third limitation on effective action on behalf of men comes from men who have been imbued with the worst of both worlds. Brought up with the traditional male stereotypes, they have at some point internalised the feminist critique of men. The result is an overriding determination to prove that they are truly penitent, that they are more willing than any woman to criticise the wrongdoings of men.

It is quite astonishing how often one comes across self-hating men in the pages of newspapers and magazines (by and large, the more upmarket the publication, the more often the phenomenon is to be found). Faced with evidence of male wrongdoing, they will report it in tones of the utmost loathing. Faced with a man who is attempting to redress the balance, they will react with the utmost contempt. Male feminism has almost become a perverse badge of machismo. It's a bit like the anti-drug campaign that featured an addict saying, 'Heroin – I can handle it,' as he collapsed into the gutter. The new motto is, 'Feminism – I can handle it.' Sure you can, pal.

Some of these men, when spoken to in private, turn out to have very different opinions from the ones they produce in public. They will tell you that – given the fact that the majority of forums for debate of sexual or gender issues tend to be magazines or newspaper pages edited for women by women – it pays to toe the politically correct line. Others seem convinced of their own inferiority. Either way, self-hatred is as poor a basis from which to start an argument as hatred of anyone else.

The result of these social and psychological phenomena is a situation in which any evidence of male advantage is treated as an anomaly requiring urgent corrective action, quite possibly legislative in nature, whilst any evidence to the contrary is believed to demonstrate the (desirable) superiority of women.

In the weeks before writing this chapter, typical newspaper stories have included the fact that more and more of Britain's spies are women, owing to the inherent advantages that women possess over men (these advantages, according to one 'intelligence source' who spoke to the *Sunday Times*, were that 'women have the right talents of analysis and concentration and a good head for keeping their eye on the ball'); that a psychologist has revealed that women make naturally better managers than men; that the preponderance of male managers in the NHS is due to an old boys' network; that men are more likely than women to be fat owing to their wilful ignorance about their own bodies, and so on.

Such stereotyping may not, in itself, seem like a particular problem when set against the enormous advantages that men (allegedly) possess. But, as any good feminist could tell you, media images and media stereotypes are hugely influential. And right now, the stereotypes are reinforcing a consistently negative impression of men. For now, by way of redressing the imbalance, here are five principles on which this book is based:

* Men's public power is matched by private disadvantage

* Equality is indivisible. Women are just as intelligent as men – and they can do just as much harm

* Only by admitting to and coping with their weaknesses will men ever become truly strong. In the words of Ernest Hemingway (which I came across, incidentally, in the pages of Gloria Steinem's *Revolution From Within*), 'The world breaks everyone, and afterwards, some are strong at the broken places.'

* If women accept that men may face obstacles to personal fulfilment, just like they do, they can make a huge contribution to genuine equality between the sexes, but . . .

* In the end, it's no good men complaining about women: they've got to get up and win a better life for themselves.

Up to now, I have concentrated on the negative side of the male position. But it is also important not to forget the positive values associated with masculinity. It is possible to be strong without being oppressive. It is possible to be assertive without being domineering. And it is possible to possess energy, determination and even aggression, without being violent or bullying.

The last thing that the world needs now is another bunch of whining, self-proclaimed victims, and no one should close this book thinking that I spend my whole time feeling miserable about being male. I have been privileged in every aspect of my life. The work I do, the family I love, the friendships I have made, the football, the sex, the laughs, the beers . . . all of that, from the profoundest feelings to the most trivial pursuits, has been affected by or dependent upon my gender, and most of it has been just fine. But that doesn't mean that I don't get angry or hurt or perplexed about some of the things that I see happening to the men around me. Nor does it alter my conviction that men, and the whole concept of masculinity, are passing through a crisis.

If we are to have a healthy society, our sons need to grow up with a sense of self-confidence and self-respect. Over the past few decades, much has rightly been done to give girls a greater sense of their own potential and to broaden their expectations of life. Writers such as Robert Bly, author of the American best-seller *Iron John*, are now reporting on the difficulties that boys are having in defining a role for themselves as they grow towards manhood.

Often deprived of the presence of a father, boys run the risk of overcompensating by becoming – as the sociologist Myriam Medzian puts it – hyper-masculine, which is to say habitually violent and desensitised. Or they drift too far in the other direction towards softness and passivity. There is a happy medium between the wimp and the terminator. It would be in all our interests to encourage it and I applaud those commentators on men's issues who are searching for a middle way. Beyond that, however, I do not think that it is enough just to deal with the psychology of manhood and the inner feelings of individual men. Banging drums and hugging have their place. But men should wake up to the fact that they can never be happy until the legal and social barriers to their fulfilment as men and as fathers have been removed. We have to get down to specifics and practicalities, and those are the issues that form the heart of this book.

Before we go any further, however, it's time to answer one important question: what, exactly, is a man?

Chapter 1

For What Is A Man, What Has He Got?

Spot the difference

The question of gender identity is one of the most controversial and divisive issues of our time. Many people feel that men and women are quite different from one another, but in what ways? And what effects do those differences have? When James Morris, the soldier, reporter and writer, became Jan Morris, the woman, she discovered that the gap between the sexes was still vast. In *Conundrum*, the story of her journey from man to woman, she remarks that, having seen life from both sides of the sexual divide, there is not one moment of the day, one event or one experience that is not different for a man and a woman.

Although *Conundrum* was first published in 1974, it is hard not to feel that Morris's observations still hold true today. Yet the endless debate between nature and nurture continues to swing back and forth: are the sexes born different, or are their differences merely the result of social conditioning?

From the start of the women's movement, this has been a vital issue. Women's leaders have needed to be able to establish that women had a right to work at the highest level in every profession. Research carried out in the early 1970s amongst large numbers of Americans showed that more than three-quarters believed that the sexes were fundamentally different. Furthermore, the majority felt that the so-called male qualities, such as leadership, assertiveness, objectivity, logic, competitiveness, self-confidence, were superior to supposedly feminine characteristics of kindness, gentleness, tearfulness and emotional subjectivity. Clearly, if women were to get anywhere in this man's world, it was vital to prove that they could, if properly brought up, be just as competitive, analytical, and so forth, as men.

To this end, academic researchers consistently sought to establish the essential sameness of men and women. So strong was their desire, that vast amounts of research from the 1960s and 1970s are now having to be reconsidered as the biases which lay behind them become increasingly apparent.

More recently, as I and other writers on men's issues have pointed out, sexism has, to some extent, been reversed. Open any women's magazine or newspaper women's page and you will read generalisations about the superiority of female qualities over male. There's a nice bit of dialogue from an episode of *Roseanne* that sums up the situation. Dan, the great big lunk of a husband, played by John Goodman, has just made an insensitive remark to one of his daughters, causing her to dash upstairs in tears. 'Oh Dan, you're such . . . a man,' exclaims Roseanne, before leaving to see what she can do to help. Dan Junior, their son, is puzzled, and has a brief conversation with his father, which proceeds as follows:

DJ: Dad, why did Mom call you a man?

DAN: Because she's mad at me.

DJ: I thought it was good to be a man.

DAN: Oh no son, not since the late Sixties.

It gets worse. Deborah Phillips, a behavioural therapist from Princeton, with a private practice in Hollywood, was quoted in the London *Evening Standard* in March 1990: 'If we just look at the female orgasm, it does not occur in the rest of the animal kingdom. It only occurs in human females. It's a much more highly evolved response than the male . . . It can be multiple. I know there are reports about multiple male orgasms, but it's nothing compared to the female. So if we just look at that, and the female's ability to communicate, I think that the female is a more highly-evolved species than the man.'

This isn't science, it's lunacy. But one often reads similar statements of female supremacy, statements which would immediately be condemned as the most grotesque sexism if they were ever made about men. It is, for example, rapidly becoming a cliché to state that women make better managers than men because they are more caring towards their staff, less concerned with pointless status symbols and possess superior communication skills. Man's apparent propensity for violence and aggression is also contrasted unfavourably with more conciliatory female qualities.

The most obvious 180° turn has occurred in perceptions of

friendship. It used to be said that women could never be friends in the way that men were, because they were too busy competing for male attention. Now it is said that men cannot be friends in the way that women are, since they lack the emotional honesty to enable them to bond with one another.

I shall be dealing with some of these generalisations in more detail elsewhere in this and other chapters. For now it is enough to note that, for reasons exactly comparable with those of the early feminists – i.e. the need to demonstrate moral and intellectual equality – some male authors have recently been as vociferous in their refusal to accept gender-based stereotyping as their female predecessors. The women did not want to be typecast as tearful, fluffy-headed sex objects. The men do not want to be thought of as insensitive, muscle-bound hooligans.

The problem arises, however, that many of the theories which seem ideologically desirable have little basis in scientific fact. This century has seen many recipes for social justice which begin with the instruction: 'First, change your human being.' Human nature, however, does not take kindly to being changed, and many authorities in genetics, physiology, neurology, psychology and a whole bunch of -ologies besides, are coming to the conclusion that there really are differences between the sexes that are innate and ineradicable.

These differences, however, must be qualified by a number of provisos. There is a feminine side to most men, and a masculine side to most women; it's just the proportions that vary from one person to another. And pre-existing differences of a minor nature may be greatly exaggerated by social conditioning. Worst of all, many individuals may be socialised to behave in ways which correspond to the natural tendency of their sex as a whole, but which do not suit their personal aptitudes or inclinations.

Meanwhile, social policies and legislation are in a state of utter chaos for want of any certainty. A company, for example, that was considering employing a woman would be accused of gross sex discrimination if it inquired into the interviewee's susceptibility to premenstrual tension. Yet that same woman, were she in court on a murder charge, might very well be able to prove that her PMT was so bad that it rendered her, effectively, temporarily insane. Few companies wish to employ people who go legally mad for a few days every month, so does PMT have a significant effect upon a woman, or not? Which are we supposed to think is the more enlightened attitude?

In sexual attitudes, as in so many other areas of our lives, our attitudes are struggling to catch up with the staggering speed of technological change. An innovation like the contraceptive pill, for example, not only has an immediate physiological effect, but it throws into confusion social attitudes that have all presumed an entirely different reproductive situation.

Meanwhile, scientists are increasingly discovering convincing biological or chemical explanations for human characteristics that have previously been thought of as moral or psychological. If a man, for example, is accused of committing an act of violence against a woman, is he evil, as traditional moralists would say? Is he the product of his upbringing, as a psychologist or sociologist might maintain? Is he, as feminists such as Marilyn French claim, merely a pawn in the continuous war waged by all men against all women? Or is he the helpless victim of his brain chemistry? Finally, could it be that he is not the guilty party at all, but merely the fall guy for a society conditioned to see men as baddies and women as their helpless victims?

The moment one starts to try to explain human behaviour, one is deluged with theories and manifestos. It soon becomes clear to anyone who, like myself, tries to look at more than one approach to the subject that few of the experts in any one field have any idea at all about what is going on in the others. On the rare occasions when they are conscious of the findings of workers in different disciplines, they seem to feel honour-bound to despise them.

I have attempted to explore some of these separate approaches. My aim is to come to some sort of understanding about the nature of masculinity and the consequent differences between men and women. Having tiptoed my way as best I can through a number of intellectual minefields, I have ended up with the simple, unscientific, common-sense belief that men and women are the same . . . but different.

We're the same because we share the human condition. We are born, we live and we die. We need sustenance and shelter to survive. We need love and companionship truly to live. We share our intelligence and we share our anger, even if we may express both of those qualities in different ways. When it comes to questions of moral worth, men and women are equal. Neither sex is more or less evil than the other, nor is the value of a man's life any greater or less than that of a woman.

On the other hand, men and women are shaped differently and sized differently. They look different; they sound different; they feel different and they taste different. Looked at that way, it's hard to believe that they are not, in fact, different.

It sounds, I know, completely obvious, but the simplest way of solving an enormous number of the problems which divide men and women is to accept that their differences are differences of type, rather than of quality. In other words, just because we may express ourselves in different ways and be motivated by different impulses, does not mean that one way, or one impulse, is better than another. They're just . . . different.

Once we grab hold of that simple truth, then it becomes possible to understand that males and females may, in some areas of their life, need to be treated in ways that recognise the needs that are specific to their gender. Boys, for example, may benefit from being taught their school lessons in a highly structured, well-disciplined and competitive environment that is geared towards one-off examinations. Girls may do better with less formal methods that recognise their greater aptitude at, and preference for, continuous assessment. There are biological, psychological and sociological reasons for these particular differences, and they are echoed throughout our lives.

This does not mean that biology is destiny, or that women should immediately be corralled within their kitchens and nurseries, making babies while their men bring home the bacon. I want to free both sexes from the prejudices by which they are dogged. But it helps to do that if we know where we are actually starting from. For far too long, we have enslaved ourselves to political theories that have, at best, a misguided view of human nature and are, at worst, deliberately deceitful.

So let's try, at least, to uncover the truth, starting with a spot of science . . .

Why, Oh Y?

To any scientist, the political battle between nature and nurture is entirely futile. According to Dr Steve Jones, a geneticist at University College, London and the author of the BBC's 1991 Reith Lectures, 'The mistake is to suppose that there exists a cake of human behaviour that can be cut into slices called "genetics" and "environment". But every genetic attribute has some environmental component, and vice versa.'

Think of a finely woven carpet. Imagine that all the genetic influences are the warp, running in one direction, and that the environmental factors are the weft, running in the other. These are intermingled with such subtlety that it is no longer possible to tell which is which. All that one can see is the pattern that they produce together.

The phenotype of any given species – i.e. what it actually is – is the product of its genotype, or characteristic DNA sequence, acting in a particular environment. The Siamese cat, for example, can have either a predominantly black or cream-coloured coat. The difference looks like a straightforward genetic mutation. But the DNA stays the same and the difference occurs because of changes in temperature. The hotter the environment, the lighter the coat. Same DNA, different phenotype.

Environmental factors can alter an individual's physical nature during his own lifetime. Studies carried out with tropical fish, for example, show that the dominant male in any school of fish possesses a number of disproportionately swollen cells in the area of his hypo-thalamus (a neural control centre linked to the brain) that is responsible for controlling sexual functions. But should he lose his dominance to another fish, that area shrinks. Is his behaviour influenced by his hypothalamus, or vice versa?

Even when links between behaviour and physiology appear obvious, sexual politicians should hesitate before using them as the basis for value judgements. Studies have shown that testosterone levels in children, both male and female, can influence their behaviour. Crudely speaking, the more testosterone the child possesses, the more likely he or she is to be aggressive, irritable and boisterous. Such children, particularly the girls, do not necessarily translate their behaviour into actual violence, but it is tempting nevertheless to link testosterone, which is a male hormone, with levels of antisocial or aggressive behaviour in men so as to suggest that masculinity is, inherently, a violent phenomenon.

Except that there's a catch. Recent experiments suggest that when testosterone passes through the human brain, it is metabolised into estradiol, which is a female hormone. From which one might, assuming that one wanted to rush to hasty and unsupported conclusions, deduce that violence is actually a female phenomenon.

In other cases, misguided conclusions can be drawn from seemingly straightforward evidence. Take the question of deter-mining human sex. This is done by two chromosomes, the X and the Y. A baby born with two X-chromosomes will be female. A baby born with one of each – i.e. XY – will, unless anything goes wrong during pregnancy, be male. Sometimes, however, boys are born with an extra Y-chromosome and thus have a pattern that reads XYY.

Some years ago, researchers noticed that the inmates of institutions for the criminally insane tended to show an unexpectedly high incidence of additional Y-chromosomes. So, too, did prisoners jailed for violent offences in regular jails. This observation was irresistible to those who sought to show that men were inherently more violent and criminal than women. The more male your chromosomes, the more psychopathic your behaviour. *Ergo*, masculinity was once again, by definition, violent.

Others set off on a different, if related, track. Dr Jones tells the story – which may well be the scientific equivalent of an urban myth – of how Richard Nixon wanted to launch a programme to screen children for XYY patterns at birth. Any boy found to possess the condition would then be followed for life by the FBI to prevent him doing anything too shocking to the American electorate.

Then researchers noticed that the additional Y-chromosome had another, even more obvious side effect. It made people much bigger and stronger. So if they hit someone, they did far more damage than they would have done if they were small. As they say in boxing, 'A good big 'un will always beat a good little 'un.' But there was no evidence that they had a greater predisposition to hit anyone in the first place. Mr Nixon might just as well have had the XYY kids followed by coaches from the Washington Redskins: they would have made excellent football players.

A similar confusion explains much of the apparent difference in male and female criminality. By all conventional measurements, men commit much more crime than women, a fact to which our overflowing jails pay testimony. But is that because men are actually worse than women, or simply because – when it comes, for example, to acts of violence – they are more effective? In any fight between a man and a woman, the man is usually the big 'un. He may well land the final blow. And he will almost certainly be the one that ends up in jail. But that does not necessarily mean that he started the fight in the first place.

Consider the matter of intention, and a very different picture emerges. Women are just as capable as men are of feeling anger, hatred and hostility. They are just as prone to feelings of resentment or the desire for revenge. Just because women do not always express those feelings physically – although they do so more often than is commonly supposed – that does not mean they are free from the need or desire to harm other people. In the US, for example, the proportion of fraud and embezzlement committed by women is roughly parallel with the proportion of women in the workforce as a whole. They may be different, but, once again, they are also very much the same.

That, however, is to get ahead of ourselves. We cannot leave genetics just yet. If he looks at a human cell under a microscope, Dr Jones can tell within seconds whether it comes from a male or female body. Given time, he could also determine the racial origins of the cell. But the difference between black and white is tiny compared to that between male and female. What Dr Jones cannot do is tell one why there should be any such thing as a male at all. Because, as he explained to me, no one can. There is no necessary or sufficient scientific reason for the existence of the male sex. The most efficient form of repro-duction, parthenogenesis, occurs within a single sex. Given that this single sex produces offspring it is, essentially, female, rather than either neuter or male.

So why does nature complicate matters? It is possible to argue that the existence of two sexes, pooling their genes in an infinite range of combinations, offers an opportunity for diversity, flexibility and adaptability. But one might also say that it doubles the number of things that can go wrong, too.

Similarly, it might be argued that the struggle that some male animals go through before being able to mate sorts out the weak from the strong, thereby ensuring the survival of the fittest and enriching the gene pool. Amongst deer, for example, stags fight amongst them-selves, thereby establishing a hierarchy and, or so it has always been assumed, reserving all the most attractive young does for the Monarch of the Glen. But as Dr Jones explained to me, it doesn't necessarily work like that. Scientists have recently discovered that the sex life of deer (and some other combative male mammals) follows a rather different pattern.

With modern techniques of genetic fingerprinting, it is possible to follow bloodlines with extreme accuracy, so that one can determine exactly which stag in a herd fathered a particular fawn. What has become clear is that while the dominant male of the herd is off fighting other males, digging up turf with his mighty hooves and bellowing his masterful cries throughout the length and breadth of the forest, other, altogether more wimpy males, are having it off with compliant does behind their master's back. This is known, with all the calm, considered categorisation for which the scientific community is renowned, as the Sneaky Fucker Theory.

The same theory applies to human life as well. Much aggressively male behaviour is predicated on spending as much time as possible apart from females, except for brief periods of sexual activity. Traditionally, men who spent too much time in the company of women, talking to them and taking an interest in their affairs, have been considered effeminate. The fact that they may actually have enjoyed a much higher sexual success rate does not seem to have reduced the opprobrium they faced for not concentrating on more appropriate activities, principally killing other men in the service of king and country.

Students of Hollywood will note that the muscle-bound heroes of all those blast-a-minute action movies are generally far too busy blowing up downtown Los Angeles to waste any time on mere women. On the other hand, wimpish comedians like Dudley Moore and Woody Allen always seem to end their movies in the company of an adorable, and adoring, female mate.

Those of us whose physique (if not our taste in young women) is closer to the Allen model than the Arnie can be grateful that nature blessed us with the attributes of the Sneaky Fucker. But what's the point of fucking in the first place? Or, to put it another way, why does the fuckee have to be put to so much trouble when she could manage perfectly happily on her own?

Were there only one, female, sex, it would exist – biologically speaking – in an atmosphere of calm, peaceful stability, adapting gradually to its circumstances over long stretches of time. On the other hand, life would not, in all probability, be particularly exciting. As Camille Paglia has remarked, much to the fury of many of her fellow feminists, if the world were run by women, we'd all still be living in grass huts. So one might think of the male sex as the irritating bit of grit in the great oyster we call life. But is this really a valid justification for its existence?

Could there, perhaps, be an explanation based on the cock-up, rather than the conspiracy theory? Maybe masculinity is an accidental side effect of some other process, rather than an intended part of nature's plan. One possibility is that she had no choice. Steve Jones suggests that man might be a form of genetic parasite. The idle male layabout, slumped in front of the telly with can in hand, expecting to be waited upon hand and foot by an overworked woman, may not be an indolent git who could do with a kick up the backside. He may just be expressing a fundamental truth about human genetics.

The process works as follows: we are now discovering that many human diseases, from haemophilia to certain types of cancer, are caused by viruses that have infiltrated the human genome – that is to say, the genetic blueprint for the human race, which is carried within every cell of every human being on this planet. These viruses are a bit like secret agents, dispatched into enemy territory, living lives of apparent normality, but just waiting for the signal that will order them into battle against the host community. In the same way that we all are threatened by external viruses, to which we have varying degrees of resistance, so we all possess a number of parasitic, genetic viruses, which we 'caught' at our conception. Whether or not they ever act upon us is determined by our environment, stress, general health and so on.

In 1990, teams of scientists led by Dr Robin Lovell-Badge of the Medical Research Council and Dr Peter Goodfellow of the Imperial Cancer Research Fund announced that they had found the actual DNA trigger that sets off the chain of genetic events that leads to the formation of a male foetus. It is a substance known as SRY and it acts as a sort of switch, sending development along a new, male, pathway. This crucial piece of genetic material is tiny. If one imagines the human genome as being the distance between Land's End and John O'Groats, then the critical section determining masculinity would cover much less than one footstep.

It is Dr Steve Jones's suggestion, made partly – but only partly – in jest, that SRY may well have started life way back in the mists of time as a microscopic viral organism, which wormed its way into DNA at an early stage of evolution, long, long before Homo sapiens arrived on the scene. If this is the case, then this was a spectacularly successful little bug, since vast numbers of species now have male members. On the other hand, since men may yet pollute or explode most life off the face of this planet, the male virus may yet find itself restricted to the cockroach family, which might seem like something of a comedown. Or, then again, perhaps not.

There is certainly a case to be made for the proposition that this genetic virus, if that is what it is, has a harmful effect upon the human body, because one of the reasons why scientists wonder why the male sex should exist is that it is, in many respects, much weaker and less likely to survive than the female. Some people, indeed, see masculinity as a weak, second-rate mutation of a superior female form.

All human foetuses start out female. The presence of a Y-chromosome, in conjunction with a series of hormonal reactions during the mother's pregnancy, determines that the previously female embryo will develop as a male. The first thing to note about this process is that all sorts of things can go wrong.

This partially explains why many more male than female foetuses are miscarried. It may also help to account for the much greater number of men than women who suffer from conditions such as transsexualism: in the journey from female to male there are, as it were, occasional stragglers. In some cases, the foetuses will be born hermaphrodite, with both a penis and a vagina, or with a greatly exaggerated clitoris. In such cases, the child is surgically given the appearance of a little girl and grows up to be a normal-looking, though frequently infertile, woman.

So prone to misfunction are baby males, that 120 of them are conceived for every 100 females. By the end of pregnancy, the ratio is 110:100. Since more male babies are miscarried or stillborn, the ratio of surviving births is 106:100. Mother Nature knows that little boys will suffer more diseases than their sisters and experience appears to have taught her that those who survive to puberty will then devote much of their considerable physical energy to the business of mutual self-destruction.

This leads us on to the two physical characteristics of men that appear to be an inherent part of their physical make-up. They are stronger than women, but their lives are shorter; as a sex, their motto appears to be, 'Live fast, die young.'

Matters of life and death

By and large, men are some 30 per cent larger than women. They have more muscle and less fat as a proportion of their body weight. They can lift greater weights, run faster and jump further than women. Until recently these would all have been considered to be uncontroversial statements. Whatever drawbacks the male may have, his physical power was his one incontrovertible advantage and was bestowed to him by his natural physiology, rather than any social conditioning.

This belief has been brought into doubt recently. Doctors in America who have studied world records in athletic events over the last few years have noted that women's performances have been improving at a rate far greater than those of men. From this they have concluded, by extrapolating these improvements forward into the future, that women will soon catch up with and possibly even overtake men.

These findings caused considerable news interest when they emerged in 1991, but they did not convince many women athletes, who appeared to be less confident of their chances of beating their male peers, and they should, I believe, be taken with several grains of salt.

In the first place, are women really improving at such a staggering rate? Before me as I write these words (at the beginning of the 1992 athletics season) is a copy of the *Guinness Book of World Records, 1992*. From it I glean the following pieces of information. During 1991, five new world records were set in men's track and field. This was an improvement on 1990 in which only two were set, although 1989 had seen five new records. Turning to the women's records, I see that only one world record was broken in 1991, none at all were set in 1990 and only one in 1989. In fact, performances at major championships by female athletes have been showing a decline of between 5 and 10 per cent.

It does not take long to work out two reasons why there should have been such a sudden halt to female sporting progress at the end of the 1980s. The first is that the testing of athletes for drug abuse became progressively tougher. And the second is that the sport's major pushers found themselves kicked out of business.

The vast majority of female track and field record holders are citizens of countries that used to lie within the Soviet bloc. When the Berlin Wall collapsed in 1989, so did the state-run sports teams of the East. As they did so, details emerged of the extraordinary lengths to which they had gone in order to improve the performance of their athletes, particularly the female ones. Young women were routinely made pregnant and then forced to undergo abortions shortly before major championships – women possess their greatest powers of strength and endurance during or shortly after pregnancy. They were also injected with massive doses of steroids and male hormones. This policy increased their muscle bulk, diminished their fat ratio, turned them into pseudo-males and perfectly, if repellently, illustrated the old axiom that if you can't beat them, join them.

If training methods that have been hitherto reserved for men are applied for women, the gap between the sexes can be narrowed. But the only way that it can be removed is by turning women, artificially, into men. Until that happens, it might be worth remembering Arnie

Bolt, gold medal-winner of the men's one-legged high jump at the 1992 Paralympic Games. Mr Bolt's personal best of 2.04 metres, set back in 1981, when he was twenty-four – achieved, remember, with the use of just one leg – was two centimetres higher than the winning jump in the women's high jump at the 1992 Barcelona Olympics.

What, then, of life expectancy: this, surely, is an immutable female advantage? As Dr Steve Jones remarked: 'That is one biological difference that is absolutely clear. Men live shorter lives than women. If you castrate them, they live longer . . . or, at least, it just seems longer!' This last fact is based on research done amongst American mental patients in the days when troublesome patients were castrated in the hope of calming them down. Once deprived of their testes and, more significantly, their testosterone, the patients lived, on average, for thirteen years longer than those who were still entire.

This differential, if accurate, would mean that castrati also live longer than ordinary women. So, for anyone keen on longevity, the thing to be is a eunuch. Judging by an informal poll I took amongst my former staff at *Punch*, 100 per cent of male respondents felt that life was not worth living *sans* balls, so let us proceed on that assumption.

One reason for the shorter lives of men is that the period of their lives in which they are fittest is also that at which they are most likely to destroy themselves, or be destroyed by other young men much like them. Self-destruction is a trait that is found among males of many species. The male fruit fly, for example, attempts to have sex with as many as 1,000 females, all but one of whom reject his advances. Having finally found a compliant female, he mates . . . and then he dies.

We may consider ourselves to be a few rungs up the evolutionary ladder from the fruit fly, but sometimes you have to wonder. Old men may start wars, but it is young men, of all nations, who fight and die in them. Oppressed by poverty and corrupted by drugs, young Afro-Americans buy guns and shoot one another on the streets with such regularity that murder is the most common form of death for young men in the inner cities. It is also true that, all over the world, young men buy or steal cars and then drive them at high, often fatal speeds.

Middle-aged men are little better, except that they choose different means of annihilation. Men have traditionally drunk more than women and smoked more, so they score high marks for liver diseases and smoke-related lung and heart conditions. One of the reasons that they turn to nicotine and alcohol is that they need an emotional anaesthetic. They feel unable to express their fears or worries to others. This tendency not only has addictive side effects, but also adds to stress and is harmful to their health.

Finally, men work too hard. In Japan, the country whose white-collar workers work longer hours with fewer holidays than anywhere else in the developed world, they are beginning to recognise a condition called *karoshi*, or death through overwork. More and more of their clerks, accountants and junior executives are devoting lunatic hours to jobs offering little prospect of creative satisfaction or self-determination. The result is that they drop dead at an early age, thereby ensuring that the famous Japanese system of a job for life ensures a job for death, too.

Even if one discounts man's self-destructiveness, the ravages wrought by nature have always been thought to be enough to ensure that women aged seventy would continue to outnumber men of the same age by a factor of two to one. In his book *A Question of Sex*, the British psychologist Dr John Nicholson cites research done amongst 40,000 American monks and nuns. Both sexes were leading low-stress lives with minimal physical danger and no smoking or drinking (apart, presumably, from communion wine). The results showed that the men still died an average five and a half years before the women.

The fundamental reason for this weakness surely has to be our old friend the Y-chromosome. Compared to the X-chromosome, it is a sorry creature, and does little but make a man male. The X-chromosome, however, carries a wealth of information. Some of this may, like a faulty piece of computer software, become corrupted. It may carry a tendency for genetically linked diseases, such as diabetes, rickets or haemophilia. A woman, however, always has a safety mechanism: she possesses two X-chromosomes, and the odds against both being identically flawed are extremely long. The man, lumbered with his useless Y-chromosome, is left with what he's got on the one, faulty chromosome.

That said, I do not think that one need assume that the differences between the sexes will always be as pronounced as they are at the moment. Just as women can become stronger, if not quite as strong, so men can live longer, if not quite as long. Funnily enough, that is just what they appear to be doing. The British life-expectancy figures, issued in June 1992 by the Office of Population Censuses and Surveys, showed that the gap between men and women had narrowed. Between 1980 and 1992, the life expectancy for women had increased by a little less than two years, from 76.6 to 78.5 years. But the male figure had jumped by more than two and a half years, from 70.4 to 73 years.

If, like those scientists who extrapolated athletic performances, we project those trends into the future then, by the year 2088, male life expectancy, which will then be 93.8 years, will have overtaken the female figure of a mere 93.7. The odds are that I will pre-decease my wife. But if I ever have a grandson, he may be given one lonely month in which to gloat over the premature demise of his nonagenarian spouse before he too finally kicks the bucket.

On a more serious note, women might care to consider the possible reasons for the narrowing of this hitherto immutable gap. Although increased living standards, improved nutrition and breakthroughs in medical technology are giving us all a prolonged stay on this planet, women are, it would seem, benefiting from these improvements less than men. The reason is simple: now that they are acting more and more like men, so they are managing to kill themselves with a near-masculine efficiency.

Rates of female alcohol abuse and smoking are on the rise. Teenage girls seem to be far more susceptible than their male peers to the lure of cigarettes – perhaps because they believe that smoking will keep them thin – and, as more and more women work, so they go out for more early-evening drinking sessions. At these, they will encounter another physical difference between the sexes: man's greater bulk and lower fat ratio enables him to handle and process much more alcohol much more quickly than the woman sitting next to him at the bar.

Armed with their wage packets and fortified by booze and the new, fashionable female machismo, young women are now taking to the road with all the mad abandon of their boyfriends and beginning to kill themselves with increasing frequency. Before they do, they should consider one important fact which sober, health conscious, emotionally open men have cottoned onto: the traditional male life style is hazardous to your health. It doesn't carry a government warning, but it should. Once women start to behave like men, and work like men, and earn like men, they may well start to die like them, too.

The mind of man

An old calypso song states that 'Man Smart, Woman Smarter', but it is generally agreed by most researchers that men and women are indivisible in terms of their average overall inteligence. In *A Question of Sex,* Dr John Nicholson summarises the history of research into intelligence, much of which had presumed the intellectual superiority of men. He concludes with a sentence from which there has been little subsequent dissent: 'The most important fact is that men are not more intelligent than women – the average man's IQ score is indistinguishable from that of the average woman.' Yet, as Dr Nicholson points out with the aid of a few simple experiments, the sexes do differ in the types of mental tasks at which they excel.

In the words of a *Time* magazine cover story, published in January 1992, 'Psychology tests consistently support the notion that men and women perceive the world in subtly different ways. Males excel at rotating three-dimensional objects in their head. Females prove better at reading the emotions of people in photographs. A growing number of scientists believe the discrepancies reflect functional differences in the brains of men and women . . . some misunderstandings between the sexes may have more to do with crossed wiring than cross-purposes.'

Women are also better at verbal tasks. If given two minutes in which to come up with as many synonyms as possible for a series of words, they will, on the whole, score better than men. In both of these tests, however, some individuals will do much better or worse than their sex suggests that they 'ought' to.

Do we, however, make the best of what nature has provided when the time comes to educate our young? Over the last few years, nationwide school exam results have shown an increasing gap between the performances of girls and boys, in the girls' favour. Many more boys than girls leave school without any form of qualification. And amongst those who do pass GCSE and A-Level exams, girls are getting the higher grades. The introduction of course work into the GCSE syllabus appears to favour girls, who tend to be diligent and less rebellious. Boys appear to prefer the one-off competition of the examination hall. These preferences may be due, in part, to differences in the male and female brain, which will be discussed anon. However, since white working-class boys now score more poorly in England and Wales than almost any other racial or sexual grouping, and since highly privileged public schoolboys can be coached and coaxed into achieving astonishingly high marks, the possibility must be considered that there are social forces at work.

Much has been written in the past about the difficulties girls face in mixed classrooms. It has always been assumed that boys tend to speak up more forcefully than girls, and tend to be spoken to more frequently by teachers. If so, this reflects life in society as a whole. In both Britain and America, researchers have found that a woman who speaks as much as a man in a conversation, class or meeting will be thought, by both male and female observers, to have been hectoring and domineering: we are, quite simply, used to men taking the lion's share of conversation.

Recently, however, suggestions have been made that question this view of the classroom. At kindergarten and primary-school level, in which little girls out-perform the boys, the vast majority of teachers are female. Surveys by the now-defunct Inner London Education Authority showed that women teachers consistently praised girls more than boys, and equally consistently criticised the boys' behaviour, often regarding it as a serious problem requiring remedial treatment. In the words of Tony Mooney, a secondary-school headmaster, writing in the *Independent on Sunday*: 'Women teachers find boys too noisy, too aggressive, too boisterous. Unconsciouslyor not, they consistently reinforce and reward more "feminine" behaviour. If all this is true, it is understandable that boys should not be as advanced as girls in the hands of women junior school teachers. There is a direct relationship between a child's academic achievement and a favourable response from the teacher.'

Mooney was first alerted to this possibility by the behaviour of his own son, whose performance and self-confidence at school altered markedly when he was taught by a woman, rather than a man. When the boy's mother asked him why this should be so, he replied, 'Because the men teachers never shout at me as much as the women teachers.'

Research evidence, from an experiment at the University of California, Los Angeles, appeared to support Mooney's anecdotal experience: 'Seventy-two boys and sixty girls at kindergarten ... learned reading with a self-teaching machine. There were no differences between the sexes in their reactions to the mechanical gadgetry. Yet when the girls were tested on their reading progress they scored lower than the boys. Then the children were placed under the normal classroom instruction of women teachers. The children were tested again on the words they had been taught by the teacher. This time the boys' scores were inferior to the girls'.'

Mooney noted that boys' exam results at secondary-school were declining just as the number of women secondary-school teachers was increasing. Boys, however, continued to out-perform girls in scientific and technical subjects where teaching was still dominated by men. The issue here is not just the favouritism that teachers may show to pupils of their own sex, but the instinctive understanding that an adult will enjoy with a child who is going through a process which he or she went through too.

The notion that boys might in some way be disadvantaged was too shocking for at least one reader of Mooney's article. As far as Christine Cosker – a correspondent to the *Independent on Sunday*'s letters page – was concerned, it was partly the fault of the boys themselves. 'If girls achieve higher standards than boys,' she wrote, 'it is not the result of sympathetic female teachers: it is that boys fail to be motivated because of their attitude to women. Boys' early experience is almost entirely one of a society which regards women's traditional roles as trivial, dull and second-rate and dismisses their opinions. If girls have a positive role model in the female teacher, they will do better than boys. But if boys, unencumbered by society's prejudices, valued their female teachers, then their progress would match that of girls.'

It is worth examining some of the prejudices revealed by this letter in some detail, because I suspect that they would be shared by a broad swathe of supposedly progressive opinion.

In the first place, note that she has found it impossible to accept that female teachers could, in any way, be responsible for the situation. It has to be the fault of males and an anti-female social order. Specifically, boys are to be blamed for their own disadvantages.

Secondly, she has misinterpreted the article. Mr Mooney indicated that his son's problem was not that he did not value his teacher, but that she did not value him. He was frightened of her because she shouted at him.

Thirdly, although it is extremely important to primary-school-aged boys not to be seen to act in any way that might be interpreted as cissy or girly, that is not necessarily to say that they regard women's traditional roles as 'trivial, dull and second-rate'. The most traditional role that women have is to be a mother. And the mother of a small boy is still one of the two most important people in his life. In the experience of most 'traditional' housewives I know, it is other, career-minded women who hold them in the greatest contempt. Their children value them above all else.

Finally, observe the double standard applied to girls and boys. Cosker maintains, and few would disagree, that girls benefit from a 'positive role model'. There is, however, no need for boys to be given the same benefit. Instead, they must pull their socks up and change their attitudes. Heaven forbid that they should be given any consideration or compassion. Heaven forbid that the prejudices of the new age should be challenged. If you ever doubted that feminists have taken over from apoplectic old colonels as the great reactionaries of society, just read this letter.

Alternatively, look at the facts. One of the few generally accepted differences between boys and girls is that boys are, across all cultures, much more boisterous and overtly competitive than girls. Boys enjoy games of rough and tumble. They play with guns, real or imaginary. They seek out physical competition, whether through sport or informal bouts of playground warfare. This makes them harder to control than girls, particularly if, as is the case in the majority of state primary schools in this country, they are being taught in an open-plan classroom. Janet Daley, writing in the *Independent*, has observed that, 'Anyone who visits an open-plan infant-school classroom, where the children organise much of their own time, will notice a pattern. Groups of little girls will be absorbed in quite orderly work or play . . . requiring little supervision. A few of the boys will be engrossed in solitary creative or constructive activity. A large number of children will be noisily participating in some loosely directed project which needs guidance and some of those will be boys who are persistently disruptive and out of control.'

Daley ascribes this behaviour to the fact that the neurological development of boys is slower than that of girls, and thus boys are 'physically and mentally unstable for much of their childhood and adolescence'. Are they? Or does Ms Daley share a prejudice – unintended, no doubt – with the boys' teachers, who are trained to define the relative maturity of their charges by their ability to sit quietly and be attentive? By those standards, boys may appear backward, troublesome and even threatening. All that has happened, however, is that we are criticising boys for their failure to be more like girls.

It has for some time been recognised that girls do better in single-sex education, where their particular needs can be catered for exclusively. Having spent ten years in single-sex boarding-school education, I have mixed feelings about its benefits for boys, but I am absolutely certain that there are great social benefits to be had from recognising that boys may need specially tailored treatment to at least as great an extent as their sisters (a point with which Janet Daley concurs).

In the years before puberty, boys are, I suspect, perfectly happy to be left to themselves. At the age of eleven or twelve, I doubt whether I would have been at all pleased to see girls getting in the way of my games of football, or intruding in the serious business of building huts and encampments in the woods behind the school. By my teens, however, I was painfully aware of the distorting effect that an all-male institution was having on my own emotional development and that of my classmates.

Despite that, however, I was taught in a system that was designed to bring the best out of boys, intellectually, creatively and on the sports field. It was certainly a world away from the non-achieving atmosphere that has been prevalent throughout much of English state education over the last twenty years. Of course, the boys with whom I was educated came from privileged backgrounds. But one of the mistakes made by critics of the public-school system is to under-estimate the efficiency, not to say ruthlessness with which its pupils are programmed to perform to the best of their ability. We were constantly tested, constantly ranked and constantly urged to do better. And, on reflection, I suspect that it is better to accept that boys are not, on the whole, docile creatures who wish to live in harmony with one another, but are, instead, highly competitive, physically energetic creatures who hunt in packs.

Some boys will suffer in that sort of environment, and they need to be respected and protected. I can remember all too well what it is like to be on the receiving end of bullying and oppression. But I also know that there is no point in deciding that, since traditional male behaviour is politically unacceptable, boys must somehow be conditioned to behave in ways that are not natural to them. That process leads only to disaster.

Boys whose lives are led without structure and discipline do not find themselves liberated. Instead they become bored, frustrated and maladaptive. They fight. They misbehave and they perform badly, both at school and thereafter. However much it might want boys to change, any society that wants to limit the antisocial behaviour of young men should start by accepting the way they are. Then it should do everything possible to make sure that their energies are directed towards good, rather than evil. When Yoda sat on his rock in *The Empire Strikes Back* and told Luke Skywalker that he had to choose between the dark force and the light, he knew what he was talking about.

Wounded people

There is one educational characteristic about boys which does bear further examination. Once they get to university, the pattern of their examination results is observably different from that of female undergraduates. Crudely put, women receive the bulk of second-class honours degrees, while men get the firsts and the thirds. Why? Taking the thought a stage further, why is it that there are certain fields of academic and intellectual endeavour – typically those concerned with engineering, architecture, mathematics, music and abstract thought, whether scientific or philosophical – in which women are almost entirely absent from the highest ranks? Most educated people could name at least one great female author, but a female composer? Or philosopher? Or architect?

The obvious reason for this disparity is to be found in the social conditions prevalent throughout history. Women were barred from entry into the universities at which scientific research was conducted. Nor would they have been given the opportunity to carry out works of building or engineering, even if they had been trained and even if – in an age before effective birth control – they were not hampered by the demands of pregnancy and motherhood. By contrast, a novel can be written in private. It does not require the support of an academy or institution. It was, in other words, the one field in which women could excel . . . so they did.

Nowadays, women claim to be similarly disadvantaged at university. Arguments for this proposition include the disproportionately stressful effect of examinations upon female students; the confrontational nature of male-dominated academic tutorials; the unwillingness of women to articulate or have confidence in their own opinions; the positive prejudice of examination markers in favour of men; the lack of female role models; and the additional social pressures faced in college by female students.

Yet it is hard to avoid the conclusion that there really is something different about the ways in which men and women like to work that goes deeper than mere conditioning. Certainly, the way we are treated will exaggerate differences, but if similar trends are at work at every stage from kindergarten to PhD and on into the outside world, there must be more to it than that. This is another pattern whose threads run in more than one direction.

Despite the vast and continuing growth in the number of female students as a whole, it is still proving very difficult to attract women into certain academic fields. You find women throughout medicine, genetics, psychology and sociology. They make up the majority of legal students in both Britain and America. But you still do not find them in quantum physics or mathematics to anything like the same extent. So are there inherent reasons why men are so dominant in certain subjects? What does this have to do with their passion for train-spotting? And what has it got to do with Mozart, Jack the Ripper and victims of domestic violence?

The answer may be found in a deeply repressed psychic agony known as the Male Wound. This is a concept whose effect is comparable in psychological terms to that of the Y-chromosome. It gives men some qualities of undeniable strength. But it may also leave them fatally flawed.

The idea of the wound is much in vogue amongst men's movement gurus like Robert Bly, but the most level-headed account of its development is to be found in Dr Liam Hudson and Bernadine Jacot's *The Way Men Think*.

In their view, the wound arises from the fact that, at a very early age – approximately eighteen months – boys make a psychological transition away from the female norm, which echoes the genetic and physical transitions they made as foetuses in the womb. For, in order to establish a sense of the identity as males, they are impelled to move away from their mother, towards a suitable father-figure, who, with any luck, is their biological father as well.

If this transition happens successfully, in a loving family with a stable, well-adjusted father and a caring, but not over-possessive mother, the boy experiences what Dr Hudson describes as 'a dislocation'. He has gained a sense of his male self, but the price is a loss of some of the comfort he derived from his mother. This dislocation, Hudson believes, may act as a motivating force: emotional energy, which might have been spent on the mother, is reassigned to other areas of the boy's life.

The tremendous emotional commitment which boys and men have to abstract ideas, or inanimate objects, or institutions, is an example of this phenomenon in operation. Boys collect stamps and support football teams in a way that most little girls do not. Having learned at an early age that profound feelings towards other people may carry with them a heavy emotional cost, they choose to direct their emotions towards non-threatening targets.

If the wound is little more than a dislocation, this tendency may not be particularly marked, and it may even give males part of their externally directed drive or sense of purpose. But what if it goes wrong? The mother may hold onto the child too long. The father may be absent or dysfunctional in some way, so that the child learns to associate masculinity with violence or alcoholism. The father's image may be tarnished by the mother's hostility or bitterness, after a divorce or breakdown.

The whole process may even prove so painful for the child that he decides that deep emotional attachments to people are simply too painful to be risked. Instead, he sublimates his emotions completely, transferring all his energies away from people and into areas of his life that are more open to control.

Although women are quite capable of possessing immense ambition, few possess the single-minded, almost manic energy that is characteristic of those men who build great fortunes or conjure up towering academic theories. These men – who must, I believe, be regarded as suffering from profound imbalance (how often the biographies of great men reveal massive emotional or familial dysfunction) – are often prepared to take much greater risks than women in order to achieve their ends.

Men are, by and large, the great entrepreneurs and they are also the great bankrupts. As academics, they can be characterised by a desire to stamp their theories upon the world, forcing the evidence to fit, whereas women scientists tend to let themselves listen to the evidence and go where it leads them. So men come up with the most spectacular discoveries, which may turn out, on further examination, to be spectacularly wrong, while the more reticent approach of a woman may lead her, in the longer run, to knowledge that is more secure. (In this context, the development of feminist theory may turn out to be the exception that proves the rule.)

Sexually speaking, the wound's distortions mean that men are much more likely than women to become fetishistic or perverse. Nervous of genuine intimacy, not only do they turn people into sex objects, they also turn objects into sexual beings, be they high-heeled shoes or inflatable dolls. Intellectually, they are often fascinated by abstract concepts, rather than human ones. Some fall in love with mathematics, music or theoretical physics, fields in which relationships between numbers, notes or particles are predictable, beautiful and unable to cause pain.

Hudson and Jacot cite research conducted amongst scientists in the 1950s by the American psychologist Anne Roe and followed up a decade or so later by David McClelland. They noted that the successful physical scientist tended characteristically to be male; to come from a puritanical family background; to avoid personal relations, preferring to work with great single-mindedness; to avoid complex emotions; to prefer music (which is based on rational harmonic patterns) to painting or poetry (which are not); and to develop a strong interest in analytical thought by no later than the age of ten.

Men of extreme genius, including Newton, Descartes, Schopenhauer, Tolstoy, Kierkegaard, Goethe, Ruskin and George Bernard Shaw, share a common desire to retreat from human intimacy in favour of formality and abstraction. They tend, too, to be sexless, since sexual activity, with its threat of engulfment by the woman, is too painful to contemplate. When there is a strong sex drive it is often, as in Beethoven's case, acted upon in as basic a way as possible, so that brief encounters with prostitutes or servants take the place of any deeper, more troublesome relationships. One of the most interesting aspects of real brilliance in abstract thought is that it is not passed on. Newton, Locke, Pascal, Spinoza, Kant, Nietzsche, Wittgenstein . . . you could fill an encyclopaedia of philosophy with the names of men whose children were their ideas, rather than any human offspring. Nor has this tendency been confined to men of such extreme genius. Until 1877, dons at Oxford University were specifically forbidden to marry.

Finally, there are those such as Freud or Skinner, the Harvard behaviourist who believed that all organisms, including humans, could be manipulated by means of systems of punishment and reward. They resolve their difficulties with personal and sexual relationships by attempting to master them by means of their intellect. For them, understanding or, more to the point, organising according to their own theories, is a form of control. In its most extreme form, this need to sublimate sexual fears by means of control leads to that uniquely male creature, the serial sex killer, who transfers his own pain onto his victim, terminally.

In her book *Sexual Personae*, the American academic Camille Paglia makes an observation whose concluding sentence is destined to be one of those quotational clichés, along the lines of Andy Warhol's dictum about fifteen minutes of fame: 'Serial or sex murder, like fetishism, is a perversion of male intelligence. It is a criminal abstraction, masculine in its deranged egotism and orderliness. It is the asocial equivalent of philosophy, mathematics and music. There is no female Mozart because there is no female Jack the Ripper.'

Before one leaps to any conclusions about the implications of the Male Wound for sexual politics, a few caveats are in order. It may be that campaigners who are hoping to increase the proportion of female physicists, architects and engineers are, to some extent, wasting their time. If the characteristics required of them may be described as on the extreme male end of the spectrum, there will never be a high proportion of women, or even of emotionally sensitive men, amongst them. On the other hand, there may be other areas of research – genetics and psychology are two which come to mind – whose human component is attractive to female academics. The key thing is to make sure that no one is excluded from a field just because they do not conform to the sexual norm.

Another vital point is this: the Male Wound may cause what Hudson describes as 'the depressing side of men – the behavioural perversions, the driven promiscuity and the eruptions of violence'. But whatever Camille Paglia may say, men have no monopoly on anti-social behaviour.

In Hudson's words: 'There is an argument that says that women are locked into a relationship with their mothers in a way that men are not, because they haven't taken the step away by identifying with their fathers. That means that all the beneficial elements of that relationship become part of themselves and so do all of the grim bits – all of the rage and anger and frustration and rivalry are carried into the growing girl and become part of her personality.'

Hudson believes that there are 'powerfully perverse elements' in both men and women. However, he notes, 'Men tend to act out, especially aggressively, their perverse needs. Women create perverse situations.'

In interviewing men who had been in relationships which had gone badly wrong, often violently so, I found Hudson's observations being repeatedly borne out. Men from a wide range of backgrounds whose wives had either been abusive, or exceptionally vindictive – over the issue of child custody, for example – repeatedly told me that their wives had intense, highly problematic relationships with their mothers. Some had inherited personality disorders. Others passed on to their partners pain that had been inflicted on them in their childhood. Often, the mothers still exerted enormous influence over their daughters' lives. The wives were bitterly resentful of their mothers' suffocating attention, but were unable to direct their anger towards its actual source. They transferred it instead to their partners.

They did this by means of verbal, psychological and even physical harassment, filling their homes with an atmosphere of anger and tension. This was the 'perverse situation'. The man might be driven to a point at which he was faced with a choice between leaving the relationship or lashing out – the 'perverse act' – but his violence would merely be the physical expression of a hostility that was common to both partners. Marriage guidance counsellors now see some acts of domestic violence as fulfilling a need that is common to both partners. In this scenario, the woman satisfies her need for violence, not by enacting it as a man might do, but by drawing it upon herself.

There are three lessons one can draw. One is that, in Hudson's words, 'Women are different. Sometimes they're different in a complimentary way to men. And sometimes they're just plain different.'

The second is this: that difference may be manifested in practical ways, but it does not mean that women are incapable of violence. They may simply choose different methods. There has never been a female Jack the Ripper, but thirty years before he made his bloody way through the streets of London's East End, Mary Ann Cotton poisoned some fifteen victims, including her husband, her lover and her child, in the mining towns of County Durham.

Finally, if the boy has to travel from the mother to the father, he has to have a father to whom he can travel. Rocketing rates of extramarital births, divorce and deliberately chosen single parenthood are rapidly making the conventional father an endangered species. The net effect of that, in Hudson's view, will be that one can expect to see consequent increases in rates of delinquency and behavioural disorders amongst young men. This is by no means the only evidence that we will uncover of the relationship between paternity – or its absence – and delinquency, but this is as good a time as any to set that particular ball rolling. It has a long way to go.

No comprendo

At one point in our conversation, Dr Liam Hudson observed that, 'One would like to feel that there are two clear lines of argument: (i) what men get up to, and (ii) what women get up to. But there are powerfully perverse elements in both, and the scenarios are mutually incomprehensible. Some sort of deal is done, but the rewards and the costs are mutually inscrutable. Even if you live with someone for a long time, they're still slightly inscrutable.'

We had been talking about the psychological background to date-rape and the possible causes of a situation in which both parties sincerely believed their own stories. In other words, the woman was certain that she had been raped, while the man truly thought that she had consented. This is an issue that will be gone into at much greater length in Chapter Seven, but what Hudson said about it was relevant to many of the disputes between the sexes.

Describing a hypothetical couple, he said, 'Both might have had romantic and pragmatic systems of need at work, but they were in some way differently deployed. The ingredients may be alike, but the brew is different. It's a bit like the relationship between two languages – an act of translation has to take place. You could translate the boy's feelings into the girl's feelings and elements would be alike, but often you would be stuck for a translation.'

The linguistic analogy is apt, because different languages do more than substitute one word for another – they embody entirely different systems of thought. English, for example, may be distantly related to Italian, since they both share a common ancestor in Latin. Yet the character of the two languages could hardly be less similar. Here is a translation, printed in *The Times*, of the introduction to an Italian comic book, written by the Marchesa Marina Ripa di Meana, wife of the European Community's environment commissioner: 'Only recently I learned that comics represent the dimension of adventure for me, the true possibility of continuous hyperbole . . . I felt exactly like a comic character: dilettante, exhibitionist, excessive, making continuous incursions into the sacred gardens of the arts, where severe priests see me as smoke in their eyes.'

I am quite certain that the original passage made perfect sense to any Italian reader. I am also sure that every word in it has been accurately transferred from Italian into English. The result, however, is gibberish. Exactly the same process is present in the gulf between men and women.

In her best-selling book, *You Just Don't Understand: Women And Men in Conversation*, the American academic Deborah Tannen takes a close look at the differences in the way that the two sexes communicate and the difficulties that this may cause. It is a scrupulous, even-handed and admirable book. In no way would I wish to describe it as deliberately biased or distorted. But, reading the book as a man, my reaction was, 'But Professor Tannen ... you just don't understand.'

Her basic point, which is echoed by other researchers such as Michael Argyle, is that female-to-female communication is essentially affiliative, whereas male-to-male communication is essentially competitive. So when two girls, or women, talk, they are seeking intimacy and inclusion. They will look one another in the eye. The non-speaker will nod in agreement. Their bodies will be aligned with one another. And they will swap experiences as a means of establishing empathy. That is not to say that women do not compete, or fight, or have intense rivalries, but they do so in ways which do not overtly threaten that sense of intimacy – hence the catty remark disguised as a compliment, or the looks which flash between one woman and another.

Men, however, learn from boyhood that the subtext of all their conversations is a competition for status and control. Unless they are very close to one another, or very secure in their hierarchical relationship, they do not look one another in the eye, since such an invasion of the other person's space might be seen as a challenge or threat. They sit with their bodies at angles to one another. They do not reinforce. And their conflicts are overt and clearly displayed.

This means that, for example, men will frequently miss 90 per cent of the communication that goes on between women, or even between women and men. A couple return from a dinner party. The wife says, 'Did you see the way that Margaret was looking at Emma? She was furious with Jack. He could hardly keep his eyes off Emma's body all night.' And the husband replies, 'Really? They seemed all right to me.'

To be fair, this is not necessarily men's fault. The English journalist and author Celia Brayfield went on assignment for the *Mail On Sunday*'s *YOU* magazine, armed with a false beard and a man's suit, to see life from the other side. Sitting in a London cocktail bar, 'I discovered why men always fall for blatantly obvious girls. They don't notice the others. From the receiving end girls put out such extraordinarily low-key signals to a man they want to know that most of the time the fella probably never notices. A come-hither glance is very hard to spot, even if you know exactly what you are looking for ... The kind of behaviour which feels outrageously bold and provocative to a girl still looks faint and covert to the man whose attention she is trying to attract.'

Tannen gives several examples of the confusion that our different patterns of communication can cause. For example, if a woman is talking to a friend who is going through hard times, she may very well say, 'I know just how you feel. I had exactly the same thing happen to me once . . .' and then start an anecdote. She is thereby endorsing her friend's experience and empathising with it. As a consequence, says Tannen, when a woman is faced with a man who is down in the dumps, she may employ the same tactics, only to be rebuffed, whereupon she feels hurt and rejected. What she does not know, however, is that the man has interpreted her anecdote as a form of challenge. He does not hear, 'I am sharing your sorrow.' Instead, attuned as he is to competition, he hears, 'My story is much more powerful than yours.' The result is mutual incomprehension and anger.

Looked at in reverse, a man may greet a friend's depression with a brisk, 'Never mind,' followed by a joke or story about an altogether different subject. To a woman, that sounds like callous indifference. To a man, it is an attempt to lift his friend out of depression by reminding him of the positive side of life. Again, the consequence is confusion.

Elsewhere, Professor Tannen describes her own experiences as a lecturer. When she speaks before students, she says, women's questions tend to be supportive, asking for clarification or personal explanations, but not challenging her hypothesis. Men's, on the other hand, are challenging, demanding that she justify her ideas. 'The women's questions seemed charming to me, but the men's seemed cheeky,' she remarks.

Tannen then reports that, in conversation with her husband and other men, they saw the men's questions as a form of respect. By being tough they were taking her seriously. But, concludes Tannen, 'I liked the women's questions better: I felt they reinforced my authority. I didn't even mind the intrusive one about my marriage, which allowed me to be wry and amusing in response . . . I doubt whether I am unusual among women in seeing challenges as somewhat more real than ritual, and to take them personally as attempts to undercut my authority rather than to bolster it by "grappling" with me.'

It may be that Tannen is making an honest attempt to give a personal example of the confusions that can arise between the sexes. But it is hard, when reading the whole section from which the extracts here have been taken, to avoid the conclusion that she feels that there is something fundamentally wrong, or unpleasant, about the male approach. I suspect, however, that she is right when she says that her feelings would be echoed by many women, and the implications of that fact go to the heart of many of the workplace and political quarrels between the sexes. More than that: she has hit upon a fundamental distinction between the way in which the sexes view the world and their place in it.

Professor Tannen believes that, having achieved authority, she deserves automatic respect. Well, up to a point, she's right. But in a democracy, authority must always justify itself, and the way that it does so is by proving its right to power on the basis of achievement. We continue to vote for governments because their policies stand up to time and interrogation. We should continue to respect professors on exactly the same basis.

One might ask how much the cause of academic understanding is advanced by cosily supportive questioning and mumsy gossip about married life. I am pleased that Professor Tannen should be 'wry and amusing', but I am surprised that she should feel so outraged by questions such as, 'Doesn't much of the material in your book fall more easily into the realm of rhetoric and communication than linguistics?'

That doesn't sound particularly offensive to me. On the contrary, the student might well have thought that he was helping understanding to develop by moving the debate forward. One of the most enjoyable elements of speaking before university audiences is precisely the fact that carefully nurtured ideas are going to be challenged by bright, youthful minds intent on tearing them apart. It is a form of conflict, but one from which the supposedly senior partner should emerge invigorated. Professor Tannen's desire for the quiet life seems to me to be a worrying one, since it leads inexorably to Camille Paglia's vision of placid women living in grass huts, unwilling to face up to the challenge of working in stone.

This is a typically male response. I see competition and challenge as part of the natural order of things. And, if one looks back through human history, and across at other species, it is hard to avoid the conclusion that this is a universal male experience. The leader of a political party, the head of a tribe and the dominant male in a pack of chimpanzees all share the knowledge that their leadership is always under threat from below. Sooner or later, a younger male will take their place. The king must die.

The archetype of female power, however, is very different. The matriarch can never be deposed, since her authority derives from the fact that she has given birth, an event that cannot be undone. Every father will, sooner or later, be eclipsed by his son, if only over a game of tennis, or a round of golf. But mother will always be mother, and neither her sons nor her daughters can ever overthrow her in quite the same way. Women, therefore, do not expect their authority to be under threat in the way that is automatic for men. Tannen felt that her male students' attitudes were inappropriate in part, I would suggest, because they were so unexpected.

Given this paradigm, daughters are not brought up in the expectation that they will have to fight and compete for the things they want. Even now, they are still raised by parents who are much more gentle to them than they are to male offspring. They are not given the training of casual brutality and emotional suppression that are the lot of most young boys. When they grow up, however, young women have to go to work in professions which are still run along male lines. They encounter the challenge-driven systems of masculine culture. Cocooned in a communication system whose values are so different, and inclined to perceive intellectual attacks as personal affronts, is it any wonder that some women are ready to see themselves as victims of harassment and discrimination? Equally, however unpleasant it may be, we should hardly be surprised if men treat women with crudeness. That, after all, is how they have been trained to treat each other.

There is one final observation I would make about Professor Tannen's remarks, which is that her picture of docile, helpful female students, ever eager to support their elders, turns a blind eye to the manner in which feminism itself was propagated on the campuses of the Western world. The challenge which successive generations of young feminists have made to the established, patriarchal authorities is like a large-scale version of the student who challenges his or her professor.

This process has had a massive impact upon the way that people think, and for that it deserves applause. But here's the rub: feminist orthodoxy has since become as touchy as Professor Tannen. It is no more happy to have its authority challenged than she is. Men are constantly being told to express their feelings, but woe betide them if those feelings do not fall within the politically acceptable norm. The result is that men and, for that matter, many women, feel themselves to be excluded from the debate, and little real progress is made towards either progress or a common ground. Still, who knows . . . maybe we men are simply speaking the wrong language. Perhaps the professor is right, after all. Perhaps we just don't understand.

The brain machine

It would be nice to think that the two sexes could become, as it were, bilingual. There is a lot to be gained for both sides from making the attempt to see the other point of view. But there may be biochemical roots to this particular problem which render it fundamentally insoluble.

It has recently been suggested that, neurologically, women link the two sides of their brains more effectively than do men. It is thought that the corpus callosum – the bundle of nerves that links the left and right halves, much like a cable links the units of a hi-fi – may be as much as 23 per cent thicker in women than men. As a result, women may be able to 'access' much more of their brain at any one time, bringing a wider range of intellectual and emotional faculties to bear on a problem. This might account for feminine intuition and also for the traditional female trait of adding an emotional element to problems which men believe are purely rational.

This effect is reinforced by small-scale differences within the cortex of male and female brains. The brain works on the basis of excitation and inhibition. You need to excite nerves and muscles to make them work, but you need to inhibit that activity in order to control the work that they do. After all, we want our arms and legs to move, but only when we tell them to.

The inhibition is performed by Gamma Amino-Butyric Acid receptors, otherwise known as GABA-urgic cells. They filter and inhibit brain activity, eliminating extraneous 'noise' in order to concentrate the required 'signal'. Men have a higher density of GABA-urgic cells than do women, so their brains are thereby more inhibited. One of the effects of this may be that the fabled inability of men to get in touch with their emotions arises not from their conditioning, but from their brain chemistry. The brain filters out emotional noise so as to concentrate on the intellectual signal.

Of course, this can be greatly exaggerated by the way in which a boy is brought up, and one would not want to encourage the idea that men are inevitably devoid of emotions. The current obsession with getting men in touch with their feelings, however, may not be a desirable form of progress so much as another example of the way in which an increasingly feminised society makes demands upon men so as to make them more like women.

Even allowing for their brain chemistry, men's real problem is not an insufficiency of feeling. Most men feel quite enough as it is. Their problem is that they can't express themselves. Again, this may have less to do with inability than with prohibition. Men are convinced that if they reveal their fears or weaknesses, they will be perceived as unmasculine. The cure for much of the male malaise lies in letting men be the people that they know they are, not the people they think they are supposed to be. They don't need improving. They need freedom.

In any case, the current idea that women are superior to men as a result of their greater emotional sensitivity is less an objective judgement than a reflection of social fashion. If you value male qualities, then you will see men as superior. If you value female ones, the situation is reversed. Neither judgement is valid. In *My Fair Lady*, Professor Higgins asks, 'Why can't a woman be more like a man?' Nowadays, Higgins wears a skirt. Now she wonders why men can't be more like women. One question is as foolish as the other.

One way of looking at the male and female brains might be to imagine that they are two different types of computer – an IBM and a Macintosh, for example. Overall, they perform roughly similar functions, but they do so in different ways and each has particular strengths and weaknesses. The basic principles that govern them are the same. The actual wiring, however, is different. Nor can they read one another's software without a great deal of trouble.

The only trouble with this analogy is that one cannot update and improve the human brain quite as easily as one can a computer. Man has been around for a long time. The earliest primates appeared about 70 million years ago. Remains found near Salonika in Greece indicate that hominoids, which may be the link between men and apes, were present 10 million years ago. The earliest tools yet found – simple, sharpened stones – are some 2.5 million years old. And the oldest known example of Homo erectus, the ancestor of Homo sapiens, found near Lake Turkana, Kenya, by Kamoya Kimeu in 1985, is thought to be about 1.6 million years old. Brain-wise, not a lot has happened since then.

We are investigating the Big Bang and creating artificial genes using brains that were designed for simple tasks of hunting and gathering. Men are characterised by powers of high concentration, focusing on a particular task for a limited period, because that is the kind of ability required by the successful hunter. Women are characterised by emotional sensitivity, less intense concentration, but greater powers of mental endurance over time, because that is what a mother needs if she is to perceive and tend to her child's needs. In modern terms, men make better fighter pilots (intense, highly concentrated activity), but women make better radar operators (less intensive diligence over a longer term).

Men are able to analyse three-dimensional objects moving in space, because that is what a huntsman has to do with his target. Women are able to recall the arrangement of objects because that is what a gatherer, searching the ground for edible plants, needs to be able to remember from one harvesting trip to another. Modern men find it easier than women to drive a car through a narrow opening; but, unlike women, they can never remember where anything in the house is kept.

These differences suggest a biochemical explanation for one of the most pervasive causes of misunderstanding between men and women. From the male point of view, women seem to require a phenomenal amount of attention. I can remember, when I first went out with girls, being amazed by the amount of constant communication they seemed to expect. My male friends didn't behave like that. You could do something with a bloke – whether it was building a model aeroplane or going off to a cricket match – but he didn't expect you to talk to him all the time.

I'm sure my girlfriends were equally baffled. They, like most other women, would be infuriated by the male habit of disappearing behind a newspaper or sitting silently in front of the television. They wanted more active companionship.

This social pattern fits exactly into the biological pattern described a little earlier. Men, being built for short bursts of high concentration, seem, in women's eyes, to alternate between sexual frenzy and indifference. Women, being built for long-term, low-intensity activity, seem, in men's eyes, to want too much chatting and cuddling, and not enough basic sex.

I am both simplifying and exaggerating. Everything that one says about women applies to some men, and vice versa. And all of us contain individual mixtures of male and female characteristics. Just to take my final point, many sex therapists point out that their biggest problem these days is that men seem unwilling to have as much sex as their female partners require. But perhaps that supports my general thesis. Maybe if the therapists spent less time making men behave unnaturally by getting in touch with their feelings, they might start behaving a bit more like men again, instead of spending all their time moaning and groaning . . . like a bunch of old women.

Artifice and initiation

The picture that has been emerging of men to this point is by no means entirely positive. For every advantage which they appear to possess – advantages which are themselves open to considerable debate – there is an evident disadvantage. And the very fact that scientists cannot come up with a convincing reason for the existence of the male sex in the first place suggests that there is, at the very heart of man's existence, a fundamental insecurity.

My mother always used to say that a woman knew *that* she was female, and *why* she was female, every time she had a period. It was put to me another way at a men's group I attended, when one of the men remarked that women were the trunk of the tree of life, whereas men were just the branches. By this he meant that there was an unbroken flow of life through the female sex as one generation gave birth to another. Men, on the other hand, were left on the side. They served a function, but they weren't the main event.

This observation may help to explain one all-pervasive aspect of being male, which is that sense of being slightly cut off, or alienated, from the rest of the world. This feeling is, I am sure, explained in part by the sense of prohibition referred to earlier. Men cannot be themselves for fear of ridicule or even emasculation, so they put up a barrier between themselves and the outside world. Once again, the problem is not that they do not have feelings, but that they repress and deny the feelings they possess.

The poet John Donne may have written, 'No man is an island, entire of itself,' but sometimes it can seem that he is. In the words of the American writer Don Hanlon Johnson, 'Alone, we ache for contact. That ache, we now know from various medical studies, is a major factor in male patterns of illness, addiction and death. Even in groups working, hunting, drinking, or playing cards, we men often feel alone. We talk a lot, but from a distance. With only a handful of men do I experience the presence of eyes, transparency of facial expression and punctuating touch that show that we are truly listening to each other.'

My personal belief is that men do not need to imitate female speech patterns in order to free themselves. As anyone who attends a men's group soon discovers, just saying what's really on your mind, as a man, will do the trick. But, in general, Hanlon is surely right. Men are engulfed in a sea of uncertainties. They cannot afford to let their guard drop with one another for fear of compromising their continual need to define and prove their masculinity. The most obvious example of this can be found in the sex act itself. The man has to display his potency, visibly and tangibly, in a way that has no parallel for a woman. 'Getting it up' is the absolute *sine qua non*, and an inability to perform that feat strikes at the heart of a man's sense of being male.

His performance anxiety is fully justified, to judge by a two-part feature entitled 'What Women Want', published by the American edition of *GQ* magazine in October and November 1987. The piece was a transcript of a ten-hour talkathon in a Manhattan hotel room, conducted by a sex therapist, Stephani Cook, and six women aged 25–33, five of whom were single or divorced.

At one point, Cook asked her panel, 'What happens if the guy has everything else going for him but is temporarily lacking an erection?'

To this, answers included:

It makes me feel unwanted and so I lose my desire for him.

Good luck and good-bye. That's his job and he's failed.

I would have to regard any erectile failure as crucial. It would be very important to do something about it.

If a man wasn't consistently potent, I'd think he was pulling something on a woman, and that's not fair.

Once a man has successfully penetrated a woman, he faces a further uncertainty. A mother needs no reminding that she has given birth and her offspring are unquestionably her own. But how can a father be sure of his paternity? Nowadays, DNA tests can be conducted, but until recently, artificial codes of naming and inheritance had to be established to enshrine a succession from father to child that could equate with the natural descent from the mother.

Men have constantly to create, by the force of their own will, what is naturally self-evident in women. Femininity is automatic, but masculinity is a concept which requires active definition. Nowhere is this more clear than in the initiation rites with which male societies, from jungle tribes to college fraternities, test and greet their new members.

Again, the comparison with women holds true. Girls pass into womanhood by the simple act of menstruating: the process may be a mysterious one and surrounded by mythology and taboo, but the evidence is clear to see. For males, however, the transition from boy to man is not a matter of growing pubic hairs or acquiring the ability to ejaculate. Instead, it has always been marked by a series of artificial, ritual experiences. These mostly attempt to confirm the boy's departure from the soft, over-sensitive world of women, into the hard, fearless, active world of men.

As if to prove that an obsession with the phallus is common to men everywhere, many of these rituals involve circumcision, a practice made all the more agonising by the fact that this is physically, as well as psychologically, the most sensitive part of the male anatomy. Coming-of-age ceremonies often also include elements of separation, isolation, starvation, pain and, thereafter, learning. As any good torturer will tell you, starvation, solitude and sleep-deprivation are all aids to extracting information, or replacing it with ideas you wish to impress upon your subject. In the course of initiation, boys learn the tribal lore that will enable them to become fully – even if artificially – male.

A few examples follow of the ways in which young males around the world are expected to prove their manhood. Men may wish to cross their legs at this point.

The Gisu, from Uganda, expect young men aged in their teens or early twenties to stand perfectly still while their foreskin is cut and the flesh peeled away. This proves that they can conquer pain and fear through inner strength and it gives them the status of *basani* – men – as opposed to *basinde* – boys – a term which is also applied to all members, as it were, of uncircumcised tribes.

In the Sudan, certain tribes cut concentric circles around the shaved heads of their young men. Once again, no sign of pain may be shown. The resulting scars are a sign of the adult male.

The Iban of Borneo take their young men away into the forest, where their teeth are blackened and holes drilled through them. Brass plugs are inserted into the holes and the teeth are filed down to sharp points. The resulting piece of cosmetic dentistry is regarded as the very height of fashion and beauty.

It is, however, to the Aborigines of Australia that one must look for the most fully developed use of agony as a fire in which the male steel is forged. Once village elders have determined that a boy has reached an appropriate level of maturity, he will be taken away from the village, to the accompaniment of the wailing of tribal women, who physically resist his removal. His teeth or penis will then be mutilated in ways similar to those described above, ways which reach a peak of sadistic sophistication amongst the Mardujara Aborigines.

Their initiates go through a five-star process which begins with the initiate (who is already fasting) eating a dish of nettles cooked in bamboo with pork fat. This unappealing recipe causes a painful stinging in the throat, accompanied by swelling. Two days later, a nose-bleed is induced by hammering sharp pegs into the nostrils with a mallet. Small wedges of flesh are then cut from around the tip of the penis, producing deep lacerations which penetrate the urethra. The penis is then beaten, repeatedly, with the handle of the circumcision knife. Finally, the penis is rubbed vigorously with salt and nettles.

This mutilation represents the killing off of the Aborigine's old life, after which he is ready to enter his new existence. He is then taught his tribal lore for a period of six to eight weeks, whereupon he is ready to return, as if from death, to his village, where he is treated with the respect owed to a man who has displayed both his courage and commitment to his tribe.

Before one mocks these apparently primitive and outlandish customs, it is worth considering the degree to which they mirror our own experience. After all, Christianity is based upon a story of suffering, followed by resurrection, redemption and ascent into a better life that is an uncanny parallel of the narrative enacted in almost all ritual initiations. And, on a far less elevated plane, boys of all sorts are put through tests by their peers to confirm their right to the status of full group member.

Wherever you find groups of men, be they sports teams, motorbike gangs, college fraternities or army regiments, there you will find rituals whose purpose is to solidify the unit and distinguish its members from outsiders. American college fraternities greet initiates with alcoholic binges; tarring and feathering; beating with ceremonial paddles. In the British Army, the Coldstream Guards once blow-torched a new recruit's testicles.

At Eton College, Britain's most famous public school, boys carry out much of the disciplinary action of the school via a series of self-electing bodies. Every house has a group of junior prefects, known as Debate, and above them a senior group called the Library. The school as a whole is governed on a day-to-day basis by the Eton Society, or Pop, whose members wear special braided coats, coloured waistcoats and sponge-bag checked trousers. In each case, the members of the group elect new members and initiate them into the ranks by means of well-planned acts of ritual humiliation.

When I attended Eton in the 1970s, boys had their pubic hair sprayed silver, were thrown into hot baths or stripped naked and smeared with potions whose recipes do not bear repetition in public. Over the next few decades, these boys will go on to become Cabinet ministers, generals, bishops, bankers and pillars of the establishment in quantities unmatched by any other school in the country. Perhaps the initiation is more effective than may at first appear. Or perhaps our establishment is even more perverted than has ever been imagined.

Cynics might add that the ritual buggery practised amongst certain New Guinea tribes has traditionally found favour within the English boarding school system – a system which also encouraged the ability of boys to stay silent whilst being beaten with canes. And they might also be interested to know that the same island is home to tribes whose initiations consist of the eating of particularly potent vegetable curries. Anyone familiar with the typical British high street on a Friday night will be aware that this test of manhood is equally prevalent on this island.

Even in groups that appear to be anarchic, clear patterns of ritual will exist, which reinforce the hidden structure and hierarchy of the group. Young boys going to football matches, for example, will often devote more time to watching older supporters than the game itself. They learn the rules of their 'firm' or 'posse', along with their chants, gestures and songs. Within the crowd, there are clearly defined power positions, such as chant leader, or aggression leader. Only once they have the support and confidence of their tribe are individuals allowed to initiate chants or acts of aggression against rival supporters.

Masculinity has to be confirmed by outside approval, and men will go to great lengths to construct social groupings which give them a *raison d'être*. Men have exploited their advantages – physical strength; their pack instincts; their ability to exclude emotion and even humanity from their considerations and, most significantly of all, the fact that they do not spend any time either being pregnant or nursing – to establish patriarchal structures in which they feel safe from the threat of women, whose inherent powers remain much stronger and more mysterious than their own. Men, in other words, have constructed a world which justifies their own existence.

Paying the price

The price men pay for their power is a heavy one. Faced with the need to stay within the boundaries of masculinity and to preserve the patriarchal status quo, little boys are brought up to conform to rigid guidelines of acceptable masculinity. A simple illustration of this occurred to me when my little daughter first started to watch Walt Disney videos. Entranced by *Peter Pan* and *Robin Hood*, she took to making herself jaunty caps, with paper feathers stuck in the rim, arming herself with a sword made out of a drumstick, and setting off to fight baddies (most notably her little sister). Then a craze for Batman swept through her kindergarten, so she had to have her black cape and mask and yellow belt.

The sight of a little girl wandering round in a Batman outfit is a profoundly endearing one. And given the extreme care with which, at the age of four, she styles her hair and chooses her dresses in the morning, not to mention her professed intention of marrying her favourite little boyfriend, I have no doubt at all about her essential femininity. But imagine that I had a son who dressed up as Maid Marian, Wendy or Catwoman – what would I think then? Here I am, a child of the glittering, glam-rock 1970s, a teenage Bowie fan whose rebellion took the form of shocking my elders with mascara rather than motorbikes, but I'd still be worried if my little boy started bending his gender too avidly. For all that I know the harm that it does, I'd still want the poor little chap to be a man.

The truth is that masculinity can't take the strain. It is so fragile and so delicately balanced that it cannot withstand the shock of non-conformity. A modern woman can, like my little daughters, play any number of roles in her everyday life. Her persona is as flexible as her wardrobe. But you do not have to venture far from the beaten path of masculinity before becoming trapped in the thickets of what society sees as effeminacy or perversion. Men have to keep any internal deviations from the straight and narrow locked up within their psyches. It is no surprise that so many men, unable to express themselves in normal circumstances, turn instead to deviancy and perversion. Countless broken lives, and careers cut short by scandal, testify to the damage that is done as a result.

A man has freedoms that a woman does not have. He can walk into a pub or a hotel dining room without being ogled or propositioned. He can go out alone at night without the fear that dogs a woman who walks alone down a city street (even if he is, if statistics are to be believed, in far greater danger of physical assault). But he lacks one vital freedom. He cannot be himself.

I do not think it is possible to exaggerate the degree to which male behaviour is motivated by the fear of other people's disapproval or contempt. All over the world, there are millions of men acting in overtly macho ways in order to demonstrate a form of masculinity which they personally find alien and even repugnant. Yet not one of them dare let down his guard for fear of losing face, even though the person whose scorn he dreads probably, if he did but know it, feels exactly the same as he does.

In researching this book I interviewed a transsexual called Diana, who had been a designer of weapons systems for British Aerospace. During the Gulf War she said that she had found herself being chatted up in pubs or wine bars by men who would wax technical about military hardware and strategy, unaware that the smiling blonde opposite had once been one of the men who had built the missiles and bombs in the first place.

The corporate culture in which she used to work was an extremely masculine one. Backs were slapped, fists were smashed onto tables and voices were raised in anger. This was unquestionably a man's world. So when she revealed that she was having a sex change, she prepared herself for a storm of insults and contempt. Instead, to her amazement, she was approached in private by a number of her colleagues who confessed that they had always felt completely unnatural behaving in the way they did, but believed that they dared not do any different for fear of compromising their masculinity. In a way, she said, they envied her for her courage in freeing herself from the burden of unbearable social conventions.

Sometimes, men can use praiseworthy activities as a smoke screen for emotions which might otherwise be disallowed. Sport, for example, is a vital component of the mythology of masculinity. Irrespective of the efforts of female athletes, sport simply does not play as important a role in female life as it does in male. It is, if you like, the mirror image of fashion. All men wear clothes, but very few of them read *Vogue*. Many women take exercise, but very few could give a damn about the contents of the sports pages.

Every winter, the men of America's two finest football teams run out onto the pitch of whichever stadium has been chosen for the Superbowl, cheered on as they go by pom-pom-waving cheerleaders. The men wear tight pants and huge shoulder pads which exaggerate their physiques to an almost comic degree. The women wear leotards, lipstick and sequins. This is the single event which, more than any other, unites the most powerful nation on earth, and it is sex-role-stereotyped to the nth degree.

At its worst, sport exemplifies the least appealing aspects of men in general and its host culture in particular. American football is materialistic, hyper-aggressive, territorial and competitive to the point of inflicting permanent physical harm on almost everyone who plays it professionally or even in college. But it is also noble, creative, graceful and dignified.

Sport, any sport, deals with the issues that are at the heart of a man's being. A true sportsman, be he golfer, football player, grand prix driver or jockey, works to make the best of what he has got, fighting against the ravages of nature, time and his fellow men. He fights to impose his will on his surroundings. He must be as gracious in victory as in defeat (the tabloid gutter press are as damning as any public school headmaster about misbehaviour on the part of stars). The writer Colin Welland, giving a radio obituary of a rugby league hero of his youth, observed that no matter how old a man gets, he always feels younger than the men he sees on the sportsfield: their genius makes him look with the eyes of a boy once again.

Sport may be, as others have observed, a pursuit as trivial as it is magnificent, but it allows men to free their emotions. The whole world saw Paul Gascoigne break down in tears during the 1990 World Cup semi-final, but no one thought him any less a man. Some newspaper columnists dived in to announce the arrival of the New Man in sport, but a man more unreconstructed than Gazza it would be hard to imagine. On the contrary, the incident illustrated one of sport's most primitive functions. Here was a young man who came from a community in which extreme, self-conscious masculinity is the sole defence left against forces of technological and social change that are making the traditional unskilled working man as redundant as the carthorse. Being 'hard' is everything. Yet within sport he could express creativity, sadness, joy, loss, even tears . . . and still remain a man.

In the world from which Gazza emerged, lads walk around Tyneside bars on freezing nights in February dressed in sleeveless shirts. In that world, no man would dare cry if he lost his job, or his wife, or his kids. But if his football club was relegated, he would weep buckets and everyone would understand. Sport justifies his tears. Sport is masculine, therefore anything connected with it is masculine too. So men who would sneer at poetry will go into raptures about a move on the football pitch.

Many people like to sneer at sport and men's passion for it. They feel that it is indicative of men's essential childishness that they should care so deeply for something so unimportant. I would argue against this on both counts. In the first place, the expressive powers of sportsmen (and women) at their best rival anything that an actor or dancer could come up with. They produce a magic that expresses the very best that a human being can be. But even as the powers fade, the terrible decline of Muhammad Ali, or the stubborn refusal of Jimmy Connors to give in to the passing years, expresses a struggle against time which all of us must share. More than that, however, sport does not illustrate the comedy of man's immaturity. It illustrates the tragedy of his imprisonment. We are trapped by the demands of masculinity. Sport offers the illusion, at least, of escape.

For some, the urge to flee from the prison of their gender becomes overwhelming. Those who have made the journey from one sex to another tend to tell similar travellers' tales. Stephanie-Anne Lloyd began life as a boy called Keith. By his mid-thirties, Keith was a balding man in a suit. He worked as an accountant, was married and had two children. But he was convinced that there was something profoundly wrong with his life. He began to suffer from near-total sexual impotence. Other men seemed like aliens, rather than members of the same sex.

Eventually, he was diagnosed as a transsexual – one of those people whose physical form is at odds with the gender to which they feel they actually belong. Following a sex-change operation, dull, mousy Keith became the flamboyant Stephanie-Anne. The suits and bare scalp made way for dresses and luxuriant locks. Strapped for cash, she was, for a while, a prostitute, servicing at least one Tory Cabinet minister as a regular client (he liked, she said, to be spanked), before founding her own business, Transformations, which caters to the needs of male transvestites.

Stephanie and Keith may have been the same person underneath, but they were treated very differently. As a nondescript but efficient executive, Keith was used to being taken seriously at business meetings. But in the commercial world of the north of England, Stephanie was looked on as an accessory rather than a protagonist: 'I went to a meeting when I first formed Transformations. I went with a man and we walked in and they immediately started talking to him, thinking that he was in charge. They automatically assumed that I was his secretary or assistant because I was female. I found it quite amusing, but I can understand women getting very, very cross about that.'

On the other hand, Stephanie says, 'Society does put a lot of pressure on the male species from all sorts of different points of view. Life is hard for men. Career-wise, work-wise, it may be much easier in most professions for a man. But on an emotional level, life is much, much richer for a woman. Women can let down barriers and can get much closer to people. Men have to maintain barriers. As a man, you can't go and cry on a best friend's shoulder when things go wrong. The first thing he'd do is edge away if you touch him.'

People may patronise women, but they certainly treat them with greater kindness and consideration. Such, at least, was the experience of a young man named Graham Flander, whom I interviewed some years ago for the *Guardian*. He worked as a waitress, complete with fluffy pink tutu and white fishnet stockings, at the Hippodrome nightclub in London.

During the day Graham lived as a man, but once he had got to work and put on his costume, wig and make-up, he was, quite simply, one of the girls. He shared a changing room with the other waitresses, who had come to look upon him as one of their own. Out on the floor of the club, after all, he received exactly the same treatment that they did. 'People see my long hair and my outfit and assume that I'm female. I get chatted up an awful lot. If I speak, they know that I'm a man, but you can get away with just smiling and laughing. If men see a blonde, they don't expect any intelligence.

'You start thinking of men as a separate sex and treating them as women do. You learn when to laugh, when not to. You have to be more modest if you're a girl. You tend to let men hold the conversation and you just return it. You give opinions, but you don't hold them too strongly – you tend to take second place to a degree.'

Graham also had to put up with the cruder side of male behaviour. 'A guy walked past me one time and he slapped my arse really hard. I asked him to stop and he did it again. It gets to the point where it's sadistic and not done for fun.

'But I don't want to sound as though I hate men because you also get treated nicer if you're a girl. If you're a man they slap you on the back and say, "'Allo, mate." But if you're a girl they're more gentle and give you compliments. Men will tell me I look sexy or gorgeous. If I look like a girl I like it, but I'd hate it if I was dressed normally.'

Towards the end of her book *Conundrum*, Jan Morris describes the ways in which her life has altered as a result of her change of sex. It is possible that some of her readers might find her an unreliable witness. How, they might ask, can anyone who was brought up as a man and who has never, for example, had a period, truly understand what it means to be female? Others might say that Ms Morris, along with all other transsexuals, is merely conforming to a fantasy of femininity – one to which she has chosen to aspire – rather than its reality. They might protest that there is, therefore, a sort of sexism about her, or their, opinions. Nevertheless, there is a lot to be said for first-hand experience: the observations of one sensitive human being may be worth more than all the theoretical textbooks in the world.

Morris remarks that the more she was treated as a woman, the more woman she became. She found herself more and more in female company and she discovered that she preferred women's conversation and the sense it gave of belonging to a school of thought that was quite distinct from male-dominated society. As a man, Morris had enjoyed all the privileges of upper-middle-class male life. James was a public schoolboy, who served as an officer in the 9th Queen's Royal Lancers, before going up to Oxford and then becoming a correspondent for *The Times*. He was a member of the Travellers' Club. Had his personal identity allowed it, a glittering establishment career awaited him. As a woman, however, Jan was treated very differently. Men assumed that she was their inferior. They expected her to be less well-informed than they were and they presumed that she would wish to remain quiet while they took the lion's share of conversation. By and large, like so many women before her, she found it simplest to oblige them.

In this respect – what she calls 'the subtle subjugation of women' – the experience of Jan Morris, moving in the smart, intellectual circles of London and Oxford, was no different to that of Graham Flander, teetering through the Hippodrome in his pink tutu. And, like Graham, Jan discovered that there were compensations. People were more courteous to her than they had been to James. They treated her more kindly and with greater tolerance. In a sentence whose relevance will become ever more evident as this book progresses, Jan Morris remarks of womankind, 'Her frailty is her strength, her inferiority is her privilege.'

Tellingly, Morris found that the differences were more than merely social. She found that the physical changes in her had dramatic effects.

The loss of her penis and the softening of her body made her, she says, more passive and more willing to be led by others. She became more emotional and more easily moved to tears. Even her interests changed. She lost her fascination for the great, impersonal sweep of history, preferring instead a smaller, more personal scale upon which to focus.

What of those who journey in the other direction? Celia Brayfield, living as a man for *YOU* magazine, found that the male world gave its inhabitants greater respect, but exacted a heavy toll in return. She found that, as a man, other motorists would give her more room on the road. Complaints to waiters were dealt with more promptly. Policemen were respectful, rather than flirtatious. But, she remarked, part of the reason that she was granted space was out of fear. People resisted contact in case it should lead to an implication of intimacy, or a provocation of violence.

I began to have a distinct sense of isolation. Without the rapidly exchanged, insignificant glances to which I was accustomed I had a greater sense of distance from the people around me . . . Living as a man was rather like living in a plastic bubble as far as relationships were concerned. A man's world seemed a harsh, lonely place where most relational behaviour was mysteriously taboo. I felt cut off from other people, distanced from them simply by the assumptions they made about manhood. As a person I had a sense of pitching from further back, needing to be louder and tougher in order to be acknowledged.

However the sexes start out, they end up living lives that are differentiated by gender at every possible juncture. Stephanie-Anne Lloyd remarked to me that, 'Men and women are so different that they could have been designed for different planets. But maybe the very fact that they can't understand one another is what keeps them interested.'

How much longer, though, must men put up with concepts of masculinity which diminish them as individuals? Why, for example, should we sacrifice so much of our lives upon the altar of work? It is to that central experience in a man's life that my attention now turns.

Chapter 2

This Working Life

'Every man's work,' wrote Samuel Butler in *The Way of All Flesh*, 'whether it be literature or music or pictures or architecture or anything else, is always a portrait of himself.' Butler knew what he was talking about. Work is how a man defines himself. Of course, work matters to women too, and a woman may also be judged by her professional status, or whether she has such status at all. But, as any cocktail party conversation illustrates, work is not such an over-whelmingly determining factor for the identities of women as it is for those of men.

Even before they begin to talk, two women will have judged one another in terms of their appearance, their clothes and their accessories. Later on in a conversation, they may exchange information, which is, in its own way, as competitive as it is solicitous, about their lovers, husbands and/or children. Men, however, exchange endless clues about their professional status, their earnings and their access to power or information. Their anecdotes are designed as much to reinforce or establish status as they are to inform or amuse. They are positioning one another on a ladder. They want to know which one of them is really the chief monkey.

One illustration of this occurred several years ago to a showbusiness reporter for a Fleet Street paper. A friend of his was in London, on leave from his duties as a pilot in the Royal Navy. The reporter offered to take him to a big rock industry party, at which the two men ended up sitting next to a pair of superstars – legend has it that they were David Bowie and Pete Townshend. The pilot, overawed by the presence of these musical demigods, remained silent until one of them asked him what he did for a living. Somewhat reluctantly, he confessed that he flew Harrier jump jets. In fact, he added, he had just returned from the war in the Falklands.

At this, the musicians' attitudes changed completely. This apparently insignificant person at their table was, in fact, a fighter pilot who had seen active service. His machismo ranking, therefore, was even higher than that of a rock star. In professional terms, at least, he had the biggest dick at the table. A man's work, after all, is his very identity.

More than that, it is a compulsion. Even now, many women regard work as something that will take a different role in their lives as time goes by. They may give up work altogether, either temporarily or permanently, in order to have and look after a family. They may work part-time or on a voluntary, charitable basis. Although the majority of women who work need to do so for the sake of their own or their family's finances, only 11 per cent of working women are the sole breadwinners within a married family. Others may be single parents. But the majority of women do not experience or, perhaps even more important, expect the lifelong responsibility for the financial wellbeing of a family that is the expectation of every man.

All men carry with them a form of gender-memory, handed down from grandfathers, fathers and elders. It tells them that their work is the way in which they become fully male. But it also speaks of the price that must be paid. Most of us have seen our fathers go grey or even die in the service of their work. We know that we, too, will be enslaved by the tyranny of the wage packet. We know, in other words, that work is a burden as much as it is a benefit.

For all that women fight, quite rightly, for equality in the workplace, it tends to be equality of rights, rather than of responsibilities. The aim is to achieve a fair deal for those women who choose to take advantage of it, not to force it upon them, whether they like it or not. Much has been said, for example, about the role of women in the armed services. In the wake of the Gulf War it is increasingly clear that the only way in which a woman is any less effective on the battlefield than a man is that she is unlikely to be able to carry the physical burden of weaponry, equipment and supplies that is loaded onto the modern frontline infantryman. Where brute strength is less important – on a warship, for example – her performance will be as good as any man's. As a consequence, the demand has arisen for equal treatment for women within the forces. No one, however, has suggested that women be faced with the possibility of conscription. For men, the onset of an all-out war would entail the duty, if called upon, to die for one's country. For women, that peculiar privilege would only be an optional extra. To paraphrase Lord Byron: 'Woman's work is of woman's life a thing apart. 'Tis a man's whole existence.'

In her book *Backlash* Susan Faludi reports on the Yankelovich Monitor Survey, an annual American poll, as follows: 'For twenty years the Monitor's pollsters have asked its [male] subjects to define masculinity. And for twenty years, the leading definition, ahead by a huge margin, has never changed. It isn't being a leader, athlete, Lothario, decision-maker, or even being "born male". It is simply this: being a "good provider for his family".'

Faludi cites this link between masculinity and bringing home the bacon as one of the major causes of the threat men feel from the presence, and success, of women at work. After all, if a man is not a worker, what is he? At a time when the combined forces of technological change and prolonged recession have devastated the traditional industries that have employed the bulk of the male labour force, replacing men's work in steel mills or coalmines by 'women's' jobs in shops or silicon-chip manufacturing plants, men are being doubly emasculated both by unemployment and by their replacement in the workforce by women.

Nor can men retaliate by migrating into female territory. However much a man washes dishes, shops or takes care of the kids, he can never do what a woman can. He can never give birth. In these circumstances, it is hardly surprising that men might feel a sense of crisis. In fact, given the degree to which male power is threatened, the surprising thing is not that there has been a 'backlash' – evidence of which is, even after the 592 impressively researched pages of Faludi's book, pretty sketchy – but that it hasn't been infinitely more virulent. It is not often that a dominant class legislates its own downfall with quite as much thoroughness as the parliaments of the Western world, filled as they are with men passing equal opportunities legislation in favour of women, have done.

What Faludi chooses not to mention, although to be fair she has done so in subsequent interviews, is that there is plenty of evidence to show that the men surveyed by Yankelovich have every reason to stress the importance of their ability to provide. A five-year study of 10,000 men and women from around the world, carried out by the American publication *Behaviour and Brain Sciences*, showed that while men in all cultures see beauty as the most important quality in a prospective mate, women base their decisions on their man's earning power and ambition. Commenting on the survey's findings in the

Daily Express in May 1989, Professor David Buss, a psychologist at Michigan University, remarked, 'It appears women throughout the world, whether they be Zulu, Brazilian or British, look for the same traits when it comes to choosing a partner. In every case, women prefer their mates to be older – British women by an average of three years – and value the ability to provide very highly. A woman will tend to look for a strong, prosperous male because he will be better able to support a family.'

A more specific view of the degree to which a man's profession can affect his desirability was provided in June 1991 by a survey conducted for the British edition of *New Woman* magazine. More than 200 women, aged 20–45, were asked which profession their ideal man would work in and what traits they valued most. Once again, security, stability and intelligence were seen as the greatest male virtues, and in this case the legal profession was judged most capable of providing them.

Lawyers were felt to have sex appeal, a good social background and plenty of brains. More than two-thirds of the women sampled felt that their own status would be increased by dating a lawyer. 'The idea of a man fighting for justice in the courts is powerfully sexy,' one particularly idealistic woman remarked, a notion that will surprise many people who have come into contact with lawyers, few of whom are noted for their over-acute sense of justice – not, at any rate, compared to their finely developed feeling for how much they deserve to be paid.

Second on the list came architects, who, it was reckoned, 'dressed like Italian love gods', a gift which placed them narrowly ahead of doctors and designers. The survey was, however, strongly dismissive of MPs (they talked rubbish, dressed badly, had terrible haircuts and cared only for themselves), 'boring' librarians, 'brain-dead' bus drivers and – voted 'least sexy' by 70 per cent of respondents – milkmen. In a neat parallel of the usual bimbo stereotype, women thought that male models were 'drop-dead gorgeous . . . but thick as two short planks'.

The main point here, apart from the institutionalised sexism and light-hearted misandry displayed so carelessly, not to say gleefully, by *New Woman*'s respondents, is the degree to which their hopes and expectations are still those of women of days gone by. Forget sensitivity, caring, sharing and all the rest of the New Man package – a man's status and salary are still the key to his attractiveness to women.

And yet, at the same time that men are being asked to make money and reach the top, they are also being told that they must abandon their grip on the upper ranks of the professions in order to let in more women. As I write these words in the late spring of 1992, I have before me a pile of newspaper cuttings collected over the past couple of weeks. From them comes a typical smattering of soundbites from the gender battleground that is the modern workplace. By the time that you read them, these stories will be out of date. But I doubt very much whether the issues that they raise, and the ways in which those issues are treated, will have altered in the slightest.

I read the news today – Oh boy

Gillian Shepherd, the Employment Secretary, has interrupted her campaign against EC legislation imposing a maximum forty-eight-hour week in order to set forward her plans for the promotion of women's issues. Under the banner, 'Women: Strategy for Success', she is preparing to monitor all government policy plans for their effect upon women; to set up a working party to report on 'some of the most intractable barriers that hold women back'; to advise on improving child care, better training and public appointments for women in the regions and to lobby the Treasury for money with which to implement her plans.

Mrs Shepherd reports that her Cabinet colleagues have responded to her plans well: there have been 'no cries of anguish'. Not from any men, perhaps, but Petronella Wyatt assures the readers of the *Sunday Telegraph* that, 'Any body designed to help women must assume that women are in need of help, poor dears. Instead of placing us on an equal footing with men, it diminishes our stature. If women are to be the objects of positive discrimination, the implication is that we are incapable of getting along on our own. This is no better than the Victorian idealisation of us as weak, vaporous creatures, whose only solace was to be found in the support of a strong man.'

Support for the Shepherd position, however, comes from Mrs Joanna Foster, chairman of the Equal Opportunities Commission, who has just announced that firms will lose out when European trade barriers are swept away unless the position of women in the labour force is strengthened. More effort needs to be made to ensure that companies provide proper child care, job sharing and appreciation for the women who will fill most of the 1.5 million jobs created between now and the end of the century. 'If Britain is not to miss out . . . we must go for the high quality/skills scenario,' comments Mrs Foster. 'The government faces a choice: ignore the gender aspect and lose out economically or have a strategy for women at work and make enormous gains.'

And what have those women at work been up to over the past fortnight? Well, dinner ladies whose pay was reduced by North Yorkshire County Council have been appealing to an industrial tribunal in Leeds, claiming that male workers in the highway department have suffered no such losses . . . Woolworths have been forced to pay out £10,000 after an industrial tribunal decided that a manager conducting a security search had no right to inspect a handbag belonging to Mrs Jackie Taylor, a forty-four-year-old shop assistant . . . A New York secretary, Ms Kathy Abraham, has settled out of court after suing her former boss, Mr Lewis Eisenberg, a Wall Street investor with whom she had had a seven-year-long affair. Claiming sexual harassment and the intentional infliction of emotional distress, she had asked for damages of $107 million. Now she has dropped her allegations without any money changing hands . . . Back in England, a legal secretary called Donna van den Berghen has – in a case we shall consider in more depth later – been awarded £5,000 after being fired by a boss whom, she alleged, made sexual advances towards her and fondled her breasts . . . Paula Abbott, a fifteen-year-old girl from Tyne and Wear, has become Britain's youngest ever winner of a sex discrimination case after being unfairly dismissed from her £14-a-week post as a part-time shop assistant. The shop claimed to have a policy of last in, first out, but the manageress, Ms Patricia Swaddle, dismissed Paula ahead of two boys who had, in fact, been hired after her.

Moving from fact to opinion, Anita Roddick has returned from Ghana to reveal that women there work twice as hard as men, who just sit idly by watching them labour. Luckily, she reveals, the Ghanaian women do not envy us in the West because, even though they are 'living in huts, eating simple food and struggling to make a living, there's no Western influence and every family loves each other'.

Black women in Britain are equally dismissive of the work-shy African, or Afro-Caribbean male. In a *Sunday Times* piece that causes serious offence among black acquaintances of mine, Donu Kogbara examines a new trend in which successful black women are supposedly choosing to have relationships with white men, rather than consort with unsuccessful black men. A black TV researcher, Marie Davis, is reported as saying: 'We have worked hard to get where we are. We have somehow outgrown the black men of our age. Putting it crudely . . . there just aren't that many middle-class black men around. [We] just don't want to marry bus drivers.' One's initial reaction is that the piece is unpleasantly racist. But then, the predominantly white readers of *New Woman* don't want relationships with bus drivers either. Perhaps modern women are simply job-ist.

Meanwhile, the *Sunday Telegraph* continues a debate sparked off by a recent report by Women in Management in Publishing – WIMP, for short – which claimed that only 23 per cent of all the book reviews in British literary pages are by women, thereby denying women . . . etc., etc. Ironically, the article does not mention a review, by Fiammetta Rocco, of a book called *Up and Running: Women in Business*, by Jane McLoughlin. This repeats the prediction that the majority of new jobs in this country will go to women – 85 per cent is the proportion given – and makes the claim that the managers of the future will need qualities and people skills that are mostly associated with women. 'All well and good,' comments Ms Rocco.

These stories represent a typical cross-section of contemporary debate about the workplace. You will note a number of themes, equal opportunities, wage discrimination and harassment being the most common. There is an overwhelming concentration on the needs, problems and sufferings of women. This is accompanied by the suggestion that there are a number of qualities specifically associated with women that would, if allowed to flourish, give them a distinct, inherent advantage over men.

On 8 January 1992, the *Guardian* opened its report on a conference on occupational psychology with the words, 'Women are the natural business leaders of the future because they have personality traits which motivate and encourage staff, an occupational psychologist said yesterday.' The shrink in question was Dr Beverly Alimo-Metcalfe, of Leeds University. If she had said exactly the same thing about men, she would never have been reported with quite such unquestioning acceptance.

Put it another way. Suppose I said that, 'Men are often much more efficient than women and get things done quicker. I have always worked for women, which has been great because they tend to be on the lazy side. What they call delegating responsibility actually means getting somebody else to do the job for them. Another reason that there are so many successful men around is that they have far greater stamina. They're much stronger mentally and physically . . . women will take to their beds at the first sign of flu.' I'd be hung, drawn and quartered.

I, however, have never said any such thing. The words above are taken from an interview given by the television producer Linda Agran, speaking to the *Daily Express* in February 1990. Except that she did not say them quite like that. She said, 'Women are much more efficient than men . . . [Men] tend to be on the lazy side . . . [Women] have far greater stamina . . . men will take to their beds at the first sign of flu.' This is female sexism at its most blatant, with Ms Agran revealed as a classic female chauvinist sow.

Mind you, there seem to be plenty of men willing to support the new stereotypes which show their fellow males in the worst possible light. Here, writing in the London *Evening Standard* in August 1992, is the psychologist Oliver James, who believes that, 'Men are far more concerned about the size of their desk or office, the flashiness of their company car and the grandness of their organisation than their sisters.'

Dr James, however, has not spent as much time as I have done in the magazine business, in which women bosses are the norm, rather than the exception. Had he done so, he would know that there are plenty of power-crazed, status-symbol-laden female executives around the place, whose demands for office redecoration, clothes allowances, chauffeur-driven cars, Concorde tickets and endless designer freebies are at least as avaricious as anything a man would ever consider. Re-read Dr James's words. Now consider the following . . . Leona Helmsley, Fergie, Madonna . . . think about their oh-so modest, entirely un-flashy life styles . . . see what I mean?

This is, in my experience, little to choose between male and female bosses. Some are good, some are lousy, others drive you crazy but happen to be successful enough to be forgiven. They don't make your life better or worse in the same way, necessarily, but you end up at the same place, regardless. The drives which impel a man or a woman to the top may, as Dr Liam Hudson suggests, arise from different sources. But the manically ambitious, of either sex, have much more in common with each other than they do with those of their fellow men or women who possess a more low-key outlook on life.

This is seldom said in the media. But then, balance is not the intention of the people who write and edit most features about the two sexes, whether they are about working habits or anything else. These stories appear, by and large, on pages intended to attract female readers (even if they are given names like 'Living' or 'Style'). So, naturally enough, they support the female perspective.

This may seem strange, given the enormous publicity that has been accorded, over the past few years, to women writers who maintain that the media wages a war against their sex. I can only make this observation. If you want to show that the media are biased against women, you have to prove that articles which appear to be even-handed are actually sexist. You have to look at the subtext and the hidden agendas. But for those of us who want to demonstrate media prejudice against men, life is much easier. We just open the papers and there it is. Nobody bothers to hide it because no one thinks that it matters.

In the same edition of the *Evening Standard* that contained Dr James's remarks, fashion editor Lowri Turner revealed that men are frightened of women who wear red lipstick – 'They feel threatened' – while columnist Nigella Lawson announced that, 'Men, poor victims of testosterone, would be far better off out of the boardroom and safely in the bedroom, to which they are obviously more biologically suited.'

Why do we not react to female sexism in the same way that we do to the male variety? Simple: we are convinced that women are society's victims. That being the case, they are entitled to complain. But are they really quite as hard done by as we have been led to believe? Let's take a look at women's working lot . . .

Male boss: female victim

The assumption of female victimisation is deeply embedded, so much so, in fact, that we take it for granted that women get a raw deal. After all, if they did not, why would we have all these charters and committees fighting to protect and enforce their rights? Clearly, since this phenomenon is true – or so we suppose – of society in general, and since the workplace is the font of male power, work must be the area in which women get the roughest treatment of all.

They certainly think so. I remember talking to a middle-ranking executive on a national newspaper. She had just come from an editorial conference, which the paper's editor had interrupted to take a call from one of his children. 'A woman could never have done that,' she said. 'The moment people saw her talking to her family, they'd stop taking her seriously as a boss.'

As it happened, however, I used to work for the man's wife and had been present at several similar conferences or meetings during which she had taken family phone calls. No one on the staff had thought anything of it. The reason was very simple: the woman in question was an extraordinarily successful editor. Whether or not she chose to speak to her teenage daughter while in conference was irrelevant. The magazine's circulation and advertising revenue were rising by leaps and bounds. The numbers told you everything you needed to know about her value.

Conversely, I suggested, had her husband been perceived as a poor boss (which, I might add, he was not), it would not have mattered if he had never interrupted a single conference in his entire life. His staff would still not have respected him. In the end, loyalty is earned by competence – gender does not come into it.

The same misconception applied in a rather different way to another woman I knew. Talented, ambitious and energetic, she had deservedly become one of the company's youngest heads of department. The problem was, she said, the other department heads would not take her seriously because she was a woman. If she made suggestions to them concerning their departments, they tended to dismiss them out of hand. This, she thought, would not have happened with a man.

As any man who has ever achieved a high position at an early age could have told her, it would have happened and it does. The issue here was not her gender, but her youth. Senior members of staff, whatever their profession may be, do not take kindly to being, as they see it, lectured by young whippersnappers, particularly if the whipper-snapper happens to be right. Given the choice, middle-aged men may even be less inclined to react angrily to an attractive young woman, by whom they may well be charmed, than they are to a younger man, by whom they will undoubtedly feel threatened.

The culture of victimisation, however, is hard to eradicate once it has been put in place. In the late spring of 1988, I visited Somerville College, Oxford, a women's college which has since become the scene of a great controversy concerning its plans to become co-educational. The purpose of my visit was to write a newspaper feature about a special EC dispensation that had been given to the college in order that it could continue to advertise for female-only fellowships. This was a practice that would, under normal circumstances, be banned on the basis of its sex discrimination.

Following an interview with the then Principal of Somerville, Daphne Park (since created Baroness Park of Monmouth), I had lunch with Miss Park, some of her college colleagues and a number of members of the Junior Common Room Committee. Most of them were graduating that year and, this being the tail end of the Thatcher–Lawson boom, they were expecting to go on to well-paid jobs in the autumn.

One would have thought that these intelligent, articulate, middle-class young women would have everything to look forward to. Instead, their conversation consisted of a litany of anticipated prejudices. Their careers, they felt, could expect to be blighted by harassment, discrimination and injustice. Everything from management training to maternity leave was going to conspire to do them down.

Anyone listening in on our conversation would never have known that these nice, but self-pitying creatures were about to become graduates of one of the country's most powerful and prestigious universities. They were incomparably better off than 99 per cent of their contemporaries, male or female. It was, in fact, offensive to hear them bemoaning their lot, when their lot was so wonderfully privileged.

After a while, even Miss Park, a redoubtable former diplomat, who lists the Special Forces Club in her entry in *Debrett's Distinguished People of Today*, began to wonder out loud about what had gone wrong in these women's education. She found it astonishing that, with all the opportunities that were laid out before them, they still chose to focus on a series of real or imaginary drawbacks. That, one suspected, was not the attitude that had taken Miss Park to the top of the tree.

One could hardly blame those whingeing Somervillians for their opinions. They had, after all, been brought up to look on themselves as unjust victims of social prejudice. Every magazine and women's page that they had ever read had underlined the fact of their oppression. But they might, perhaps, have been surprised had they known the results of a survey into attitudes at work that was conducted some two years after our interview.

Commissioned by, of all people, Royal Crest Dutch Bacon – whether on the grounds of chauvinist piggery, or the need to bring the bacon home, I do not know – it examined the way in which men and women were treated in the workplace. Four hundred British workers were interviewed, and, as a spokesman for Royal Crest told the *Daily Express*, 'We were frankly surprised at the results. We expected that workers throughout the country would experience the same sort of treatment but our survey clearly shows bosses are much tougher on their male employees.'

Men were more likely to be bullied or sworn at in public; more likely to have rows with their boss; more likely to feel ill-treated and, as a consequence, far less likely to feel a sense of loyalty to their superiors. Respondents gave the following answers to a series of questions beginning with the phrase, 'Do you . . .'

Question	Men	Women
Have rows	79%	33%
Swear/get sworn at	60%	18%
Get blamed in front of others	50%	26%
Feel no loyalty to the boss	17%	5%
Get treated well by the boss	41%	58%
Feel taken for granted	59%	40%

Looking at these findings, you would have to conclude either that men are inclined to exaggerate their problems, and/or women minimise theirs, or that men are demonstrably treated with less kindness than women. Since it is the case that, from their earliest babyhood, males are given a rougher ride than their sisters or female playmates in the hope that this will make them the tough, forceful, independent men of the future, it would not be at all surprising to see the same disregard for their humanity displayed when they are adult.

Nor should one be surprised by the way in which the *Express*'s report was phrased. The survey showed that male bosses are nice to women, but beastly to their fellow men, so much so that men were increasingly bursting into tears at work. But reporter Belinda Beckett and the paper's subeditors were not going to be distracted by that minor detail. 'Sexes go into battle on the office frontline,' the headline read, before Beckett's breathless introduction, which ran: 'Women can kiss their New Man goodbye when he leaves for work in the morning. He might be great at cooking breakfast. But when it comes to bringing home the bacon, Nineties Male reverts to that old Eighties cliché – the chauvinist pig . . . The battle of the sexes is still being fought on the office front-line.'

That, of course, was the very opposite of what the survey said. Men were, in fact, being nice to women, but foul to their own sex. But why let the facts get in the way of a really good, old cliché?

Money: how it's earned . . .

The worst sin committed by the male worker is that he earns more than his female counterpart. I have no desire to argue that this is a laudable state of affairs. If two people do the same job, working for the same number of hours, at the same level of seniority, and to the same degree of competence, then they should get the same pay, irrespective of gender, race, sexual proclivities, shoe size or anything else. The market, however, may take a different view and sometimes those examples of unequal pay which appear to be discriminatory merely reflect the simple laws of supply and demand, rather than any evil, masculine conspiracy.

Over the next few pages, I will attempt to demonstrate the reasoning behind one apparently discriminatory situation; to question the steps towards equality in another; and to give an example of a third profession in which the traditional male/female pay differentials are reversed. All three of the activities that I look at – acting, professional tennis and modelling – are far removed from the lives of ordinary folk. This may suggest that they are irrelevant. My contention, however, is that they illustrate principles which apply equally well to businesses that are far less glamorous.

In the first instance, actresses on both sides of the Atlantic have complained in recent years about the disparities between the salaries given to male and female performers. Meryl Streep, for one, has pointed out the unfairness of playing a leading role opposite a male star whom she knows is being paid two or even three times as much as she is. When Sigourney Weaver was signed to recap her role as Ripley in the third installment of the *Alien* film series, she was promised $4 million, plus a percentage of the box-office take. At the time this was the highest fee ever negotiated by a female star. Yet it was a third, or less, of what a male superstar such as Arnold Schwarzenegger might expect to receive for an action role. And no actress has ever come close to the sort of deal that enabled Jack Nicholson to pull in an estimated $50 million from *Batman* and all its associated merchandising.

In Britain, the actor's union Equity published a report by Dr Helen Thomas of Goldsmith's College at the University of London, on the disparity between male and female pay within the acting profession. An average TV actress earns a mere £13,178 a year, whereas her male equivalent can expect to take home £26,466. Within TV commercials, women earn an average £6,650, whereas men receive £18,031.

The gulf is undeniable, and there's no denying that straightforward sexism is one of the reasons for its existence. Yet it can also be explained in ways that have little to do with gender *per se*, and everything to do with the marketplace within which the acting profession operates. For example, the key determinant of a film star's value is the ability to 'open' a picture: that is to say, to draw in enough people to its opening weekend to create box-office momentum.

At the time of writing, there is a small group of male stars who have this proven ability, including Arnold Schwarzenegger, Kevin Costner and Mel Gibson. Actresses such as Michelle Pfeiffer, Julia Roberts or Geena Davis shift magazines when their faces appear on the cover, but they do not guarantee bums on seats. Sigourney Weaver can open a film but only so long as it has the word 'Alien' in the title (just as Sylvester Stallone can open anything called *Rambo* or *Rocky*, but absolutely nothing else). Meryl Streep, meanwhile, is a splendid actress. If payment were allocated on the basis of quality, she would be as rich as Croesus. She does not, however, set the box office on fire very often. And in Hollywood, that is the only talent that counts.

In Britain there is no significant movie business, so the market works in a different way. The membership of Equity is more or less evenly divided between men and women. Yet women have only half the roles on television that men do. It is, therefore, a buyer's market: there is always an oversupply of actresses, so TV companies can afford to pay women less.

Why, then, is there such an imbalance in roles for women? Well, no one can doubt the degree to which both the American movie business and British television are dominated by men. Of the hundred most powerful people in Hollywood, as listed by *Premiere* magazine in May 1992, only five were women. The BBC may be making special efforts to promote women into senior management posts, but the vast majority of decision-making executives in both public and commercial broadcasting are men and 90 per cent of all advertisements are written by men (even though 80 per cent of them are aimed at female consumers). The argument seems overwhelming: male control means female deprivation.

Except that it isn't quite so simple as that. The people who make films into blockbuster hits are, roughly speaking, young men. If you want to make $150 million, lots of young men have got to see your film lots of times each. And, just to make sure, they need to take a young woman along with them on as many occasions as possible. Young women, either because they are naturally keen to please, or because they get off on seeing Arnie blow people up just as much as their boyfriends do, are happy to go to action adventures aimed at a male audience. Young men would rather pull their own entrails out with a blunt fork than be seen going to the gentle, relationship-based stories that are traditionally defined as women's pictures. They will go and see Sigourney slug space monsters. And they'll just about tolerate slush like *Dying Young* in the hope of seeing Julia Roberts without any clothes on. But otherwise, forget it. Once again, the marketplace has spoken.

Fine, you might say, so change the marketplace. Since anything that makes young men more sensitive to the value of their emotions is greatly to be applauded, I'd be tempted to agree. But before you do, check to see that it's okay with Madonna. In the music business, she has exerted a hold on the public that has given her a worldwide sales power, in terms of both recordings and live appearances, that is the equal of any of her male peers.

The music industry needs no lessons from Hollywood in the art of corporate sexism. But record company executives can read a balance sheet just as well as anyone else. If Madonna, or Janet Jackson, or Whitney Houston shifts units and keeps record companies in business, she gets paid accordingly and her whims are happily indulged – hence Madonna's personal record label, Maverick, which was set up for her by her parent corporation Time-Warner. If their sales start to slip, so will their money. Gender doesn't come into it.

On the other hand, an obsession with achieving equality can sometimes lead to situations in which the desire to help women completely obscures, or even helps to create, an equal unfairness towards men. For many years women tennis players have been campaigning to achieve parity of prize money with their male counterparts. As a result, women's prize money at, for example, Wimbledon, is within 10 per cent of the men's. This near-equality has been widely applauded, although some players, such as the current world number one, Monica Seles, have stated that they will not be satisfied until full parity has been achieved.

Few men have dared make any public complaint about the way in which things are moving, although one who did was the Australian Pat Cash. Some years ago, he incurred the odium and contempt of many a female critic by stating that it was absurd to pay women the same as men since they were neither as good as men, nor spent as long on court.

Shortly before the 1992 Wimbledon tournament, a Dutch tennis player called Richard Krajicek went even further when he told a radio interviewer that, in his opinion, 80 per cent of women players were nothing more than unfit, overweight pigs.

Mr Krajicek soon found himself in trouble, not least because the formidable Martina Navratilova threatened to give him a personal demonstration of just how fit and strong she was. This was little more than he deserved, if only on the grounds that there is no excuse for bad manners. But there are scarcely any rational grounds for disagreeing with a word of what Pat Cash said. And what's more, a very strong case can be made to support the proposition that current prize-money policy actively discriminates against men.

Starting with the question of ability, the sheer physical power of the top male players is such that no woman, not even one with the enormous talent of a Monica Seles or Steffi Graf, could hope to take anything more than a game or two per set off any one of the top 100 men. Within the two sexes, there is also a disparity. There is little depth of talent in women's tennis. At any one time, the top half-dozen women tend to be so dominant that there is little chance of any of them being beaten by anyone outside the top ten. And even if the female players should not be described as fat pigs, the BBC's radio commentator Barbara Potter – a former professional tennis player in her own right – has estimated that no more than 50 per cent of the women on the circuit could be described as fully fit. The men, however, tend to be in much better shape and for a good reason: they cannot afford not to be. After all, they face far tougher competition and are always liable to be humbled by a supposedly lesser player.

As a consequence of this, the route to the final of a tournament is likely to be much more arduous for a man than a woman. This will be particularly true in those tournaments – most notably the ones comprising the Grand Slam – that require the best of five sets for men's matches.

The 1991 Wimbledon Championships perfectly illustrated this point. The winner of the men's title was a relatively unknown German, Michael Stich. His triumph was as hard-earned as it was well deserved. In the course of his seven matches, Stich played 257 games, spread over twenty-six sets.

The women's title was won by Stich's compatriot, Steffi Graf. Returning to her most imperious form, Miss Graf proceeded to play all but one of her matches, the final, without losing a single set. All but one of those sets was won to three games or less. As a result, she played a total of 128 games, almost exactly half the number played by Michael Stich. To emphasise the different demands placed upon men and women, André Agassi – who would win the title in 1992 – was defeated in the fourth round having played a total of 166 games, thirty-eight more than Graf required for the entire tournament.

How, then, were these three athletes rewarded for their endeavours? Well, their winnings were as follows:

Stich	£240,000
Graf	£216,000
Agassi	£16,800

Let us, as a rough measurement, take each game played to represent one unit of work, comparable, for example, to an hourly rate in an office or factory. If we divide the total amount earned by the amount of units required to earn it, we find that our trio were being rewarded on the following sporting piece-rate:

Stich	£933.85 per game
Graf	£1,687.50 per game
Agassi	£101.20 per game

The last figure represents the low value placed on a loser, rather than any gender-based calculation, but even restricting ourselves to the winners, it is clear that a much higher value is placed upon Graf's work than Stich's. This would be further emphasised if any note was taken of the length or closeness of games. Given her domination of her opponents, it is reasonable to assume that Graf spent little time fighting over deuces. Stich, on the other hand, was taken to eight tiebreaks, each of which is only counted as a single game for the purposes of our calculation, but which must have been considerably longer and tougher than a regular game.

It would be reasonable to suggest that the closeness of Stich's games – the semifinal, for example, was decided by three consecutive tiebreaks – provided a greater degree of excitement for the spectators than the smooth progress of Miss Graf, however impressive that might have been. So what we have here, in essence, is a man playing much more tennis, to a much higher standard, in a more entertaining context than his female equivalent and yet being paid a sum that is only 10 per cent higher in absolute terms and at least 40 per cent lower when measured against the amount of effort required to earn it. A clear case of sexual discrimination, wouldn't you agree?

But wait. Perhaps there is some hidden market mechanism that I have overlooked. After all, I have been unshakeable in my insistence that quality is of no financial importance if allied to a product or person in whom the public has no interest. Michael Stich could play a thousand tiebreaks. But if the punters don't want to watch him do it, he doesn't deserve to be paid a bean.

Except that they do. The BBC TV ratings for the 1991 Wimbledon finals were as follows:

Men's final	8.1 million viewers
Women's final	7.0 million viewers

So much for armchair fans, what of the paying public? Wimbledon Centre Court tickets are, almost by definition, sold out. So the way in which one judges public appeal is not by the quantity of tickets sold, but the amount one has to pay to obtain one on the black market. A survey of ticket touts conducted in June 1991 for *Punch* magazine revealed the following range of prices for a single seat at that year's finals:

Men's final	£650–900
Women's final	£300–450

There is, in other words, no qualitative or quantitative reason why Wimbledon's women should be paid as much as the men. The only reason that they are is because women are willing to make demands and men are unwilling to oppose them.

Men seem equally unable to stand up for themselves when the tables are turned: that is to say when they are operating in a female-oriented environment. In the modelling business, social conditioning acts to women's huge advantage. We have all been told about the ways in which the flood of visual images of perfect female bodies places intolerable pressure on normal women. Equally, the reduction of women to sex objects is one of the oldest complaints in the feminist book. But there is another way of looking at our society's obsession with the photographic depiction of women.

Walking past a magazine-stall shelf, the most obvious conclusion to be drawn is not that we despise the female form, but that we worship it. Stalin, Saddam and Kim Il-Sung may have littered their nations with memorials to themselves, but none of them was as regularly glorified as any one of the supermodels who are the paragons of female glamour today. These women are as powerful in their field as any Hollywood stud. If you want to sell large numbers of women's magazines, bottles of scent, tubes of make-up or pairs of jeans, then the best way to do it is to advertise them with a picture of a world-famous model.

As a consequence, those women who are, by a freakish coincidence of genetics, diet, exercise and, occasionally, plastic surgery, at the very top of the modelling tree can charge enormous sums of money for the use of their face. At twenty-three years of age, the entirely unreconstructed Christy Turlington signed a four-year, $5 million-plus deal with the American cosmetics company Maybelline. The company felt that Ms Turlington embodied 'the heart and soul of the Maybelline woman – savvy, self-assured and surprising'. For someone with so many marketable qualities, a deal that worked out at some $100,000 for every day of actual modelling seemed eminently reasonable.

According to *Time* magazine, deals such as Turlington's, or Paulina Porizkova's reputed $6 million contract with Estée Lauder, ensure that, when catwalk, editorial and other advertising fees are taken into account, the very top half-dozen models can earn around $2.5 million per annum. Another thirty or so can make around $500,000. And, away from the LA–New York–Paris–Milan axis, top models in a city such as Miami can pull in a cool quarter of a million bucks for a job that consists, in many people's opinion, of standing around and saying 'cheese'.

The same cannot be said for male models. Although men need to wear clothes, they consume a fraction of the cosmetics that women do, nor do they need accessories such as tights, handbags or jewellery. Furthermore, heterosexual men are, by and large, extremely unwilling to admit to any interest in studying pictures of other men in search of tips on how to make themselves more appealing. As a consequence, the fees for male models are far less than those paid to women. Typical rates for a male model at the Paris shows are between £500–1,000 per show. The very top men might, just might, make £2,000 – a fraction of the five-figure sums earned by the female superstars. Nor are there male cosmetics contracts comparable with those awarded to Turlington or Porizkova. If a man has made £15,000 from a jeans commercial he's been doing very well.

As yet, there have been few complaints from male academics about the gross inequalities – far greater than any in the acting profession or the game of tennis – that exist in modelling. Everyone understands that our culture is not particularly interested in looking at men who aren't actually doing something, or who haven't already established a reputation in another field.

Yet the fact that men do not actually deserve to be paid as much as their female counterparts should in no way inhibit them from demanding that their rates be equalised. If Steffi Graf can pull down 90 per cent of what Michael Stich makes for winning Wimbledon, then Maurice the model should hold out for 90 per cent of what Christy Turlington collects from Maybelline. At something in the region of $4.5 million, it sounds as if it's well worth holding out for.

. . . and how it's spent

Earnings are one way of judging relative prosperity. But there is another measurement, which is the access one has to money after it has been earned. If, for example, one class of person does all the work and another does all the spending, you do not have to be Karl Marx to conclude that the second of those two classes is the more privileged. Except that, in real life, it isn't a class, it's a sex.

The economics of a typical British household make an interesting subject for examination. To begin with, there are more men in work than women. Men comprise about 48 per cent of the population as a whole, but they occupy roughly 56 per cent of all jobs. They also get paid more. The average female wage is just 77 per cent of the average male wage. There is always the possibility that this disparity may, in part, be due to the many mothers who choose to work part-time in order to give themselves time with their families, or who choose to sacrifice pay and promotion in exchange for reduced responsibilities and greater flexibility – a group with which, as will become clear, I have a very great degree of sympathy. But let us, for the sake of argument, agree that the system appears to be working in favour of men.

Once that money reaches the family bank account, however, it's a very different story. In November 1991, a survey by the Britannia Building Society revealed the extent to which women controlled the family purse strings. The report's author, Rachel Vining, wrote: 'Women emerge as the primary decision-makers in most areas connected with money. About 75 per cent decide what to buy and how much to spend on the home. They also rule over presents and children's clothes. For holidays and larger items, most women make a joint decision with their partner. Even when it comes to the traditional male preserve of the car, joint decisions are more common than the man deciding alone.'

Specifically, 77 per cent of domestic purchasing choices are made by women, 70 per cent of whom also decide how much to spend. The figures are roughly similar for gifts and children's clothes. But only 35 per cent of men decide which car to buy (31 per cent determine how much to spend). In other words, they are less than half as powerful in their sphere of influence as women are in theirs. Similarly, the survey also showed that in two-thirds of the respondents' households, both partners held cheque books. However, three times as many women (24 per cent) held the only family cheque book, as men (8 per cent). Whichever way you look at it, this survey suggests that the British family purse strings are firmly clasped in Mummy's hand.

Nor is Britannia the only company to have come to this conclusion. The research organisation Mintel also asked women a series of questions relating to decision making in matters of domestic finance. Mintel asked respondents to express their influence on a percentage basis. If the woman questioned felt that she had sole control of a decision, she should claim 100 per cent. If she discussed it with her partner, but then made the final choice, she got 75 per cent. If they discussed and chose together, the figure was 50 per cent; if they discussed, then he chose, 25 per cent; if he decided unilaterally, 0 per cent. Mintel then averaged out all the responses to arrive at a percentage figure which described the typical degree of female influence in any given area. The results were as follows:

Choice to be decided	Female influence
In-store credit card	80%
General credit card	65%
Current account	62%

Other bank, building society accounts	57%
Endowment assurance	51%
Whole life insurance	47%
Stocks and shares	43%
Mortgage	43%
Pensions	41%
Health insurance	38%
Motor insurance	36%

From this one can see that although men have marginally more influence in six out of the eleven categories, in none of them do they have the dominance enjoyed by women in their most influential areas. The overall average works out at a marginal advantage for the female partner by 51 to 49. It is also worth noting that the two strongest areas for men – motor and health insurance – have to be considered in the light of the fact that, for white-collar workers at least, both may well be included as part of a man's professional remuneration. So the women's lack of influence should not be taken to imply male power: it's just that he's abandoned his wife's decision-making in favour of his boss's. Either way, he's the junior partner.

This phenomenon is by no means confined to British society. In fact, it might even be true to say that the more that a society appears to be financially biased in favour of men, the more the reverse is actually the case. In Japan, for example, men still hold the vast majority of positions of executive and political power; feminism has made nothing like the strides there that it has in the West. Japanese wives are seen by their occidental sisters as hapless servants, waiting hand and foot on their male masters, like geisha girls ready to provide everything that their man might require. The truth, however, appears to be rather different.

As a Japanese salary man slaves away at the absurdly long hours that can, as we have seen, induce premature death, or *karoshi*, his wife is out enjoying the fruits of his labours. A Japanese woman has the same lock on the family finances as her Western counterparts, a privilege that merely adds to the traditional power that she enjoys as the matriarchal ruler of the family home. For the purposes of public consumption, she may play the dutiful helpmeet. But in private, she's the boss.

The Japanese name for a domineering, dictatorial wife is *obatalian*. So common is the species that in 1992 Fuji Television launched a series called *Obatalian Watching*. In the words of Joanna Pitman, reporting from Tokyo for *The Times*: 'A group of scowling harridans were unwittingly filmed on one of their power-shopping sprees, swarming through sales like locusts, dolling themselves up in Chanel suits and Italian shoes. The cameras then followed them onto a crowded underground train where they were seen doing battle for seats armed with designer handbags and umbrellas. The obatalian gets what she wants.

'The comedy of the series depends on the gap between social pretension and reality. Everyone knows that if the cameras were to arrive at her home, the obatalian would slip into her public role as the simpering wife who selflessly tends to the needs of her husband.'

Social attitudes towards the family's supposed patriarch can be guessed from the title of a popular Japanese comic book series (the Japanese consume *manga*, or adult comic books, with a voracity and seriousness unknown in the West). It is called *Stupid Dad*. Its hero – if that is the right word – is eerily reminiscent of the hopelessly inadequate male to be found in so many British TV commercials (and Japanese ones, come to that). After a hard day of ritual humiliation at the workplace, he comes home for more of the same at the hands of his wife and daughters: virulent shrews who would give Regan and Goneril a thoroughly good run for their money. Bossed at work and bullied at home . . . no wonder the poor old Japanese male spends so much time getting drunk in *karaoke* bars.

Logically, one might imagine that if patriarchy at work led to matriarchy in the home, the reverse would apply as well, so that equality in one arena would necessarily lead to a similar liberation in the other. In fact, contemporary ideology merely reinforces the notion that the woman must be the mistress of her own household – overtly, as well as covertly.

In the summer of 1991, the British advertising agency Lowe Howard-Spink revealed the existence of the Self-Regulating Household. This was defined as one in which the female partner earned at least 60 per cent or more of her husband's salary and was thus able to become a Successful Negotiator, who used the bargaining power of her income to whip her once indolent husband into line.

There's no doubt who wears the trousers in the Self-Regulating Household. Ninety-seven per cent of Successful Negotiators (all of whom are female) manage the family finances, while 70 per cent initiate sex. Meanwhile, the man is busy with the housework: 80 per cent do the shopping (although not very well, according to the survey, since they eschew reliable products in favour of 'novelty and gadgetry'); 66 per cent do the vacuuming and 50 per cent do an equal amount of cooking. The result? 'Having actively and consciously renegotiated their roles, they are happier and respect each other more.'

This is the voice of the new orthodoxy. But is it really telling us anything particularly novel? One might equally well argue that we haven't come very far from the days when a man would come home from a hard week at the mill, hand over his pay packet to his wife and then hope she'd bung him some beer money. Men seem to be dismally willing to bring home the bacon to their families without keeping any for themselves.

Part of this is nothing more than willed incompetence. After a hard day's work, it seems like more trouble than it's worth to sort out the bank accounts and credit cards. But women, accustomed as they are to having to do more about the house in any case, have clearly understood that the effort is justified if it brings with it control.

In the old days there may have been some justification for the male point of view. 'Er indoors ran the house and hubby let her boss him about within the confines of their own four walls, secure in the knowledge that once he stepped out into the big wide world, everything was run to his advantage. But now that life at work is not nearly so cosy as it was, it may pay him to reclaim some of the territory he has forfeited back home. Once he's done that, he might like to bring his mind to bear on the single, massive and inexcusable injustice faced by men when they finally come to leave the workplace and clutter up their homes on a full-time basis: the pensions scandal.

Retired and ripped off

Nothing epitomises the way in which men have become unwilling or unable to stand up for their rights more than the inequality of their treatment as pensioners. Before touching on the recent legal history of this sorry saga, here – as of October 1992 – are the facts.

In order for men to qualify for a full state pension, they must pay contributions for forty-four years, up to the retirement age of sixty-five. Between the ages of sixty and sixty-four, they must continue to make payments, even if they have already contributed for the full forty-four years. Women, on the other hand, need only contribute for thirty-nine years in order to receive their full pension and cannot contribute after their retirement age of sixty. So, the first thing is, men pay more and have to work longer.

This anomaly is compounded by the difference between male and female life expectancies. As we have already seen, men die younger than women. An average man can expect to reach the age of seventy-three, while a woman soldiers on to a ripe old seventy-eight and a half.

The disparity between male and female retirement dates means that men, who work longer, but die younger, spend some 11 per cent of their lives in retirement. Meanwhile, women, who work less but live longer, can look forward to those golden, sunset days taking up a full 24 per cent of their time on this planet. The net effect of all this is that men work for at least forty-four years in order to receive eight years of pension. This works out at five and a half years of payments made for every single year of pension benefit received. Meanwhile, women work for thirty-nine years to receive eighteen and a half years of pension, a ratio of 2:1.

Roughly speaking, then, every year of a woman's working life brings her two and a half times as much pensionable benefit as her brother, husband or male colleague receives. If that is not a blatant case of gender-based discrimination, it's hard to imagine what is.

Surely, you would think, the men who control the system would ensure that their fellow males would not suffer unduly from it. What, after all, is the point of power if you do not use it to your advantage? We live, do we not, in the age of the backlash, in which men everywhere are fighting back against the threat to their position posed by uppity women? In actual fact, however, the history of the struggle for equal pension rights illustrates the lengths to which men in positions of authority will go to protect advantages bestowed upon women and prevent themselves having to bear the costs associated with extending them to men.

The situation regarding company pension schemes, as opposed to those organised by the state, is marginally better, but only after a bitter struggle. The crucial case was that of Mr Douglas Barber, a former deputy claims manager with Guardian Royal Exchange in Sheffield. He was made redundant in 1980 at the age of fifty-two. Under his company's non-contributory pension scheme, the normal pensionable age for employees like Mr Barber was fifty-seven for women and sixty-two for men. He was given his redundancy payment, but told that he could not claim a pension for ten years, even though a woman with the same length of service would have been able to claim immediately she was made redundant. When he died in 1989, Mr Barber was still below the age at which he should receive a pension. All his years of work had benefited him not a jot.

But Mr Barber had not died in vain. For during his years of forcible and unpaid early retirement, he fought a series of court cases against GRE in the hope of winning back the £50,000 that represented the difference between what he received, or rather, did not receive, and that given to female employees. The case went all the way to the European Court of Justice in Luxembourg before being decided, on 17 May 1990, in Mr Barber's posthumous favour. The grounds for the judgement were that pension rights were part of an employee's remuneration and therefore covered by Article 119 of the Treaty of Rome, which guarantees equal pay for men and women. In the words of the judges, 'The principle of equal pay must be upheld in respect of each element of remuneration . . .'

The judgement, however, specifically stated that no retrospective claims could be made on any pensions except those which were already the subject of court action. Even so, there was a brief flurry of excitement as courts in Britain struggled to interpret the meaning of the ruling: did the judgement apply, for example, to the full pension rights of all men who retired after 17 May 1990, or merely to that part of the pension accumulated since then? Politicians pontificated on all the various options available. Men might retire at sixty. Women might work on till sixty-five. Both could quit at sixty-three. Perhaps a sliding retirement period could be brought in between the ages of sixty-two and sixty-seven.

The British government's posture throughout the pension debate was typically British: let's wait and see. It was summed up by Sir Geoffrey Howe, then still deputy Prime Minister, who, in July 1990, remarked, 'The Government certainly supports the principle of equal treatment for men and women. But it is a very complex issue where change cannot be introduced without careful study of the financial implications, demographic projections and expectations based on existing arrangements. That study is going on.'

In 1991, the Social Security Secretary, Tony Newton, told the House of Commons that the Government was introducing a 'senior citizen's charter', which would sweep away sex discrimination in pension rights. He told MPs that the Government was determined to 'establish in practice the equality to which we have long been committed in principle'.

There was little sign of this commitment when, in May 1992, a Belgian European judge called Walter Van Gerven ruled that the British Government was not breaking EC rules by having different retirement ages for men and women. Nor need women pay pension contributions after the age of sixty, even if men had to do so. He was giving an interim ruling on a case brought by the Equal Opportunities Commission, which maintained that, 'The gap between men and women is an anachronism.'

The *Daily Express*, edited by a man and staffed with predominantly male executives and sub-editors, reacted to this ruling, which dealt a savage setback to their personal prospects of equality, with the headline, 'First Round in Pensions Battle to Britain', a line that demonstrates jingoism and stupidity in just about equal proportions.

As I write these words, the situation remains the same as it has always been. Pensions, whose value may represent the single biggest capital asset of a working man, are grossly skewed in favour of women. Amazingly enough, however, the vast majority of pension-related actions brought against companies on the grounds of sex discrimination are done so on behalf of women. Some are furious that they have to retire five years sooner than men. Others are angry about the exact opposite – being made to retire later, just like men already do. They know that the system is skewed against *them*, they just haven't quite decided how.

Still, the present situation is not women's fault. They are not responsible for the disparity between their benefits and those given to men. The persistence of the pensions scandal is due to the unwillingness of the government and employers to pay out the money required to rectify the situation, coupled with the total indifference of men towards their own interests.

Just say 'No'

If the men of this country cannot be bothered to get up and fight for their rights, then, frankly, they barely deserve to have any.

We already know that:

1. Male life expectancy is diminished by work

2. A man's powers of attraction are largely determined by his job status, which is, in turn, largely dependent on the degree to which he is prepared to devote his life to work, and

3. Once married, he can expect to lose control of the majority of his income.

So this final piece of information concerning pensions might persuade the proverbial Martian that the human male is little more than a worker bee, or a soldier ant. He's socialised from an early age to submerge his own personality in order to serve the interests of his community and he's discarded the moment that he has outlived his usefulness. Amazingly, whatever Mr Martian might think, that's not how our society sees it. We still persist in imagining that man's burden of work is his greatest privilege.

Every man grows up watching what work has done to his father. In my own case, I was profoundly affected by the knowledge that my father, whom I idolised, went off every day to work at a job which, to my young eyes, he did not appear to enjoy, purely in order to meet the needs of his family. I always swore that I would never be in the same position myself.

Yet, as I lived through my early thirties, I found myself doing exactly what Dad had done: working foolish hours at a job which, though prestigious and intellectually stimulating, often brought nothing but frustration and endless wars of corporate attrition. Nor was money a compensation: the more I earned, the greater my expenses seemed to be, until I finally had a year in which I made more money than I had ever done in my life, but still ended up £20,000 in debt. The greater my debt became, the more I had to earn. I felt trapped on an endless treadmill of perverted aspiration.

It was only when I found myself out of a job, stripped of all the status that senior position brings, but happier than I had been in years, that I fully understood the insanity of the life that I, like millions of middle-class men all over the Western world, had been leading. And the question arose: why the hell should we bother?

Faced with the loss of their automatic pre-eminence in the work-place, men today have a golden opportunity to reassess their whole approach to work. After all, for hundreds of years, work was regarded as a burden from which to escape. The middle classes were defined by their freedom from wage slavery.

The desire to free oneself from work was common to all classes and both sexes. Dr Joanna Bourke of Birkbeck College, London, has studied the diaries of 5,000 women who lived between 1860 and 1930. During that period, the proportion of women in paid employment dropped from 75 per cent to 10 per cent. This was regarded as a huge step forward for womankind, an opinion shared by the women whose writings Dr Bourke researched. Freed from mills and factories, they created a new power base for themselves at home. This was, claims Dr Bourke, 'a deliberate choice . . . and a choice that gave great pleasure'.

In recent years we have reversed the beliefs of centuries. Throughout the 1980s achievement was judged by the number of hours one worked. Friends and family were relegated to a few moments here and there of 'quality time' – that most bogus of all fashionable ideas – whilst our lives were willingly sacrificed to the great god of labour. We must have been crazy. Maybe we still are. For most office work – which is to say, most work these days – is tedious, stressful and burdened with pointless corporate politics.

Few men have the huge privilege afforded to writers, which is to earn one's money doing the thing which affords one the greatest creative satisfaction. The vast majority begin their working lives knowing that they are placing themselves upon a treadmill from which there is no release until they reach death or retirement, save that which is forced upon them by the indignity of unemployment. No wonder they care about the size of their desks or the quality of their company cars – what else is there to care about?

If they are to be successful in the terms laid down by Western society, men must work hours which can cause them to become alienated from families whom they scarcely ever see. The alternative – unemployment – is doubly harsh for men, since their identity is so dependent on their work. Stripped of their working status, some men feel as if they have ceased to exist. They may, in any case, drop dead long before they reap the full benefit of their labour. That, as the history of Florida and the growth in the cruise industry so forcefully demonstrate, is a privilege left to their widows.

The vast majority of men, of course, are no more likely to reach positions of power than are women. In Britain, for example, government statistics showed that 70 per cent of all workers, male and female, were earning £16,850 or less in 1991. But even should they finally reach the top, they will discover that their position is just as precarious as it ever was at the bottom. The great tycoons of the 1980s are the bankrupts and jailbirds of the 1990s.

Those entrepreneurs and executives that survive do so at the mercy of stockholders, fellow directors and predatory rivals. In general, corporate success teaches one that the greater rewards given to those at or near the top are almost always matched by the greater intensity of the crap they have to face when they get there.

We glorify work for its own sake. We worship all things material: new cars, designer labels, fancy gadgets, and so on. Yet here we all are, killing ourselves with stress, killing our own planet with the effluent side effects of our lust for more possessions and seemingly quite unable to free ourselves from our addictions.

Of course, it is nice to wear well-made clothes and drive elegant cars. It is rewarding to dine in fancy restaurants and stay at luxurious hotels. But are these fleeting pleasures worth the price of admission? My strong belief is that men can do the world a great service by kicking the drug of work. Do as much as you have to in order to provide the basic necessities of your life, to keep your mind or body in shape and to fulfil your need to feel involved. Then stop. You might make a bit less money, but just think of the benefits that can be derived from all that extra time – all those things that you had always wanted to do, but had never quite got around to. It is perfectly possible for a man to redefine himself in a way that involves more than work. He just has to give himself the chance to do so.

The understandable desire to achieve financial equality and independence has driven women onto the same treadmill as that upon which men have long been toiling. As women have come into the workplace, the market has adjusted so as to make their presence a requirement, rather than an option. In both Britain and America, two incomes are now needed to provide the goods and services that used to be bought by one. But if women are crazy enough to take over the burden of corporate life, terrific – they're welcome to it. They certainly can't do a *worse* job than male managers, politicians and generals have done. Meanwhile, if men can lead the way out of the mess we find ourselves in, that might prove a service to us all. It would certainly be a more constructive reappraisal of the male stereotype than some of the images of men that have been foisted upon society of late, images to which I now turn.

Chapter 3

Macho, Macho Man, Who Wants To Be A Macho Man?

So who cares about getting big, healthy-looking, good-looking muscles?
Only a pencilneck would ask such a dumb question! Who indeed!
Everyone! That is, if you have the guts to try and if you have the right
information!

The words come from an advertisement for ICOPRO, a 'professional
body building program', created by TitanSports and published in
WWF magazine, the magazine of the World Wrestling Federation.
The advertisement, whose copy is, apparently, written by one
Frederick C. Hatfield, PhD, of Stamford, Connecticut, promises 'an
integrated conditioning program' through which the would-be body
builder can achieve 'a level of muscle mass that few dare dream about,
let alone achieve. If you can visualise yourself growing massive
beyond mere convention, that is where you must go!'

But there's a price. You've got to want it bad enough to do what it
takes. You've got to use ICOPRO, which is, Dr Hatfield explains,
'something so profoundly superior to its relatively paltry predecessors, so utterly complete and powerful in its unique assemblage of both
man-made and natural forces that nothing could possibly surpass it'.
Which is just as well, if you're about to enter 'a state of being where
only the strong survive', where, my friend, 'You will have to do battle
with men infinitely wiser than the greats of yesterday ever encountered.'

The ad is illustrated with a picture of a man pumping iron. We know
he's a man because he has a man's chest, a man's vein-knotted biceps, a
man's neck and a man's face, contorted by a rictus of agony. (You've
gotta want it!) But here's the weird thing . . . he has a girl's haircut.

Welcome to the world of pro wrestling, the cultural nexus for all the
gender obsessions and confusions of our age – a so-called sport that

could, without undue exaggeration, be thought of as the single most highly evolved fictional enterprise of our time. In WWF wrestling, men who have never been near an acting class stay in character in a way that would put de Niro to shame. They become someone else for the purposes of marketing. Everyone is acting: the fighters, the TV commentators, the journalists – everyone.

For example, the same issue of *WWF* magazine features a controversy that has been dogging the wrestling world, to wit: did Ric Flair, pictured for *WWF* magazine in a pink, marabou-trimmed, sequinned housecoat, really play by the poolside with Miss Elizabeth before she got together with Macho Man Randy Savage, or were the pictures faked? In huge, eezee-read type, the kind that's normally reserved for half-blind oldsters or the under fives, Flair and Savage battle it out. Flair claims to have had Miss Elizabeth before she became Savage's wife (for which, subtext fans, read 'property'). Backing Flair is his Executive Consultant, Mr Perfect, whose thick neck, pink skin, squishy features and defiantly baffled expression put me unavoidably in mind of the starship commander from the old *Muppets* sketch 'Pigs In Space'.

Meanwhile, Savage wants to make the world eat its words. He's after Flair. He's after Bobby 'The Brain' Heenan, the florid, thickset reporter employed by WWF to spice up its TV coverage, who's photographed loosening his collar as he swears that he was just doing his duty as 'a good broadcast journalist'.

All sports reporting is overladen with myth and fuelled by bullshit. But this is Booker Prize stuff. Remember, these people don't really exist. Their feuds are pure fiction. Even their names are not their own, being, as it happens, the property of TitanSports, as is ICOPRO, as are such valuable properties as Super Wrestlemania, WWF and, indeed, 'all other distinctive titles, names and characters' mentioned in *WWF* magazine, which is itself, of course, a division of TitanSports.

Anyone who still believes in the New Man should check out the WWF. Everything about it screams testosterone fever. Managers make outrageous claims about their clients' destructive powers. Wrestlers threaten to smash one another to bits. Just look at the names: Psychotic Sid Justice, Ultimate Warrior, The Boss Man, Sgt. Slaughter, The Undertaker and, of course, British Bulldog.

This is all patent nonsense. And yet it is also, like all successful mass culture, a genuine reflection of desires and appetites that really exist out there in the real world.

The Alan Alda doll

In an appendix to his book about masculinity, *Fire in the Belly*, Sam Keen prints the results of a survey that appeared in the American magazine *Psychology Today* in March 1989. Six thousand respondents gave their views on 'What makes an ideal man?' One question asked them to name 'The Man of Our Dreams'. Amongst women, the top three dreamboats were Jesus, Gandhi and . . . Alan Alda. Men named Jesus, Gandhi and John F. Kennedy. Both sexes gave the most important male qualities as caring, loving, intelligent and moral/honest. When asked to name good men, the women came up with George Bush, Ronald Reagan and, yes, Alan Alda (please, no laughing at the back). The men named Jimmy Carter, JFK, and, believe it or not, George Bush.

Let's leave Jesus out of this on the assumption that He is the Son of God and thus exempt from criteria we might apply to mortals. And let's do our best to ignore Kennedy's obsessive promiscuity and documented links with the Mafia. Let us also turn a blind eye to the judgement American voters made on Jimmy Carter when they had a chance to vote in 1980. Let us allow a little leeway on Contragate, the hundreds of indicted Reagan/Bush officials, Dan Quayle, Nancy Reagan, the botched conclusion to the Gulf War, and America's refusal to sign the bio-diversity treaty (the last two of which would not have been known about by Keen's respondents). Let us simply ask this question: when did you last see an Alan Alda doll?

Does the one-time star of *M*A*S*H* and *California Suite* sell movie tickets like Arnold Schwarzenegger? Does he fill stadia like Ric Flair and Randy Savage? Have Nintendo created a whole range of games dedicated to his adventures? Yes, you too can play Bourgeois Angst, the ultimate on-screen challenge!

Can you find his face on souvenir backpacks, cameras, bandannas, T-shirts, posters, workout bears, painter's caps and wrestling buddies? Because you can find Hulk Hogan's there . . . and Savage's . . . and the Legion of Doom.

When they launched *WWF* magazine in Britain, with minimal promotion in the traditional media, it rocketed to sales in excess of 200,000 a month. That is more than the combined monthly sales of the three major men's glossies – *GQ*, *Arena* and *Esquire*. Those middle-class pencilnecks can go on all they like about their suits and cars and hidden sensitivities, but what Joe Public really wants is guys with gorilla muscles and skintight lycra panties beating the shit out of one another. When Wrestlemania came to London, they had to hire Wembley Stadium so 80,000 fans could get to see their hulking heroes.

There's only one other man's publication that has exceeded the success of *WWF* magazine in Britain, and that's *Viz*, the scabrous, filthy, hilarious comic whose cartoons about Fat Slags, Johnny Fartpants and Sid the Sexist have provoked bimonthly sales in excess of 1 million copies per issue. Is the picture coming into focus?

The motor that drives the WWF machine is television. The broadcasts are conducted in the same hysterical tones that echo through all the WWF's various outlets. I switched on to one wrestling show just a few days before writing this chapter. An enormous black wrestler called Kamala, who was dressed as an African witch doctor, was climbing into the ring. Two commentators were analysing his chances. This is what they said, word-for-word:

First Commentator: He's a savage!

Second Commentator: Of course he's a savage! He comes from Uganda, from the dark jungles. That's where savages come from.

First Commentator: Not everyone from Uganda is a savage, surely?

Second Commentator: How would you know?

You wouldn't. Not unless you were some weenie, pointy-headed, pinko, intellectual *pencilneck* . . . right?

Is this stuff scripted? I don't know, but that dialogue, which is, in its brutish, screw-you simplicity, much funnier than anything Alan Alda ever came up with, has echoes in it of *Terminator 2*. In that blockbusting fiesta of carefully orchestrated but caring violence (Schwarzenegger is, don't forget, trying to ensure peace on earth and goodwill to all men, even if he has to wreak havoc in order to get it), the young John Connor goes head-to-head with Arnie/Terminator, as follows:

Connor: You were going to kill that guy.

Terminator: Of course . . . I'm a Terminator.

Connor: You just can't go around killing people.

Terminator: Why?

Does it bother you that kids watch this stuff? In Britain, WWF wrestling goes out on British Sky Broadcasting, the satellite and cable network, which runs two weekly shows on its free Sky One channel, as well as showing Wrestlemania special events on its subscription channel, Sky Movies. When they showed Wrestlemania VIII – the one described above – 48 per cent of all the viewers in all of the 3.5 million homes equipped to receive BSkyB tuned in. Among children, the market penetration was 77 per cent. Just to make that plain: of all the myriad channels or videos that they could have been watching, 77 per cent of all the children who were able to watch Wrestlemania did so. What picture, do you suppose, are they getting of contemporary masculinity?

How about hyper-violent, inarticulate, judgemental, non-conciliatory and, quite possibly, steroid-addicted? How about confused, uncertain, sexually ambiguous and insecure? How about threatened, defensive and insecure? Or why don't we simply say . . . fucked-up?

Boys will be . . . what?

To authors such as Myriam Medzian, wrestling is just one element in a package of media manipulation which condemns Western boys to a life trapped within a destructive and all too often self-destructive stereotype of insensitive machismo. In her book *Boys Will Be Boys: Breaking the Link Between Masculinity and Violence*, she points out that children's weekend daytime TV programmes average 15.5 violent incidents an hour. The popular cartoon series *Transformers*, which was created to peddle a mid-1980s toy craze, averaged a staggering eighty-three acts of violence per hour.

WWF has special programming aimed at kids, who then flock to see their heroes in the flesh at gigantic arena shows. 'Some of them are only two or three years old, although most of them seem to be in the six to twelve range,' comments Medzian, who notes that when she attended a wrestling exhibition at New York's Madison Square Garden, about one-third of the audience for this school-night show was made up of children.

She further points out that whereas adults know that the whole performance is little more than play-acting, the children mostly believe that the violence is real. She says, 'The reality of the punches, the groans, the bodies falling to the ground is amplified through the loudspeakers hidden under the wrestling ring. In spite of this heightened reality no one ever gets hurt. There are no concussions, no broken legs, almost no blood. Children are being completely misled as to the effects of physically attacking others.'

I interviewed Ms Medzian on her visit to London in 1992. Confronted with the view that it's all just entertainment and that none of it actually affects young minds, she told this story about a meeting with the Terminator.

'I had a personal meeting with Arnold Schwarzenegger. It was eyeball to eyeball. I was up in Vermont giving some lectures, just before my book came out, and there were some demonstrations against him because he had been chosen by President Bush as the head of the council on physical recreation and sport and it was an extraordinary choice. Some of the people that had invited me to lecture asked me if I'd like to join one of the protests and I said, sure.

'Afterwards there was a press conference at an elementary school, where he was talking to the kiddies about health. I already had my book, even though it hadn't come out yet, so after they had finished taking photographs, I stepped out, holding my book, and said, 'Mr Schwarzenegger, I'm the author of this book and my research reveals that there have been over 235 studies done on the effects of viewing violence on the screen, and they show overwhelmingly that viewing violence encourages violent behaviour. Violent behaviour is bad for your physical fitness. It seems to me, therefore, that you are an unfit spokesman for this cause.'

'He gave me a look that could have terminated me. He said, 'It's irrelevant to my being here. When I'm here to promote my films we'll discuss this.' But then, in answering someone else, he boasted about how he had inserted seven minutes of physical fitness scenes into *Kindergarten Cop* because he knows how much films influence children.

'He went on to say that when John Travolta did *Saturday Night Fever*, people around the world were disco dancing. So he's admitting the enormous impact of these films, but somehow he can make films with endless, endless violence and they have no impact and it's irrelevant to his being a spokesperson to children.

'I don't think he's stupid. I just think he has a complete denial of the effect of what he's doing.'

Real men

But before we rush to condemn WWF, the Terminator and the makers of children's TV cartoons, it's worth remembering that the big lesson of WWF is: *people want this.* Whatever they may say about wanting men to be gentle and kind, junior Gandhis for the New Age, that's not what the punters choose when the time comes to open up their wallets.

The same applies to real-life relationships. Counsellors at London Marriage Guidance told me that one of the most common complaints they receive is from women who are dissatisfied with their husbands. They have been pestering him to participate in housework – to clean and cook and wash just as much as they do – but when he complies, they discover that they start to find him unattractive. By doing 'women's work' he has forfeited his masculinity. Suddenly, they are filled with an overwhelming desire to run away with the utterly unreconstructed garage mechanic down the road.

I remember once doing some research for a magazine feature about the way in which the traditional male habit of dividing women into virgins and whores was echoed by a female propensity to split men into two camps, wimps and bastards. (In the end, incidentally, the editor of the magazine had to subedit, check and proof the story herself, since her staff refused to work on a piece that was based on such a grossly sexist concept, even if it happened to be true.) Anyway, I talked to a friend who had just ditched her latest lover. The reason she gave for this was that she had rung him up one Sunday afternoon and asked him to come over and help her decorate her flat. He did. This willingness to drop everything at her beck and call, she decided, was so pathetic that she could no longer respect him and she cast him off immediately.

'But,' I said, 'he was probably just trying to be nice.'

'Exactly,' she replied.

More recently I've heard it said by commentators such as Joan Smith, the critic and author whose book *Misogynies* is such a fascinating read, that society is tending towards androgyny. One can quite understand why she should feel this. The 1980s, for example, were the years in which Mrs Thatcher ruled Britain while Boy George put ribbons in his hair. And yet, when you cruise around our TV channels and feel the beat of popular culture, it's impossible to ignore the unquenchable desire for differentiation.

Look at *Studs* or *Blind Date*. Check out those giggling girls in high heels and low dresses and those beefcake hunks with neck measurements bigger than their IQs. Then listen to the things they talk about. The young women want their men to be kind and considerate, but they also want them to be real men. The young men want big tits, good laughs and great sex. They both, in their own sweet ways, want each other. *Nothing's changed.*

Of course, one can claim that this is just an example of the way in which media moguls manipulate our sensibilities. We could all be the victims of some vast male plot, designed to trap us in outmoded sex roles for the benefit of the patriarchy. It's an intriguing theory, but it's low on reality. The point missed by many critics of the media, on both right and left wings, is that the mass media are not driven by socio-political imperatives. It just doesn't work like that. What gets on the air is, by and large, what sells.

Personally, I see no problem in any of this. Or I wouldn't, were it not for the fact that there is something so obviously problematic about the sex-role caricatures for which we have all so happily fallen. I will leave it to others to reiterate women's difficulties. For now let's concentrate on men. More specifically, let's look at the archetypal masculine hero as he's developed in Hollywood movies over the past few decades.

In particular, I want to focus on three figures: John Wayne, Clint Eastwood and Arnold Schwarzenegger. Sure, there have been many, many others. Just among the tough guys you could include Mitchum, Douglas, McQueen, Bronson, Stallone and all those new-wave European body-building types, like Lundgren and van Damme. Then there are the all-American decent men, from Gary Cooper to Kevin Costner. And somewhere in there you've got Bogart and even the hero-as-schlemiel, Woody Allen. But since the subject here is machismo, let's keep the focus tight.

The Duke

John Wayne, the all-American cowboy, was shown fighting battles for clearly defined moral causes (always assuming that one regards the slaughtering of Japs and Apaches as morally worthwhile). He was clearly on the side of truth, justice and the American way. His violence was administered in two basic forms. The first was a manly punch to the jaw, usually of another white man. This was often seen as an act of bonding, after which both parties would recognise one another's masculinity and join forces against some mutually agreed foreign foe.

In *The Alamo*, for example, John Wayne spends several minutes exchanging punches with Richard Widmark before going off to die heroically by his side in the service of Texas. Wayne directed this film which, along with *The Green Berets*, a trenchant defence of America's involvement in Vietnam, pretty much marks his ideological card.

Wayne's second weapon was a bullet from a gun. The true effects of this bullet were never shown; bad guys or Injuns dropped dead, give or take the odd famous last word, and such extraneous details as blood, guts and agonised screams were kept to a bare minimum.

Having done what a man had to do in the big wide world, Wayne then turned back to hearth, home, and the little woman who waited for him there. In the super-conventional 1940s and 1950s, the public was suitably reassured when Wayne took Maureen O'Hara in his arms, paused a while as she beat her delicate female fists against the broad expanse of his chest, accepted her eventual submission and went off to raise a family (unspoken postscript: she became the Great American Matriarch and was left in charge of her man's life from then on).

The effect of Wayne's work was most marked on American servicemen. Myriam Medzian reports on the way in which the fantasy of glorious, righteous conflict embodied by Wayne was a major factor in the minds of men enlisting for the Vietnam War. When they discovered the enormous gulf between the portrayal of battle on the big screen and the horrors of the real thing – a horror exacerbated by the absence of any justifiable sense of moral purpose from the Vietnam campaign – their disillusionment and anger were profound.

Nor was this a new phenomenon. As William Manchester recalled in a 1987 *New York Times* magazine article (cited by Medzian), World War II soldiers felt equally repelled by the gulf between truth and fiction. When, in 1945, Wayne made a supposedly morale-boosting appearance at a naval hospital in Hawaii after the battle for Okinawa, he walked on stage, dressed in cowboy hat, bandanna, pistols, chaps and spurs, only to be greeted by a chorus of boos. In Manchester's words: 'This man was an example of the fake machismo we had come to hate, and we weren't going to listen to him.'

Clint

If John Wayne was a phoney, and everything he stood for was equally rotten, what was left for men? Clint Eastwood, whose first major film,

A Fistful of Dollars, was made in 1964, halfway between the Existentialist movement and the first burned bra, portrayed a man whose morality was generated not by social or patriotic obligation, but by his own, internal code of conduct.

As the Man With No Name he appeared, resolved a conflict and then disappeared. Barring the occasional use of a Gatling gun or two, the fights may have lacked the scenes of mass slaughter common to Wayne's westerns and war films, but when it came to one-on-one gunslinging, Eastwood was a far more efficient executioner than his predecessor.

Forget the love interest. Although he was involved with women, at no time did they appear to establish any permanent hold on his emotions: despite the greater sexual freedom available to film makers, Sergio Leone, director of the classic spaghetti westerns, scarcely ever gave his hero a significant love scene. It is as though relationships with women were becoming too problematic to be dealt with in the confines of a male-oriented action film.

As Dirty Harry, or to give him his full name and rank, Police Inspector Harry Callahan, Eastwood's belief that his first duty was to rid the city of San Francisco of wrongdoers – or, as he would put it, punks – was contrasted with the liberal (and, by implication, effeminate?) attitude of politicians and senior officers who seemed more concerned with the perpetrators' civil rights. By now, the dose of violence required to achieve an audience's arousal was beginning to rise considerably. The first, eponymous, Dirty Harry film makes do with four slaughtered punks and one dead psycho. In *Magnum Force*, Harry offs two hijackers, a couple of hoods, a pair of punks and five corrupt policemen. Having paused for breath in *The Enforcer*, whose body count drops to nine, Harry peaks in 1983's *Sudden Impact*, in which his score includes three black punks, three white hoods, one gangland boss, three white punks in a car, one further hood, a brace of punks on foot and a solitary token psycho.

In his prime, Clint was the absolute epitome of masculine cool. But he represented a fantasy figure for men in an age beset by insecurity. His fans would never be inspired to sign up to fight for their country as a result of seeing his films. Instead, they dreamed that the next time the boss gave them hell, or they got jostled on the street or ripped off by a garage mechanic, they would not simply mutter some feeble excuse and run away, but clench their jaw, give an ominous twitch to their narrowed eyes, pull out their great big Magnum and say, 'Go ahead. Make my day.'

Their identification was reinforced by the fact that Eastwood was still, like Wayne, a good, all-American hero. While much of the certainty about both man's and America's place in the world had been eroded, enough confidence remained for Eastwood to be recognised as the embodiment of masculinity. That he appeared to have a certain real-life sense of style and was prepared to make films like *Every Which Way But Loose*, which satirised his popular image, only added to his appeal.

But what of women? For Wayne, they were one of the two reasons – the flag being the other – that a man did what he does. They needed protecting. They were, with the occasionally feisty but tameable exception, gentle and loving and could be relied upon when a guy had just taken a bullet in the gut and could do with a cold compress across his fevered brow. Women were patently inferior to men but they were, nevertheless, very much a good thing. For Dirty Harry, however, the whole situation was much more complicated. He had girlfriends, but, like so many movie characters of the past two decades, he was divorced. So we knew that there had been a fundamental breakdown in his dealings with the opposite sex. Work, too, got in the way. Whereas Wayne could count on his girl's understanding, Eastwood operated in a world in which women competed with his duties for his attention. They refused to take second place.

In his own, self-directed films, such as *The Gauntlet* or *The Outlaw Josey Wales*, Eastwood tended to be more tolerant of emotional entanglement. In fact, *Josey Wales* ends on an almost pastoral note as the hero finds peace and tranquillity. The drawback for Eastwood *aficionados*, however, was that the woman with whom he settled down, in real life as on screen, was Sondra Locke – Clint's answer to Linda McCartney. In any case, by the time that their ardour had cooled, on both sides of the camera, the man himself had fallen from his perch at the top of the box-office charts.

His decline was due to two mutually reinforcing concepts. The first and most brutal was time: when a man approaches pensionable age (Eastwood was born on 31 May 1930) he may, as Sean Connery has discovered, carve out a new career as a cinematic father figure, but his days as an action-movie lead are numbered. To add to his box-office woes, Eastwood as a man discovered that his interests were more varied and more subtle than his screen persona would allow. As an actor and/or director of films like *Bird* or *White Hunter, Black Heart*, he has revealed himself to be a mature, intelligent film-maker of the highest quality. It's just a shame that the movie audience is predominantly adolescent and brain-dead.

In the end, Eastwood was able to recreate his box-office appeal by giving himself a Connery-style role as the grizzled old gunfighter in *Unforgiven*. In the meantime, however, his position as Hollywood's leading man had been taken – following a brief interregnum involving such major, but myth-free stars as Harrison Ford, Mel Gibson and Tom Cruise (the latter two of whom are far too pretty to be seen as true male archetypes) – by the one and only Arnold Schwarzenegger.

Arnie

As the first draft of this book was nearing completion, Arnold Schwarzenegger was reported to be preparing for his latest role . . . as the Tooth Fairy. This, one imagines, is another step in his continuing campaign to be seen as an all-round actor. But, *pace* his occasional attempts at light-hearted comedy, such as *Kindergarten Cop*, which he approaches with all the comic grace of a rhinoceros on Quaaludes, Schwarzenegger's work is notable for the ruthless eradication of all the redeeming features used to justify violent action by earlier Hollywood stars. For Schwarzenegger, brute force is its own justification. Why does he kill someone? Because he's there. Schwarzenegger is a new phenomenon, the superstar as bully.

This is not to deny his visceral appeal. When, halfway through the first *Terminator*, Schwarzenegger chops his hair and puts on a pair of impenetrable shades, the result is an icon of macho grace fit to rank alongside Brando. When, in *Terminator 2*, he equips himself with leathers, shades and a pump-action shotgun, before sitting astride a Harley-Davidson bike, he achieves a level of high-tech cool of which Eastwood would be proud. To see these scenes in a cinema and feel the twin forces of female excitement and male identification is to realise that, whatever our politics may say, our hormones have their own agenda.

In keeping with the supposedly more benevolent 1990s ethos, *Terminator 2* sees Arnie adopting the persona of a benevolently destructive robot, reprogrammed to avoid unnecessary death. But this is as unconvincing as decaffeinated coffee. If you want to know what Schwarzenegger is really all about, take a look at *Total Recall*.

This film, which may have cost as much as $70 million and will end up grossing many times that amount once foreign, video and TV sales are taken into account, is a happy hunting ground for gender deconstruction. In the first place, Arnie is very big and tough and strong . . . but he doesn't know who he is. His mind, his role and his very identity are all fake. His real self has been taken away. His new self is an invention. The metaphor for the male condition may well be unintentional – Arnie's public image is that of the last entirely unconfused male – but it could not be more apparent.

Among the many betrayals he faces during the film, the most telling is made by his wife. She is willing to have sex whenever he wants, but she really belongs to another man, the spymaster who is out to kill him. Given half a chance she attempts to kill him herself, thereby forcing him to beat her up. On Mars, Arnie meets another woman, who was – though we have little reason to believe this – his lover in the days when he was someone else. He joins up with her to defeat their mutual enemies and they end the film standing together on the newly oxygenated surface of the Red Planet.

They will, we assume, stay together, although no justification has been given for any emotional closeness, save the fact that they may have been together when he possessed his original identity. Except, as we also discover, his original self was a double agent who was working for the baddies so . . . oh, what the heck, who ever said that a movie had to be consistent?

During the course of the film, Arnie kills innumerable enemies. He breaks their necks. He shoots them. He runs them through with pneumatic drills. He rips their arms off while they're hanging from an elevator. He's very inventive.

I'm not particularly squeamish, but I was genuinely disgusted by my first viewing of *Total Recall*. The violence was so frequent and so relentless that it allowed for no real tension to develop. It was just a series of cheap thrills, based, as the journalist Toby Young has observed, on the nonstop action of a Nintendo game (a toy possessed by a vast proportion of the movie's target market), rather than any more traditional dramatic pattern. To make matters worse, the audience reacted with glee and hilarity to this display of pointless and graphically depicted bloodshed. Men and women, boys and girls, hooted with delight at every fresh atrocity.

Yet here was a film that displayed the insecurities of its parent culture with terrifying clarity. Look how frightened men are. They're surrounded by enemies. They can't trust their workmates (Arnie's best pal turns out to have been a spy, hired to keep an eye on him); they can't trust their womenfolk; they can't trust themselves. In desperation, they retreat to the last bastion of masculinity: they pump up their muscles and get out their guns. They become killing machines.

Pump it up

Is it any coincidence that America should be pouring out such a stream of bilious violence at the very time when its own identity and power is under challenge, from outside and from within? After seventy years of unchallenged prosperity and power, the United States is threatened by the economic resurgence of Europe and the Far East. The Japanese can't be killed in movies any more. They own Hollywood. And the cultural assumptions of the white heterosexual male – the breed epitomised by Schwarzenegger – are lying in tatters under the force of racial and sexual criticism.

Total Recall demonstrates that wanton violence is not a function of masculinity, but a dysfunction. It's what man resorts to when all else has failed. Violence on this scale, both in the movies and in such real-life incidents as the LA riots of 1992, is a destructive cry of despair from individuals, from a society and from a gender that are all profoundly messed up. Guns and muscles are not a demonstration of power: they're a last line of defence.

Bulking up has become Mr America's final resort. In the 1980s, rock stars abandoned the old, drug-induced emaciation epitomised by Keith Richards or David Bowie, in favour of the kind of power pectorals that would allow them to strip off their shirts on MTV. Bruce Springsteen, for example, began his career in the early 1970s looking like a street urchin and playing music of lyrical, freewheeling romanticism. By 1985, and the second leg of his 'Born in the USA' world tour, he was a pumped-up hunk, pounding out beefcake rock'n'roll to stadiums filled with young Republicans.

Springsteen pared himself down, both physically and musically, once the mid-1980s madness had passed. But what of the children of America? What was their response to the hard bodies paraded before them on their TV screens? In December 1988 the *Journal of the American Medical Association* revealed that as many as 6.6 per cent of all high-school seniors, and perhaps 500,000 teenagers in total, had taken anabolic steroids in pursuit of the perfect physique. This was the flip side of the pressures that produce countless thousands of anorexic girls (although it should be noted that the number of anorexic boys is rising dramatically). And, just as starvation has drastic effects upon the development of the female form – which, after all, is partly the point of it – so steroid abuse produces a catalogue of physically and socially abusive side effects.

In the words of *Time* magazine, 'Steroids can cause temporary acne and balding, upset hormone production and damage the heart and kidneys. Doctors suspect they may contribute to liver cancer and atherosclerosis . . . The drugs can stunt growth by accelerating bone maturation . . . Steroid abusers have experienced a shrinking of the testicles and impotence.'

Not bad, eh? But there's more. As well as leaving you spotty, bald and shrunken, steroids also provoke bouts of depression, irritability and rage, even leading to outbursts of violence. All this for the sake of looking butch.

There are other ways of achieving physical perfection. You can work out in a gym. If you really want to take it seriously, you can go to the grand-daddy of them all, Gold's Gym in Venice, California, just a couple of blocks off the beach. There you can parade the muscle tone you acquired by strapping yourself to the bright yellow torture machines that stand in long, implacable rows, like the tools on some perverted assembly line, where the finished product is pain and muscle fibre.

You can help the machines achieve the desired effect by eating Gold's vanilla nut flavour Metabolic Optimiser, the great-tasting, high-energy performance bar from Gold's Nutritional Products Division. Unlike other candy bars, it doesn't try to sell you on chocolate or toffee. Instead its wrapper tells you about the contents that count when it's body bulk you're after: amino acids, medium chain triclycerides and, best of all, chromium. Yum!

Still, if that doesn't work, and the TitanSports ICOPRO doesn't leave you feeling fit enough to fight against the masters, there is another way of getting the body beautiful. You can buy it from a surgeon.

Cosmetic surgery has traditionally been thought of as a means of making money out of female vanity. But then again, one of the weirder ironies of these post-feminist years is that, rather than women being freed from the cruel rules of appearance imposed by the patriarchy, what has actually happened is that *both* sexes have become imprisoned. The increased competition for jobs brought on by the recession, coupled with our society's deeply ingrained belief that young executives will work harder and better than older ones, has led to a boom in plastic surgery for middle-aged men.

According to America's Society of Plastic and Reconstructive Surgeons, 44,000 American men annually undergo eyelid surgery, 38,000 opt for liposuction, 14,000 have facelifts and some 14,500 are injected with collagen. There's no shame involved. When the American tabloid newspaper the *Star* claimed that singer Kenny Rogers had undergone liposuction to remove some unwanted avoirdupois, he immediately wrote to the paper.

Rogers didn't want to complain. After all, as he said, 'Cosmetic surgery . . . has made a major improvement in my life.' He just wanted to get the details right. 'Dr Martin, whom you quoted, did my first liposuction some three years ago, when he removed 3 to 4lbs of excess fat. My latest surgery was performed by Dr George Semel of Los Angeles, who has developed a new procedure which allowed him to take 4,500cc (approximately 11lbs) of additional fat from my stomach. I'm so impressed with the results I wanted to make sure he got the credit.'

Well, that's real neighbourly, for sure. But what happens if you don't want to take anything off, but you do want to put a bit on? Well, if you're looking for those mucho macho calves, buttocks or pecs that the gym just can't provide, I know just the man.

In a medical centre on Beverly Boulevard, Los Angeles, I met Dr Brian Novack (he's since moved to a suite on Wilshire, if you want to get in touch). Floppy-haired and moustachioed, this then thirty-eight-year-old flesh carver looked like a 1970s singer-songwriter: James Taylor's kid brother, maybe. As he talked, he toyed with a translucent sac, which sagged and flopped between his hands. 'It's a fun thing to play with,' he said. It was a female breast implant.

The men's ones don't behave like that. They're made of silicone, but they're hard to the touch with a slightly sticky surface. They look and feel like those giant novelty erasers kids used to have at school. Dr Novack carves this stuff. On the night before an operation, he whittles away at it, like a surgical Rodin, aiming for the shape that will give his patient total satisfaction. He knows what's wanted because he's already had a long consultation with his patient. 'They'll bring in photos of a model or someone they saw in some surfing magazine and they'll talk about what they want. And if they don't know, then I'll make them know. I tell them to go away and look at some pictures and come back. Because I want them to be happy.'

Not that Dr Novack is a slave to his customers' desires. 'I won't do anything that's against my artistic judgement or taste, because I don't want to have a bad product out there.'

For nearly ten thousand bucks, you don't expect anything but the best. And you get bespoke treatment on the big day, too. Once he has his patient anaesthetised and in the operating theatre, Dr Novack arranges him in the shape of a cross, with the arms at 90° to the body. He then cuts a tiny incision, one and a half inches long, and slices open a pocket underneath the existing pectoral muscle. Into this he inserts his hand-tooled implant.

As he explained, 'The implant goes in and out, back and forth and I'll say, "Gee, it's a little high here, or low there. I want to build it up a little bit here, or take it down a little bit there." No matter how much work you do beforehand, it still takes a little sculpting on the day.

'That takes a few hours and once it's done I make pretty close to a mirror image on the other side and make the final touch-ups. Then I close the incisions with special plastic surgery techniques. I don't have any stitches going through the skin. The patient can basically take a shower the next morning.'

Dr Novack has no ethical worries about putting lumps of plastic in people when he could be curing cancer or tending to sick refugees. In fact, he has a message for any would-be critics, which is, 'Let them eat cake. I could show you books of cards that people send me when I've done their surgery and they just feel fabulous. They can go through years of psychotherapy and they don't feel as well. People get in a bad mood, so they go to a store and blow a couple of thousand bucks on clothes. Here I'm giving them a lifetime product. They're buying a sculpture that they can wear and enjoy.'

They certainly seem to. I spoke with two of Dr Novack's patients and they were both delighted. 'I'd always been very flat-chested. I felt like the perennial 98lb weakling,' said Cloy Morton, a scientist at the University of Southern California. 'This was the answer to my dream. It really made me happier and it was well worth the money for the change in the way it made me feel about my body.

'I have some friends and I was over at their pool not long after it was done. I just walked in and they said, "My God, you have been going to the gym lately, haven't you?" '

Right now, the majority of men approaching Dr Novack for chest implants are gay. This should come as no surprise. Homosexuals are pioneers for the male sex. They experiment with attitudes and life styles that may take decades to reach the straight community. Gays are to straights as California is to Arkansas.

Still, it is one of the many paradoxes about extreme masculinity that it carries with it such a pungent air of camp. When Arnold Schwarzenegger wanted to break out of the body-building scene into general celebrity status in the early 1970s, it was the gay magazines that first were prepared to put him on their covers, or show him, naked, on their inside pages. The WWF wrestlers, with their permed, peroxide hair and their outrageous clothes, share with heavy metal music – which is, no surprise, the soundtrack of choice for their adventures – a bizarre effeminacy.

Metal musicians, who pride themselves on their machismo and sing songs about devil-worship, suicide and slaughter, will primp themselves up with leotards, mascara and those blonde, shaggy-dog hairdos more associated with the stiletto-wearing bimbos of the world's shopping malls. Wrestlers often do the same. Then they shave their chests and limbs, disposing of the body hair that is one of the male's distinctive secondary sexual characteristics, in order to achieve a perfect smoothness that is usually considered an ultra-feminine prerogative.

Ultra-masculinity seems to be so self-conscious that it ceases to be truly masculine. It's as if the muscles are really just a disguise. Maybe Joan Smith is right about our move towards androgyny. Maybe all these guys are pumping themselves up to look just like Randy Savage, when all along they'd much rather be Miss Elizabeth. There is, however, a more direct route to achieving that effect.

Chapter 4

Frocks Away

In December 1990, the British edition of *Cosmopolitan* ran the results of a massive reader survey on attitudes to sex. More than 15,000 women replied and they revealed themselves to be a lively, broad-minded bunch. To the question 'How often do you have sex?', the most common answer (34 per cent) was 3–5 times a week. On the other hand, when asked, 'How many partners have you had?' the largest single group (36 per cent) answered 2–5. So you might conclude that they were energetic, but faithful – a laudable combination.

Respondents were also asked which of a number of sexual activities they had participated in, and whether they enjoyed them (the latter figure included women who thought they would enjoy the activity if given the opportunity). The table below reproduces their answers.

	% participate	% enjoy
Cunnilingus	59	84
Fellatio	77	59
Wearing sexy underwear	53	67
Being held down	20	32
Pretending to fight	16	22
Pinching, biting, slapping partner	15	17
Being pinched, bitten or slapped by partner	14	18
Performing striptease	12	15
Anal sex	12	8
Role-playing with partner	8	9
Cross-dressing	2	1

Some of these responses will come as no surprise. Are we, for example, overly amazed that women give more head than they'd really like to, but get less than they deserve in return? I don't think so.

Other responses are rather more unexpected. I daresay that most men would be delighted to discover that women want to wear more sexy underwear and perform more stripteases than is currently the case. And the proportion of women who think that sex would be improved by a bit of good-natured rough and tumble, complete with slaps, bites and restraint, also suggests that the nation's bedrooms could soon become a lot livelier. One woman in twelve even enjoys anal sex (although one in eight has to put up with it anyway). Only one activity, it would appear, is rejected by 99 per cent of these women: cross-dressing. The moment a man puts on a frock, he can forget about having a happy wife or girlfriend. The overwhelming odds are that she'll hate it.

Over the last couple of years, men dressed as women have been a mini-trend in the nightclubs of London and New York. Films such as *Paris is Burning* have been made about Manhattan's vogueing she-males. Fashion magazines have run spreads of boys in miniskirts and feather boas. Gorgeous drag queens have even paraded upon the Paris catwalks. Ru-Paul Charles, a dazzling male Grace Jones, who stands six-foot seven in his/her thigh-high stiletto boots, has signed a record deal with the Tommy-Boy label. 'Drag isn't just acceptable now,' gushed *Vanity Fair* in November 1992, 'it's the baton-twirler at the head of the parade.'

These are all brief flickers of fashion that owe more to the dramatic traditions of female impersonation and burlesque than any more mundane motivation. In the everyday world, however, transvestism is a taboo that remains resolutely unbroken.

It is, to psychologists, a typical example of the distressing way in which men display forms of sexual perversity that are alien to women. Male cross-dressing is, they would say, maladaptive, perverse and fetishistic. Given the observations already made by Liam Hudson, it is an understandable consequence of the distortions that can be caused by a malformation or malfunction of the Male Wound. Men tend, as we have already seen, to invest inanimate objects with animate emotions. If a boy failed to make a successful transition from his mother to his father, but stayed too long on the mother's side of the fence, one might not be surprised if he were to end up having an over-intimate relationship first with her clothing and then with female clothing in general.

To traditional feminists, the transvestite is insulting and mocking women: they see transvestism as a profoundly misogynist act. But, more recently, academics such as Marjorie Garber, author of *Vested Interests: Cross-dressing and Cultural Anxiety*, have seen the cross-dresser (amongst whom she includes figures as diverse as Peter Pan and Elvis Presley) as a sexual radical who wages war on culturally predetermined notions of masculinity and femininity. The drag queen deconstructs the whole notion of gender, ending up – in Joan Smith's words – as 'an erotic rebel, a disruptive third force in the false dualism of conventional gender politics': a guerrilla in a girdle, as it were.

On the other hand, there is the view put forward by the rock singer Bono. Standing backstage at the Minneapolis Target Center, following yet another triumphant show by his band, U2, he allowed himself to be photographed wearing a diaphanous floral dress before pronouncing wistfully, 'Women get to wear all the good clothes.'

The most significant word in Bono's remark is 'all'. Women can, indeed, wear whatever they like. Women don't indulge in the 'perversion' of cross-dressing, because it's not a perversion for them. Flick through the pages of any fashion magazine and alongside the dresses you will see models in mannish suits or leather jackets, lumberjack shirts and heavy boots. In his 1992 April show, displaying the year's Fall collection, Ralph Lauren was inspired – or so that month's fashion pages informed me – by turn-of-the-century men's tailoring. His girls wore pinstripe suits, shirts, ties, bowler hats and pocket handkerchiefs. They even carried walking sticks. They looked great. But imagine, for a moment, what would happen if Mr Lauren sent the male models of his fall collection down the runway in turn-of-the-century women's tailoring, looking like the Ascot race-goers from *My Fair Lady*, complete with bustles, floor-length skirts and huge hats.

A woman only has to retain one or two visible elements of femininity in order to keep her gender identity intact. In front of me as I write these words is an advertisement for the Jaeger chain of clothing stores, published in the September 1992 American edition of *Vanity Fair* magazine. It is a three-quarter-length portrait of a woman wearing a man's charcoal grey, double-breasted suit, together with a striped shirt and woven silk tie. She is, to put it crudely, in drag. But her flowing hair and delicately made-up face reassure us that she is still unequivocally female.

For men, the opposite is true. It only takes one or two non-masculine elements to intrude upon a man's appearance for his whole identity to fall apart. He may be six foot six, bearded and wearing combat boots, but if he's got a skirt around his waist, he's no longer a man in the eyes of the world. Once again, one should note the extreme fragility of masculinity in the face of any threat to its conventions.

Women can become irate if their right to cross-dress is impeded. When the authorities at Birmingham University decreed that female students should arrive at their graduation ceremony wearing dark skirts, white blouses and dark shoes, the response was instantaneous. More than 1,000 undergraduates signed a petition demanding that the university's Vice-Chancellor, Professor Sir Michael Thompson, should reverse the order. One history student, Emma Thompson (no relation), huffed, 'We feel it is a sexist attitude to enforce this dress requirement. Many women feel in this day and age that they should be able to wear trousers.'

Now I don't give a damn whether Birmingham's young women wear skirts, trousers, pyjamas or bikinis to their graduation. I merely note this: educated young women in their early twenties, such as newly graduated students, form the core target market for *Cosmopolitan*, a magazine in which 99 per cent of their peer group announced that they would not wish to flirt with a man in a skirt. In other words, they denied their menfolk an option they would fight to preserve for themselves.

Transvestism is an unlikely mast upon which to fly the banner of men's liberation. But it illustrates two typical processes in society's treatment of men. The first is that we drastically limit male freedom of action by drawing rigidly defined boundaries around the perimeters of acceptably masculine behaviour. The second is that we then classify any action outside these boundaries as either criminal or, in this case, perverse. Neither of these processes apply to women, whose femininity is in no way compromised by the clothes they choose to wear, any more than it is by the job in which they choose to be employed.

The consequence of this is that those men who do not wish or feel able to conform to society's expectations are pushed into a cycle of denial, suppression and fear. The irony is that their initial impulse may not be nearly as kinky as is always assumed. After all, women choose between trousers and skirts on any particular day not because of any weird fetishism, but simply on the basis of how they feel. Maybe it's hot, so they wear a skirt. Maybe it's cold and they can't be bothered with finding matching tights, so they wear trousers. Maybe it just feels like a trouser day, or a long skirt day, or a short skirt day – who cares? When women put on their clothes, they automatically express themselves as the person they want to be. And if, a few hours or a few days later, they feel like someone else, well then they just express her, too.

Men, by contrast, cannot satisfy their need for expression within an innocent context, so they are forced to do so in one that is considered perverse. What may start out as an innocent desire is forced into a cul-de-sac of fetishism and warped sexuality. Unable, thanks to the male code of silence, to talk to friends lest they be exposed or ridiculed, these men carry their guilty secret like a festering wound. They long for sympathy and understanding. They know that they are unlikely to find it.

As a social spectacle, cross-dressing is gruesomely intriguing. More than that, it is a sort of metaphor for the limitations that are placed upon male behaviour as a whole. In the reasons why transvestism should be feared by the many, and desired by the few, lie many of masculinity's most delicate hidden secrets – secrets which relate to all men, even if they've never, in their wildest nightmares, dreamed of wearing a frock.

The butcher prefers him in a dress

The motivations for male transvestism vary from sexual fetishism through to sheer escapism: a man says goodbye to his burdens when he says goodbye to his trousers.

Misha Hervieu works at Madame Jo-Jo's, a transvestite cabaret in Soho. The son of an electrician who was, he says, a frustrated dancer, Misha started life as a carpenter's apprentice before going to college to study ballet. When we met in his small, south London flat, he was wearing a black lycra bra-top and micro-skirt, black stockings and black high-heeled shoes. His face was made up and his hair was painted. Under normal circumstances, he said, he'd just be wearing a T-shirt and jeans – well, you can't do the cleaning in a miniskirt, can you? – but he had some clients coming over and they expected him to dress up.

His clients are fellow transvestites. He acts as an untrained, but invaluable, counsellor to men who are just emerging, with infinite caution, from their own individual closets. He gives them a combination of a sympathetic ear and an expert's handy hints. He can advise them on how to cope with their families – the vast majority of his clients, like transvestites as a whole, are heterosexual – and he can tell them how to put on their mascara.

There is clearly a demand for Misha's services. The telephone rang continually throughout our hour-long interview. Many of the people who called, Misha said, would leave a message but then, terrified of exposure or blackmail, would go no further, not daring to make or keep an appointment. Of those who did come along, the majority were middle aged, or even older.

Younger men may know that they have strong transvestite impulses, but they will do everything they can to deny it. 'At a young age,' said Misha, 'a transvestite will say, "No way will I have my friends saying that I like dresses," so they overcompensate. They get married to prove their masculinity and they go for really male jobs. A lot of TVs join the armed services or are long-distance lorry drivers. It's only at a later stage that they say, "This is what I am. I know I'm not gay, I'm quite happy in my sexuality, but I do like to wear dresses." It's a realisation of who they really are.'

Having recognised their transvestism, these men tend to exaggerate in the other direction and are, according to Misha, far more effeminate and 'girly' than a real woman. His own transvestism is so everyday that he will happily pop down to his local shops in drag – his butcher, who knows him in both roles, apparently wishes he came in as a woman more often – as a result of which it is also less affected. 'If I was walking down the street and wanted to pass [as a woman] I used to take small steps and have feminine mannerisms. Now I don't bother. I just don't have the time. I don't do overtly feminine things, but that makes me, funnily enough, more female.'

But not completely so: 'I'm a reflection of women. I try to look good, but they're the real thing. Sometimes I do wish I was a woman. I do feel jealous now and then, but I get the best of both worlds, so they may be jealous of me. I've never wanted surgery to remove my three-piece suite, but I do feel as female as male.'

This position in the no-man's-land of gender identity has, in some ways, freed him as a man. 'In the old days I would shake hands with my father. Now I just say, I want a kiss. I love you. Bugger what people think.' Of his career as a dancer he remarks, 'There's no reason why a man can't be as graceful as a woman. There's real masculinity there.'

This is an opinion, however, that may not be shared at home, as Misha has himself discovered. '[Cross-dressing] made my ex-girlfriend feel inadequate. I wanted us both to enjoy it, but she didn't like me dressing up at all. She said, "I don't like it, I don't understand it and I don't want you doing it in front of me." We couldn't talk about it. We didn't get married because I wasn't prepared to change and I didn't want to impose on her. I'd hate for her to have to cope with friends saying, "He's a bit strange." '

The couple had a daughter. One of Misha's rules, which he gives to clients, is never to dress up in front of their children. As he says, 'They've got enough to worry about.' When, from time to time, his own daughter notices that her father is wearing make-up, she just inquires, 'Daddy, have you been dressing up as a clown again?'

His experiences with his partner were typical of those faced by TVs. 'A lot of TVs' wives never know. A lot of wives know, but don't want to. Some of the wives say, fair enough. All the man wants to do is put on a dress and have a wank, so who has he hurt? Has he hurt the wife? Maybe not, because he's got rid of stress and anxiety and he won't have a go at her because he's repressed and wound up.'

Is 'having a wank' the point of it all? 'There are a lot of men who want to get rid of their manhood, paying the bills and so forth, and just be a woman and relax and feel good. But a lot of it is to do with sex.'

To that end, most of Misha's clients want to dress up in the most blatantly sexual way possible. 'Whenever they come along, I always offer them a choice of make-up or clothes. Some of them want to dress up in clothing that would suit someone of their age, but nine out of ten want to look tarty. And nine and a half out of ten want to wear stockings.'

Some drag queens can look amazing. And women who spent the first decades of their lives as men have posed for *Playboy*. But the sight of an average man dressed as a backstreet slut is not a particularly appealing one.

'Samantha' was the *femme* name used by a twenty-nine-year-old sales manager from Manchester. We met in an unprepossessing lounge in the flat above a shop called Transformations in Prestwich, a

Manchester suburb. Here men can come to buy transvestite clothes and accessories – false breasts, man-size women's shoes, make-up – and, if they so choose, to spend a few hours as a Changeaway. For around £65 they are given a makeover, a wig and the run of the Transformations wardrobe. Then, decked out in all their finery, they retreat to the lounge where they sit and talk and watch television and gaze longingly at the world outside, wishing that they, too, could go tip-tapping down the street, just like a real woman.

Samantha arrived as a man wearing jeans and a purple T-shirt. He had brown hair, looked about five foot seven tall, and was of light build. One transformation later, she (strictly speaking, transvestite etiquette demands that a fully dressed trannie should always be referred to as 'she') was bedecked in a blonde wig and, inevitably, the TV uniform of black pelmet, seamed stockings and patent leather black stilettos. Despite the copious quantities of thick Dermablend make-up that had been lavished upon her face, her stubble was still clearly visible and her skin – this being a stuffy room and a hot September afternoon – was coated in a thin film of sweat. She looked a proper sight.

It is only fair to add that I wasn't any more gorgeous, even if, perhaps, just a tiny bit more tasteful. At least I wasn't wearing stockings and a suspender belt. Out of deference to my naturally hairy legs, I had teamed my purple Pineapple skirt (borrowed from my wife) with a pair of 'Velvet Soft Luxury Opaque Tights with Lycra'. These I had bought, in a steaming frenzy of embarrassment, at a Sock Shop concession on Euston station. As I took them off the stand on which they were displayed, my hands were shaking so much that I knocked the whole thing over, sending fifty pairs of velvet-soft tights scattering across the concourse. By now practically molten, I picked them all up, reserving the one, incriminating pair for myself. As if to suggest that the tights were, in fact, for someone quite else, I also bought a pair of regular socks for myself.

The tights came in a packet upon which was a picture of a female leg being stroked by its owner. The seven-word description of the contents was picked out in gold, copper-plate type on a rich black background. The message was one of sensuality and self-indulgence. The socks had a paper tag pinned across their tops. On it was the legend, 'Sock Shop, Men's, Shoe size UK 9½–10½.' If you wanted, in two simple images, the difference between our attitudes to male and female clothing, that was it.

The theory which I was hoping to test on my transvestite away-day in the Northwest was the proposition that men, once freed from the restraints and inhibitions imposed upon them by masculinity, and the drab uniformity that goes with it, would discover a new, richer, more indulgent, more expressive side to their natures.

I had had some evidence of this in the winter of 1979, when I was still a student at King's College, Cambridge. I ran a student nightclub there called – with a devastating flight of youthful imagination – The Club. Desperate for a gimmick with which to liven up a Christmas party, I decided to hold a black-tie ball . . . in reverse. The women would come in tuxedos and bow ties, while the men put on their girlfriends' party frocks.

At first, there was an understandable air of male uncertainty about the whole project. No man wanted to be seen being too keen to attend this event until he was sure that his friends were all going to make fools of themselves too. Eventually, the university's key, opinion-forming dudes decided that it would be a bit of a lark and an invisible seal of approval was granted. Before you could say 'Jill Robinson', suspender belts were twanging in Trinity and the solid citizens of Magdalene and St John's were squeezing into sexy little numbers in silk. In fact, once the floodgates had been opened, it soon became clear that the question, 'What am I going to wear?' was the one on every boy's lips.

On the day before the event itself, a deputation of women arrived on my doorstep. They had, they said, been discussing the party with their friends and they didn't feel that it was reasonable of me to expect them to turn up in black tie.

'Why on earth not?' I asked.

'It would be too boring. We'd all look the same.'

'So?' said I. 'We all look the same most of the time, but you seem to manage to tell the difference.'

'Ah yes,' said these liberated young ladies, 'but you're men. That's different.'

So it was that, when the big night came, the gentlemen's lavatory was filled with the studs of the university, the hard-drinking, red-blooded heroes whose conquests and adventures were the talk of the town. Standing before the lavatory mirrors they primped and preened like a bus load of Essex girls out on the pull. Oh, the care with which they touched up their eyeshadow and repaired the damage that dinner had done to their lipstick. Once legitimised by the presence of their fellow men, they felt entirely free to behave in ways that they would ruthlessly suppress in other, more normal circumstances.

And the women? Naturally, they came dressed as women as well.

Nearly a dozen years later, there I was in outer Manchester, tucking my private parts into the cache-sex (a sort of G-string that pulls a man's most distinctive features between his legs and out of sight), strapping on a vast, barmaid's bra stuffed with rubber titties, and surrendering to the tender ministrations of Judy, one of Transformations' beauticians.

She seemed remarkably tolerant of her unusual clientele. 'They're all sorts, just everyday men. They come from all walks of life. But when they get changed they become a different person. As soon as they get the clothes on, they become a she. You talk to them as if they were just another woman. They're more gentle than most blokes. They're softer.'

Did she, I wondered, think any less of them for their habit?

'No, not at all.'

What if her husband did it?

'That's a very difficult question to answer. I'd probably be concerned, but I just don't know how I'd cope with it.'

By now I was learning three important lessons. The first was that I do not look my best in a long, black, curly wig. The second was that I was not deriving any particular sexual *frisson* from the experience. And the third was that – in this context at least – the clothes made no difference at all to the way I felt. The reason, I realised, was that I was working. And be he dressed in jeans or a G-string, a working journalist is just a journalist – his story is all he has on his mind.

Luckily, however, Samantha was feeling the effects of 'her' transformation. 'I'd like to bonk. I just feel horny wearing this gear,' she said. 'I'm relaxed. And the more I do it the more relaxed I become.'

Samantha, who was married, had been dressing up for a decade or more. She didn't think much of Transformations' wardrobe, which was a blizzard of man-made fibres, but she was pleased, nonetheless, with her overall look. 'I wanted to be a bit of a tart. The girls downstairs said I looked good, but they probably say that to everyone. As soon as the wig goes on it makes all the difference. I felt embarrassed walking through the shop without my wig, but as soon as I had it on I was a right little flirt.' A pause, then: 'You know I envy women to some degree. They look great.'

Transformations is owned and managed by Stephanie-Anne Lloyd. This might come as a shock to the executives at Disney, but she believes that she is in the same business as they are. 'I've always said that our nearest competitor is Disneyland, because it's sheer escapism.

The thing of leaving that body with all its responsibilities and pressures and escape for a few hours until they go back . . .'

Both places, too, deal with cartoon stereotypes. Samantha wanted to be 'a bit of a tart' because, in his/her eyes, that was the most female she could be. She didn't want to be an ordinary woman, walking around in a pair of jeans or a cotton dress from Laura Ashley. She wanted the thrill of going to the extreme.

Of course, there are some differences between Walt's Magic Kingdom and Stephanie-Anne Lloyd's. At Transformations, it is the guests, rather than the staff, who dress up in funny costumes. 'Some want to be French maids, some want to be schoolgirls, some want to be princesses and we even have bridal wear for the ones that want to be brides,' she says. Also, few of us think of a desire to visit Disneyland as a guilty secret that has to be kept from the world at large.

For Ms Lloyd's customers, things could not be more different: 'I've had guys cry, absolutely break down and cry and say, "I've kept this secret for forty years, I've never told anyone" . . . I feel sorry for them because they've bottled it up for so many years. But I don't feel sorry [about their cross-dressing] because it's a good outlet. I think that on the scale of things that they can do . . . it's escapism, it's harmless, it's safe, you don't transmit any sexual diseases, it doesn't require emotional involvement with another person . . . I think it's healthy. It gives them a much-needed release.'

When one thinks of 'Samantha' with her hairy legs peeking out over the top of her sheer stockings, or the full-frontal nude photographs of Stephanie that were on sale in her shop on the day of my visit, along with an assortment of explicit 'she-male' transvestite videos, it's hard to think of cross-dressing as being entirely healthy. But is it any worse than the pastimes that are considered acceptably masculine? Is it any more deviant to wish to put on a dress than it is to wish to buy a 24-shot repeater shotgun and go into the forest to slaughter deer? Or people, come to that? Is it more dysfunctional to put on mascara than it is to pump oneself full of steroids, cortisone and painkillers in order to get through a professional football match? Is it really that much more weird than body building?

Perhaps the way to look at cross-dressing is to see it as a reasonable response to an unreasonable situation. The real perversion, one might say, is the definition of masculinity we insist upon for 'regular' guys. What is it about being male that forces people to act in this way? If men were kept on a looser rein, would they need to go to such extreme lengths in order to express every aspect of their personality – a form of self-expression that women increasingly take for granted?

Whatever its root causes, the fact remains that this is a pan-global activity. Transformations has expansion plans for European branches and there are transvestite groups the whole world over. Sydney, Australia, has a flourishing transvestite and transsexual community (the two phenomena are linked, but quite distinct). In Japan, where *onegata* – actors who train all their lives to play female parts, not as impersonators, but as women – are superstars, the Elizabeth Club caters for Tokyo's cross-dressing businessmen. According to an August 1991 feature in *New York Woman* magazine, somewhere between 3 and 5 per cent of American males are thought to cross-dress, and they are catered for by more than 300 self-help groups across the nation. In Kansas City, local TVs attend the annual Harvest Moon Ball, while every October Provincetown, Massachusetts, plays host to the Fantasia Fair, an annual cross-dressing convention.

To judge by the *New York Woman* report, there are few differences between cross-dressers in America and those on the other side of the Atlantic. Many had repressed their needs for years, following the pattern of compensation via displays of overt masculinity. Once dressed, they softened, becoming more gentle, relaxed and emotionally expressive: they displayed the qualities of empathy and communication more normally thought of as feminine.

Some could pass as women in the outside world without being 'read' as transvestites: they were party girls who went to clubs in tight leather skirts. But, by and large, the more they were allowed to cross-dress, the less they used it as a source of sexual excitement, preferring instead to relax and explore previously hidden sides to their personalities. As one of their girlfriends said, 'Some guys shoot pool to unwind. These fellows put on dresses.' Other women, however, found their men's proclivities more threatening. In the words of Dr Richard Docter, a clinical psychiatrist and the author of *Transvestites and Transsexuals: Toward a Theory of Cross-Gender Behaviour*, 'Not only do the wives live under the cloud of potential social rejection if the cross-dresser is found out, but they also become aware that the husband has a girlfriend on the side – himself.'

One can see how this might imperil a relationship. But why should society as a whole be so threatened by male cross-dressing? The most obvious answer is that it is a blatant challenge to the patriarchy. Men who put on women's clothing are letting the side down, forfeiting their power for the pleasures of the supposedly inferior sex. More than that, they are issuing a challenge to the very structure of masculinity.

Society has traditionally been constructed in such a way that all men make a form of Faustian pact. They sign away their emotional and sensual freedom of action and constrict the range of their personalities in exchange for the promise of power. The cross-dresser is refusing the terms of that contract and insisting on his right to be whoever he wants.

This may be an entirely logical move, given that the Devil can no longer deliver on his half of the deal. Men are losing their monopoly on power. Why, then, should women have the monopoly on gentleness and sensuality? And here we come to an important issue. Women dislike the notion of cross-dressing for two distinct reasons. In the first place, however much they may maintain that they want men who display more feminine characteristics, the truth is that they do not: they want their men to be men.

To be fair, heterosexual men feel the same way about women. However much a man may say that he wants his partner to possess such traditionally male virtues as financial independence, that desire ceases the moment that her success intrudes upon what he perceives to be her role as the woman in his life. The difference lies in the degree of tolerance. One woman, reading an early draft of this chapter, commented, 'I want a man with feminine characteristics. I just don't want a man in a dress.' Few women would disagree with her and most men (myself included) would understand her point of view. But suppose a man said, 'I just don't want a woman in trousers.' How much sympathy would he receive?

Deep down inside, the average woman is as conservative as the average man when it comes to defining sex-role stereotypes. In the words of Stephanie-Anne Lloyd, 'Women have a desire for someone strong to lean on. It allows them to show frailty and weakness because then they've got an anchor. So it passes the responsibility from them onto the man. If he becomes a New Man – I hate that phrase – the wife is liable to go off with someone she regards as being manly. And the guy's stood there with his feather duster thinking, "My God, what went wrong?" '

Secondly, the man who puts on a dress not only betrays his manhood, but he enters into the woman's sphere of influence. Those young women from Cambridge, who went on in later years to become bankers, lawyers, doctors and media stars, had no desire to be parted from their sartorial weaponry. Women often say that they don't want their men to be too good-looking or to take too much trouble over their appearance. Not only might that seem effeminate, but it might also distract attention from them and, as any traditional black-tie ball demonstrates, men are supposed to be the sombre backdrop against which women are displayed in all their glory.

No wonder, then, that men like Samantha envy real women so. But before 'she' becomes too caught up in her desires, she might like to consider the words of Stephanie-Anne Lloyd, the doyenne of Transformations: 'Our customers only want 1 per cent of femininity. They don't want the other 99 per cent. They don't want to be a real woman with responsibilities or kids. They don't want to have periods. They don't want to do the housework. They want the 1 per cent of glamour that a woman has in her life when she gets dressed up to go to a dinner party. That's the only bit they want because it's the ultra-feminine bit. It's the escapism, the pampering. It defines a man's idea of what a woman should be. But their idea of femininity is slightly different from reality.'

Maybe. But our ideas about masculinity are also a long way from being reasonable or accurate. Misconceptions about the nature of men handicap our response to some of the most serious problems currently facing society. Problems, for example, like child abuse.

Chapter 5

The Myth Of The Bad Man

When I started work on this book, one of the issues by which I was most deeply troubled was the sheer amount of evil that men appeared to do. Wherever one looked, from the pictures on the TV screen, to the words in a vast array of newspapers, books and magazines, one was confronted by the violence and abuse wreaked by man upon defenceless women and children. Men harassed and raped. They punched and abused. They butt-fucked little children, for God's sake. (I apologise for the crudity of the language, but it's only when you strip accusations of their jargon that their horrors become apparent.) There seemed to be no end to men's depravity.

I had never done any of these things, nor even wished to. Nor had I ever witnessed any of them. In all my years as a journalist, including several spent as a senior executive on a number of different publications, I am not aware that any of my female colleagues has ever been sexually harassed by me or anyone else. Nor do I for one moment believe that any of my close friends has ever beaten up his wife or sexually abused his little children. Nor does my wife recall that any of the women she knows have ever made the slightest reference to any such acts. We simply cannot afford to believe such things, because if we did, we would lose whatever faith we have in the power of love or friendship or, indeed, any of the values which make life remotely tolerable.

And yet, if the reports I read were to be credited – and many of them came from apparently unimpeachable, nay, official sources – the Western world was steadily being overrun by a plague of abusive behaviour. One in three children had experienced some form of sexual abuse. One in five women had been the victim of an attempted rape, or was it even, as some American academics claimed, one in two? One in seven university students actually had been raped. According to a respected academic authority, between 21 and 35 per cent of all women had suffered some form of domestic violence. And, in every case, the perpetrators of the terrible acts were men.

Try as one might to deny the claim that all men were rapists, or abusers, or wife-beaters, it was impossible not to feel overwhelmed by a sense of guilt. Trying to be a good man was like trying to be a good German – you could always feel the Nazis, or the perverts, in the background. Just as those Germans who were not involved in the Holocaust had to explain, both to the world and, perhaps more importantly, to themselves, how they could possibly have allowed it to happen, and then had to find some means of atoning for it, so I struggled to resolve my feelings of complicity in the crimes that men were apparently wreaking upon the rest of humanity.

My early interviews for this book – conversations with psychologists, scientists, therapists, counsellors and even the odd agony aunt – were all directed to answering the question: why do men behave so badly? Is it something which is unavoidable, a malevolence that is buried deep within the genes? Or is it a matter of conditioning, an anomaly that might, who knows, be 'cured' by changing the way in which we educate and condition little boys?

Some of these questions have been examined elsewhere in this book. They remain, I hope, central to any consideration of men today. But there's something else . . . The more I looked at the subject of male dysfunction, the more it seemed that the view that society was taking had become grotesquely distorted. This distortion took two main forms: in the first place, the accusations made against men had been inflated far beyond anything that was justified by the actual – as opposed to the claimed – evidence. And secondly, the ways in which women hurt their fellow human beings had been virtually ignored.

Just consider what happens if one takes all the claims about male malevolence at face value. Take all the estimated figures for female victimisation that I have mentioned above and add up the percentages. They come to more than 100 per cent. Now, it could be that some women suffer disproportionately, but the campaigners who come up with these figures also insist that the problems they describe are spread evenly throughout society. So, by their criteria, every single woman in the Western world has either been abused as a child, or raped, or attacked by a male partner.

Who's been doing it? Well, it could be that a few men commit many crimes each. That, after all, would be the common-sense view. But we're not dealing with common sense, we're dealing with political correctness, which insists that perpetrators are as evenly spread as their victims. So we have to conclude that every single man in the Western world has committed at least one of these acts.

Do you believe that this is possible? Do you believe that every single man you know, without exception, has actually committed some form of sexual or physical assault on a woman or child? Look round the dinner table at your friends. Are they all sex criminals? Think of your favourite football team or rock band. Fair enough, they might drive the odd car into the occasional hotel swimming pool, but is every single man on the pitch at the FA Cup Final, or on stage at a charity rock gig, really a violent pervert? Think of your father, brother, husband, boyfriend, son and workmates. Think of the firemen, ambulance drivers, air-sea rescue pilots, doctors and teachers you've come across or seen on the TV news. Think of the newsreader, come to that, and the weatherman, and the bloke behind the camera. If you believe the propaganda, you've got to believe that every single one of them deserves to be locked up.

Let's get specific and name some names. How about Michael Palin, for a start? I think one could say with a fair degree of certainty that the former Monty Python member and Phileas Fogg impersonator is one of the nicest, most popular people in show business. His image is that of a charming, unassuming and dedicated family man, and for once the image appears to be identical with the truth. Not only do Fleet Street's papers not have a bad word to say about Palin in public, they do not have any malicious, off-the-record gossip about him either. I know, because I checked. 'He lives just down the street from me,' said one media Rottweiler. 'He always says hello to my wife and my kids if he sees them on Hampstead Heath.'

Yet, if you find the estimates I have mentioned above – most of which will be examined in detail during the course of the next few chapters – convincing, then you have to believe that there is an overwhelming statistical probability that a paragon of decency like Michael Palin has either hit his wife or sexually abused his children or attempted to rape either his wife or another woman or women unknown.

Most readers will probably find that a gratuitously tasteless and disgusting suggestion. That's precisely the point, because every man has, implicitly, been put in the position into which I have just put poor Mr Palin. And the choice before us is either to believe the statistics which supposedly condemn him, along with every other man in the land, or to consider that the people who compiled them are either (a) misguided, (b) malevolent, or (c) plain nuts.

I know where my vote is going.

Before we go any further, let me get one thing straight. I have no desire whatsoever to try to put the boot on the other foot. I do not believe in some grotesque misogynist fantasy that men are the helpless victims of a vast gang of scheming, manipulative, violent bitches from hell. I just want to say that men do rather less harm than is currently believed and women do rather more. Not all of this harm takes the same form. Not all of it is looked at in the same way by our legal system: by and large, the harm that men do is illegal; by and large, the harm that women do is not. Some of it, perhaps, ought to be. But, in the end, we all work out about equal.

Their pretty little heads

There are, being simplistic about it, two classes of people who tend to disagree with this proposition. The first consists of those feminist academics and proselytisers who wish to persuade us that men are violent and violence is male. The second group to have been consistently prejudiced in favour of the proposition that men do most of the bad things in the world and that women don't have a mean thought in their pretty little heads consists of the nation's judges. Overwhelmingly male, elderly and upper-class, these eminent figures cling to a precious belief in the fragrant sanctity of the mother and wife.

In custody cases, they find it inconceivable that a man should want to look after his children, still less that he should be able to. In murder cases they frequently assume that any woman driven to murder must have been in some way out of her mind, since she could surely not have committed so vile an act of her own, independent volition. This, interestingly, is a belief which is shared by women's activists, who steadfastly contend that no woman ever attacks, still less murders, her partner without prolonged and overwhelming provocation.

Of course, there are enough cases in which the prejudices work in the other way – against, for example, a rape victim who has had the temerity to wear a short skirt – to provide plenty of ammunition to those critics who say that the judiciary is actually biased against women. In truth, I suspect that the answer is that women have a huge advantage in court so long as they conform to a distinctly outdated, indeed chauvinist, concept of ideal femininity, and a corresponding handicap when they do not. The answer to both these problems is to appoint a greater proportion of younger, non-politicised, female judges. They, as figures as far apart as John Mortimer and Edwina Currie have observed, are likely to be altogether less forgiving of women's genuine crimes, and less censorious about their imaginary ones.

In the meantime, an enormous gulf exists between the self-appointed spokespersons of womankind, and the rest of the female sex. It is my experience, and that of many of the men whose cases will be examined over the next few chapters, that most women are sympathetic to the situation of, for example, battered husbands or maternally abused boys, and are perfectly willing to accept the idea that a man can be the victim of a woman's wrongdoing.

One father to whom I spoke, whose ex-wife had prevented him from seeing his son for over three years, told me that his most vigorous supporters were all women. They could empathise with the pain of separation from a child and were appalled by the action his former partner was taking against him. Similarly, in the chapter on battered husbands, a woman police officer makes a trenchant attack on the idea that women have a monopoly on being victimised.

Throughout the research, writing and editing of this book I have found that the vast majority of women to whom I have spoken have been tolerant and broad-minded. They may not agree with every single proposition that I put forward – why should they? – but they welcome the fact that the debate is being addressed at all. Yet before I had even begun to write, I found myself under attack from female columnists who seemed convinced (usually without having taken the trouble to speak to me) that any challenge to feminist orthodoxy must be part of some misogynist plot against women as a whole.

One writer, Sarah Mower, claimed that, 'Just when we'd given up calling ourselves feminists, we're in for the fiercest, dirtiest outbreak of the sex war our generation has known . . . It's a specially aimed assault by educated, middle-class young men – in other words, exactly the sort of men we share our lives with . . . The greater the progress women are perceived as making, the more vicious the attack is likely to be. In Britain, where women notoriously still have no significant presence in boardroom or politics, we nevertheless face [an] eruption of misogyny.'

The *Independent*'s Suzanne Moore speculated: 'Maybe there are hordes of radical lesbians roaming the corridors of Eton waving their menstrual sponges in the faces of poor defenceless boys. Or maybe Mr Thomas is nostalgic for a time when men could behave as they liked and woman would have to put up with it.'

I can't say that I've ever been assaulted by the menstrual sponges of radical lesbians, but I do wonder why some women writers seem so determined to preserve their sense of victimisation and so unwilling to allow any challenge at all to their position. On the wilder shores of academia, the contrast between the majority of women and their would-be representatives becomes even more marked. In the *London Review of Books* of 23 July 1992, Margaret Anne Doody, Andrew Mellon Professor of English Literature at Vanderbilt University, Nashville, Tennessee, reviewed *Backlash*, by Susan Faludi, and *The War Against Women*, by Marilyn French.

During the course of the review, which ran over several thousand words, she set out the full list of crimes committed by society (i.e. men) against women. The media, she claimed, pumped out a continuous stream of anti-female messages. Even a TV programme as innocuous as the comedy series *Butterflies*, written by Carla Lane (a woman), was attacked for showing women's 'wistfulness, lack of assurance, uselessness and lack of direction'. The superb TV thriller *Prime Suspect*, starring Helen Mirren and written by Lynda la Plante, with technical advice from Detective Chief Inspector Jackie Malton (three more women), was not, as millions of viewers had innocently imagined, a stirring tale of one woman's triumph against institutional police chauvinism. Instead, 'The message was certainly sombre: your marriage will suffer and you won't be popular if you get involved with your work.'

The obsessive detective whose zeal affects his marriage and gets him into trouble with his bosses is, of course, an archetypal male hero. The brilliance of *Prime Suspect* was precisely the way in which the conventions of the weatherbeaten cop were transferred, with a positive feminist twist, onto a woman. To find defeat in such a triumph is really quite an achievement, but Ms Doody is not satisfied.

She wants us to know that she, like Susan Faludi, regards short skirts as an evil male conspiracy designed to infantilise women (of which misconception, more anon); that 'advertising portrays women as helpless, vulnerable, feckless, silly, so that they will have the humility necessary to take upon themselves the chains of marriage'; that Third

World men waste UN handouts on transistor radios; that 'the background to all women's lives is fear'; that 'individual "nice" men must . . . collude in woman-bashing in order to preserve the status of manhood'; that people who are opposed to the British monarchy are really woman haters who want to remove a female head of state; that 'the family is where social control of women must take place'; and that men believe that 'the proper attitude to women is one of contemptuous control, of never-ceasing vigilance, of, in short, permanent hostility.'

What comes across in this extraordinary diatribe against male misogyny is an equally powerful anger towards and hatred of men on the part of Professor Doody herself. This would not be of any great concern – the *London Review of Books*, for all its prestige, is not a publication likely to inflame the general public – were it not for the fact that these extreme ideas are influential far beyond the boundaries of university campuses and literary magazines.

Travelling through America in the summer of 1992, I repeatedly encountered writers and editors who would preface a conversation with a phrase like, 'Of course, I don't believe in political correctness,' or, 'No one takes that correctness shit seriously,' before launching into a conversation through which the fear of incorrectness ran like the red stripe through a tube of toothpaste. Whatever they may say, no serious, liberal commentator, in Britain or America, would dare make a head-on challenge to the basic premises that underpin contemporary feminism.

Meanwhile, government legislation on both sides of the Atlantic is hugely influenced by a desire on the part of male legislators to be seen to be pursuing correct policies. Needless to say, those who shout loudest are heard the most clearly: the majority stay as silent as the lambs. Furthermore, the vast bulk of sociological and psychological research into gender-related issues over the past few years has been conducted by people who have, *a priori*, determined where guilt lies.

Little attention is paid to domestic violence against men, for example, because there is almost no research into the subject. There is no research into the subject because, it cannot, politically, exist. Women are only allowed to be seen as victims, and nothing must threaten this point of view. Of course, since those deeply disturbed women who carry out assaults on their husbands or children do not – officially – exist, nothing can be done to help or counsel them, let alone their victims. But that, I suppose, is the price one pays for correctness.

One of the reasons why the current state of sexual politics, particularly in America, is so tormented is that the whole debate has become grievously distorted. To take a political parallel: the members of the British House of Commons, or the United States Congress, may divide along party lines, but most of them agree upon the basic assumptions of democracy, freedom of speech and economic liberty. The gulf between Conservatives and Labour, or Republicans and Democrats, is far smaller than that between, say, the Labour Party and the Socialist Workers, or the Republican Party and the Ku Klux Klan.

Similarly, men and women may have their disputes, which can, at times, become extremely bitter. But most men and most women have much more in common with each other – the belief, for example, that marriage should be a source of love and support to both parties – than most women do with the claim that men are engaged in a worldwide war against them. The difference between sexual politics and economic ones is that no one takes the Socialist Workers or the Klan seriously. Yet French, Doody and their like are treated as though they were offering the only valid analysis of the world in which we live.

Over the next few chapters, I will be looking at a number of social phenomena in which the man has, traditionally, been seen as the evildoer. I will be suggesting interpretations of what has been going on that are at odds with the conventions of contemporary thinking on the subject. But before I do so, let me give an example of the ways in which the exaggeration of male wrongdoing, and the denial of female complicity, have harmed our understanding of one particular crime, that of child abuse.

The child abuse industry

Towards the end of the 1980s, Britain, along with numerous other Western nations including both America and Australia, was gripped by a sense of moral panic. A clutch of self-appointed experts, ranging from doctors armed with controversial diagnostic techniques, through to fundamentalist Christians on the lookout for devil-worship, managed to persuade us that the land was rife with suffering, sexually abused little children.

The crime of child abuse as it is popularly conceived – forcible, non-consensual sex with an under-age child – is so shocking to most ordinary people that anyone who commits it should not be surprised to receive the full force of society's wrath. We know that abusers tend to be people who have themselves been abused. It is also true that abusers are, increasingly, to be found amongst the ranks of children as young as eight, boys and girls who are passing on the virus of pain with which they have already been infected. Yet to most of us, especially those who are themselves parents, the thought of little children being sexually assaulted and penetrated is almost unbearably repellent. Do not, for one second, suppose that I condone the action of the male child-abuser.

What became clear, however, as one horror story gave way to another, was that the hidden agenda behind the activities of many self-appointed guardians against abuse was at least as destructive, and as harmful, to the children as the abuse itself. The stories that came out of the Cleveland, Rochdale and Orkney child seizures, in which gangs of police and social workers made dawn raids on families, abducted their children and denied any contact between parent and child, made it quite clear that there was almost as much of a sickness in our medical and social services as there could ever have been amongst the parents whom they were accusing.

In Cleveland, children were being woken from their sleep in hospital wards, for anal and genital examination, in the early hours of the morning. Judicial reports into these cases suggested that children were interviewed in ways which owed more to the Gestapo than to child psychology. Children were verbally assaulted until they gave the 'correct' answer, which is to say the one that the investigators wanted to hear (there is every reason to believe that at least one celebrated American abuse case was distorted by similar interrogatory tactics). Parents were consistently denied the opportunity to act in their own defence. They were refused access to the media, the courts or even their local MPs. Only thanks to the determined action of MPs such as Stuart Bell, in the Cleveland case, and newspapers like the *Mail on Sunday*, which broke the Rochdale scandal, was the public at large alerted to what was going on.

By then, an unlikely alliance of anti-family and anti-patriarchy ideologues, fundamentalist religious fantasists and misguided media celebrities, ever eager for a bandwagon upon which to jump, had managed to persuade the nation that one in three children suffered from sexual abuse administered by men. What they tended not to reveal was that their conclusions were a deliberate twisting of research which defined abuse in an extremely general sense. Far from it consisting exclusively of the forcible intercourse which most of us tend to imagine, however disgustedly, in these circumstances, the term was applied to any unwanted sexual experience of any kind. Any little girl who had seen a flasher in the park had, by that definition, been abused. Any little boy whose maths teacher had put his hand on his knee had been abused.

Penetration by a penis formed a small proportion of total cases of abuse. Of those cases, many occurred between stepfathers and teenage daughters. Of the rest, most involved vaginal, rather than anal penetration. Only a minute fraction within a fraction comprised the activity alleged by the doctors at Cleveland, to wit, the anal penetration of small boys and girls by their fathers.

In my view, the obsessive search for evidence of such perverse behaviour tells you more about the people doing the searching than it does about those being searched. But, lest anyone doubt the harm that such obsession may bring, let me quote from a letter that was published in the *Solicitors' Family Law Association Newsletter*, November 1991. It was written by a lawyer, whose name and gender were not revealed, although I presume from the account given in the letter that she is female.

I was sexually abused over a period of approximately two and a half years by a male near-relative who had been adopted into my mother's family. The sexual abuse has, so far as I am aware, had little discernible effect upon me. The discovery of the sexual abuse and the trauma of the investigation by professionals have had a profound effect upon me.

When Esther Rantzen introduced her Childline, with the attendant television programmes, I watched and found, to my shock, that the description by one of the participants of the medical examination she had following discovery of sexual abuse caused me to cry uncontrollably.

I will never forget the ordeal I was put through at the age of seven. I will never forget the feelings of shame, degradation and intense physical invasion when examined by a paediatrician. I have no doubt that the same paediatrician would, if questioned, have stressed the consideration, tact, kindness and understanding he showed to me on examination.

My views were not sought as to whether I should be examined. I doubt that I would have had the knowledge or understanding to express or hold my own views. In retrospect, of course, I have strong views, but those are formed only with the knowledge of hindsight. I was seven: these were 'grown-ups' who knew best what should be done with me.

How much needless suffering is caused to children who have been sexually abused by the professionals? . . . In my own view, the sexual abuse I suffered was, to quote a judge in a rape trial, 'a pretty tepid affair'. The subsequent sexual abuse I suffered at the hands of a paediatrician will live with me for the rest of my life.

The children weren't the only ones blighted by the child abuse panic. In May 1988, shortly before the publication of the Butler-Sloss report on the Cleveland case, a book was published called *Child Sexual Abuse*. Written by Dr Danya Glaser, a consultant child psychiatrist at Guy's Hospital in London, and Dr Stephen Frosch, a lecturer in psychology at Birkbeck College, it was a handbook for social workers dealing with child abuse. Its central proposition was that the family was founded on patriarchy and the ownership of women and children by men. Family life was, consequently, inherently destructive: 'There are elements in all families that are potentially abusive – that is something inherent in families themselves,' the authors remarked.

Further to that, the abuse of children by their fathers was the inevitable result of men's 'emotional illiteracy', which meant that their 'ability to form emotional relationships is restricted'. Sex, in this world view, was little more than a means by which men dominated their partners: 'The link between such a form of masculinity and sex abuse is apparent.'

This is weasel-worded prejudice, disguised as rational opinion. To get its full flavour, merely – this is an old trick, but never mind – substitute the words 'black people' and 'blacks' for 'their fathers' and 'men' in the paragraph above. Now imagine that it ended with something like, 'The link between such a racial background and sex abuse is apparent.' These apparently sober words suddenly sound like blatant racism. So why did they not seem particularly offensive in the first instance? Because we are so used to pseudoscientific denunciations of men and masculinity that we have ceased to notice how repulsive they actually are.

Note, for example, the use of the word 'potentially'. If by 'potentially', the good doctors mean that I possess the strength 'potentially' to abuse my children if I were so inclined, then of course it is true. I have the same physical equipment as any other man. But the truth is so trivial as to be worthless. If, on the other hand, 'potential' is taken to mean an *actual*, if unfulfilled, urge or inclination to commit an act of depravity against my own children, then it is as offensive as it is inaccurate.

If men are, by definition, incapable of expressing the full range of human emotions, then they are clearly less than fully human. If they are less than human, then they do not deserve to be treated in the same way as those people – i.e. women – who are. And if that is the case, then you might as well start stoking up the ovens right now.

I do not believe that the authors are proposing a Final Solution for the gender problem. But I am quite certain that they express – perhaps unknowingly – a prejudice that is far more common than one might imagine. Lots of otherwise normal, rational people sincerely believe that men are far less sensitive or vulnerable than women, as if they walked around in a permanent state of emotional anaesthesia. Over the next few chapters, I will be discussing several different but related social phenomena, including sexual harassment, date-rape and domestic violence. In each of those areas, examples will be given of policies and conventions which only make sense if one presupposes that men do not feel pain, or fear, or emotional distress.

To this readers might say, 'But you told us yourself that the male brain is different – it's got all those inhibitors, or whatever they're called, that prevent men feeling.' Well, up to a point. The male brain may be structured in such a way that it does not permit the continual intermingling of thought and emotion that takes place in the female brain. A man's cerebral wiring is designed to limit distractions. It acts a bit like a Dolby system, which cuts out the hiss that might otherwise cloud a tape recording. But that does not mean that emotion is not present in men, nor that it cannot be just as acute as it is in women: it is simply handled in a different, more compartmentalised way.

One hesitates to think what might have gone through the mind of any impressionable young social worker who read, and believed, *Child Sexual Abuse* back in the dark days of 1988. How, for example, could one possibly write a favourable report on a father seeking increased contact with his children, knowing that such a father was, by virtue of his maleness, an emotional retard who was liable to translate his frustrated sexual urges into abuse at any moment? How could one be dispassionate about a man accused of abuse if one knew, as a matter of faith, that such abuse was 'potentially' present in every man?

These theories of male inadequacy are the intellectual equivalent of toxic waste. They poison the ground around them. And they need to be cleared away. Until they are, they will continue to affect official thinking on a sensitive subject, since bureaucrats are apt to believe the nonsense put out by supposed experts. And the feelings of individual human beings will continue to be corrupted. At the time that *Child Sexual Abuse* was published, my first daughter was four months old. Her birth had been, for me as for so many other parents, the best thing that had happened in my entire life. I was overwhelmed with love – an unconditional love that required no analysis or calculation. It had nothing to do with patriarchy. It was in no way emotionally illiterate. I just loved my child, end of story.

Except that these people, it seemed to me, wanted to sully and pervert that love. They wanted to strip it of any nobility or altruism. They wanted to interpret my actions as those of a pervert. An extreme reaction? Of course, but you have to remember the extraordinary atmosphere of the time. You have to consider the fear that the knock on the door in the middle of the night might be coming to your house next. I knew parents who were refusing to take their children to the doctor in case sore bottoms, brought on by upset stomachs, were interpreted as signs of abuse. I knew fathers who dared not bathe their children in case they were accused of improper conduct every time they washed their private parts. There was real evil abroad in the land.

Worse than that, in the hysteria surrounding abuse of children by men, abuse by women was ignored. Indeed, it was actively denied. It was, after all, impossible. It was politically incorrect.

The female abuser

Over the last few years, however, a different view of mother's abuse of their children has begun to emerge. For example, the official Home Office figures for victims of homicide in the United Kingdom show that the group most at risk is that of children under the age of one. They do not count as murder victims, since the crime that has been committed in the case of their deaths is referred to as 'infanticide'. If the American pattern holds good in this country, this is a crime that is substantially committed by women and it is, without too much shadow of doubt, a terminal form of abuse. And then there is the most common form of all physical abuse, the straightforward smack around the chops. Mothers are, by simple virtue of their incomparably greater contact with children, rather than any inherent lust for violence, far more likely to clobber their children than are fathers. Just wander round any supermarket and watch the wailing children and their mothers' flailing palms.

This leaves us with sexual abuse. Clearly, women don't do it in the same way that men do. They don't have penises with which to penetrate their children. What they do instead, as those who have suffered it will tell you, is envelop and overwhelm their little victims. The experience can leave those victims psychologically crippled.

For Kerry, a sufferer from maternal abuse whom I met at a men's group outside Sydney, Australia, the effect of his mother's abuse had been to leave him one of life's automatic victims. His mother had regularly got into bed with him, lain over and around him and fondled his genitalia. Now adult, he was the sort of man who seemed always to be getting ready to cower in the nearest available corner. All through his childhood and teens he had been mercilessly picked on and frequently beaten up by gangs at school and in the street. Teenage boys can be like animals: they smell weakness and prey upon it. It is often said that if you do not act as if you are in danger, you will not be, even in the roughest parts of town. Your body language will protect you. Kerry's body language screamed out his defencelessness. In the urban jungle, he was easy meat.

How common, then, is abuse by mothers and other women? Official Home Office figures show that only 2 per cent of sexual abuse cases in Britain involve female suspects. Of those convicted for abuse, 3 per cent are female, half of whom are charged together with a man. But how much is undetected or ignored?

As with so many other phenomena in which the woman is protagonist, rather than victim, no one really knows. The victims are extremely unwilling to come forward. They feel suffused with guilt about their own suffering, as if they themselves were to blame. Our instinctive denial of the possibility of such a crime – our atavistic revulsion at the thought that the madonna may turn out to be a whore – combined with a political refusal to accept the concept of female wrongdoing, has left this whole subject festering under a rock of ignorance.

The academic literature on the subject appears confused. In *The Sexually Abused Male, Vol. I: Prevalence, Impact and Treatment*, edited by Mic Hunter and published in 1990 by Lexington Books, Anthony J. Urquiza and Maria Capra confidently assert that 'Most boys and girls are victimised by male perpetrators who know them.'

Turning specifically to the question of sexually abused boys, the authors note that, 'The literature specifically addressing or identifying sexually victimised boys strongly identifies males as the primary perpetrators. Published studies report the percentage of male perpetrators as 97 per cent (Friedrich, Beilke and Urquiza, 1988), 88.9 per cent (Showers et al., 1983), 86 per cent (American Humane Association, 1981), 66.7 per cent (Urquiza, 1988) and 53.3 per cent (Risin and Koss, 1987). Separating the abuse into three levels of severity –

exhibition, fondling and penetration – Risin and Koss (1987) identified male perpetrators in 49.3 per cent, 60.9 per cent and 46.8 per cent of the cases, respectively.'

Hang on a minute. Just how strongly *does* the literature pin the blame on males? Urquiza himself shows a 30.3 per cent swing in his opinion between two studies published in the same year. And the only study that is quoted as categorising forms of abuse appears to suggest, staggeringly, that men do *not* commit the majority of cases of penetrative abuse, although this particular finding is not deemed worthy of comment by the authors. The same 1987 study by Risin and Koss is subsequently said to have found that 42.7 per cent of abusers were female (the missing 4 per cent were, presumably, not known), 'many of whom appeared to be babysitters, teachers, neighbours and parents' friends'.

Note that only one of these studies, all of which were carried out in America, appears to support the British Home Office's belief that 98 per cent of abusers are male. Either Americans have habits that are very different from those in Britain, or the British Government is way out of line. As we shall see, the latter is by far the more likely proposition.

One of the best ways of bringing the subject out into the open is by publicising the existence of both male victims and female perpetrators through stories in the media. In June 1991 the *Spectator* published an article by Sandra Barwick in which she suggested that child abuse may not, as had always been thought, be a purely male crime. This was, of course, a dangerous proposition. One female therapist told Barwick, 'I have had some feminists walk out of a talk when I have suggested that women also sexually abuse their children.' The therapist asked not to be named, 'or I may never be allowed in another support group'.

One researcher who would be named was Tilman Furniss, Professor of Child Psychiatry at Munster University and author of *The Multiple Professional Handbook of Child Sexual Abuse*. He said, 'At first it was thought that sexual abuse was all by men against girls ... We have increasing knowledge of female abusers assaulting children for the same reason as men – for sexual relief – though my feeling is that the total will turn out to be less than 50 per cent of all abusers.'

As Barwick remarked wryly, 'The guess of "less than 50 per cent" is a long way from the received wisdom of 2 per cent.'

Barwick went on to detail further examples of cases involving abuse by women, including the penetration of children's anuses with objects held by the mother or even, in one case, the family's much-loved female doctor. She also cited one therapist who calculated that about a quarter of all her patients were victims of sexual abuse by women. The therapist commented: 'It is no longer a surprise to me when children mention women as the assailant, but what is a surprise is this figure of 2 per cent. If that is true then the whole 2 per cent workload for the country is somehow ending up on my casebook.'

The *Spectator* article was read in Australia by Lyndall Crisp, editor of the prestigious *Bulletin* magazine. So astounded was she by its findings that she decided to investigate sexual abuse by women in Australia. Professor Kim Oates, who for fifteen years was in charge of the sexual abuse unit at Sydney's Royal Alexandria Hospital for Children, told Crisp: 'We used to think that most abuse happened within the family. Now, the indications are it's happening in pre-schools where women have the most access ... babysitters ... you don't want to think about that ... There's never been any argument that the main physical abusers are women. So there's a view around that you can say women cause physical abuse, but you're not allowed to say women sexually abuse.'

Once again, we see the bizarre coincidence of interest between radical feminist and judicial buffoon. Crisp mentions the case of a judge in the United States who dropped meticulously prepared charges brought against a woman by a social worker, detective and lawyer on the grounds that, 'Women don't do those kinds of things. Besides, the children need their mother.'

But what kind of mother would abuse her own children? Lyndall Crisp interviewed Elizabeth McMahon, a doctor from Denver, Colorado, now working as a counsellor of abuse victims in Melbourne, Australia. McMahon told her: 'In the case of women who sexually abuse, the victim is in years of sexual bondage before telling anyone. The mother is a fairly ruthless, dominating woman. Whereas with female victims it is anger that motivates them to report a male abuser, the male being sexually abused by a female is usually a very vulnerable personality who feels absolute shame and worthlessness. There isn't much publicity, it isn't talked about, so it's very hard for them to report it. They don't think they will be believed.

'Thanks to the women's movement, women have formed support groups for each other, but that hasn't happened with men ... The prognosis for males who have been sexually assaulted by their mothers or another female is not good for three reasons. One, because there are no clinics to deal specifically with their problem. Two, it has been going on a long time. Three, child victims of abuse who do best are those with strong, supportive mothers.'

Turning blind eyes

Crisp published her story in August 1991. On 31 March 1992, Kidscape, a British childcare charity, organised a conference on female sexual abusers. It was prompted by the extraordinary response to a single phone-in programme on women abusers on a London radio station, which had resulted in a flood of calls from victims. How did journalists respond?

Sarah Nelson, writing in the *Guardian*, got her retaliation in early. In a piece published before the conference she asserted that this interest in 'a tiny minority of women' was not due to genuine public concern, but because 'During the eighties professional literature strove to show the preponderance of male abusers was accidental or incomplete . . . It ignored any implication that sexual abuse was a problem of male attitudes [Really? We can't have been reading the same books – DT] . . . Powerful establishment forces merely went into brief retreat under the weight of feminist evidence. Today's stress on female sex offenders is part of the fight back on behalf of "gender-free" theory [as opposed to] demanding a radical look at men's responsibility to challenge other men's behaviour and at power relations between the sexes.'

Over the next few hundred words, Ms Nelson considered the professionals' 'anti-woman basis', the 'dynamics of male–female power and domestic violence', and the need to consider our 'deep-rooted prejudices about women'. She ended, 'Many child protection staff will feel this conference is fiddling while Rome burns and will ask that the urgent interest lavished on it is also given to 95 per cent of the problem of sexual abuse.'

The *Independent*'s report on the conference, perfectly fair in itself, concluded with a quotation by one Jan MacLeod of the Glasgow Women's Support Project: 'There has been a disproportionate amount of interest in female abusers. There is a danger that attention will be distracted from the main abusers: men.'

I wonder whether the Glasgow Women's Support Project has a copy of a fact sheet called 'Child Abuse and Neglect Data' published by the American Humane Association, whose offices can be found at 63 Inverness Drive, East Englewood, Colorado, USA. Admittedly, it comes from America, rather than Britain. But the members of the GWSP would surely agree that men in America are not likely to be any less satanic than their brothers in Britain. Please forgive this one last piece of number-crunching, but it is the best guide I have found to the numbers of all forms of abuse, on all types of children, by all kinds of perpetrators.

The following is a summary of data prepared by the AHA's children's division, the American Association for Protecting Children (AAPC). It concerns reported cases of child abuse and neglect collected throughout the USA between 1976 and 1987, when the Reagan administration – the one that cared so much about family values – cut their funding. By the time this book appears, there will be new information covering the period until 1990, assembled by the National Center on Child Abuse and Neglect in Washington, DC.

Preliminary estimates from that information indicate that the total number of abuse cases reported in 1990 was approximately 2.5 million, a 267 per cent rise on the figure for 1976, which was 669,000. As always in these cases, one has to be careful in drawing apocalyptic conclusions from such an apparently horrendous increase: much of it may be due to improved reporting, rather than an actual increase in activity.

In 1987, the last year for which accurate statistics are (at the time of writing) available, 2.2 million children were reported to have been abused or neglected. Of these reports, some 40 per cent were substantiated after investigation. The remaining 60 per cent were not, it should be added, dismissed as false; they were merely not proven, or not fully investigated.

Going back one further year, 1986 was the last year in which the AAPC was funded to collect data on each individual case. In that year, 2.1 million children were reported abused, of whom 737,000 were shown to have been maltreated. Of these, the form of maltreatment was broken down as follows (NB: the figures add up to more than 100 per cent since some children suffered multiple forms of abuse):

Type of maltreatment	Percent of children	(Actual numbers)
Major Physical Injury	2.6%	(21,000)
Minor Physical Injury	13.9%	(115,000)
Other (Unspecified) Physical Injury	11.1%	(84,000)

Sexual Maltreatment	15.7%	(132,000)
Deprivation of Necessities (Neglect)	54.9%	(429,000)
Emotional Maltreatment	8.3%	(71,000)
Other Maltreatment	7.9%	(61,000)

The AAPC's figures, however, do not stop with the forms of abuse, they also cover characteristics pertaining to its victims and perpetrators. They conclude that:

The average age of a child involved in an abusive or neglectful situation is 7.23 years old.

The victim is female in 53.5 per cent of the cases.

The perpetrator of the abuse is a parent in 81 per cent of the cases.

The average age of the perpetrator is 31.7 years and is male in 46.7 per cent of the cases.

Stress factors acting on abusive families include health problems (42.8 per cent of cases), financial worries (40.8 per cent) and family interaction difficulties.

You will notice that one staggering finding of this research, whilst it is clearly implied by the figures above, is not actually stated in explicit terms. In fact, it is specifically hidden. The finding is that, according to an authoritative study of every single case of child abuse in the entire United States – a study which requires no extrapolation whatever since it covers 100 per cent of the population, and whose findings I have personally checked with staff at the American Humane Association – slightly more than half of all child abuse (53.3 per cent, to be exact) is carried out by women.

Let me run that by you one more time: more than half of all child abuse in the United States of America in 1986 was carried out by women.

Now, what the survey does not specify is the proportion of individual forms of abuse committed by men and women. It could still be that men commit the majority of acts of sexual abuse. But that begs another question: why are we so obsessed by that particular means of doing harm to a child? Is a child who has been beaten, or starved, or verbally humiliated any better off than one who has been sexually assaulted?

It is generally agreed that a child who is compelled to have sex with an adult against his or her will suffers lasting damage. Certainly that would be the common-sense view, and one with which, as a parent, I would instinctively agree. In August 1992, however, the *New Statesman* published a special issue devoted to opinions that were politically incorrect. One of its articles, by Edward Barrie, suggested that the after-effects of sexual activity might be less traumatic to children than had previously been supposed. In particular, he said:

An enormous investigation was carried out for the German police by Dr Michael Baurmann, who reported his findings in 1983. His team carefully assessed 8,058 young people of both sexes (more girls than boys) involved in illegal sexual relationships. They found that in many cases no harm was done – neither emotional nor physical. About 1,000 boys under the age of 14 took part in the study, and not one of those was found to have been harmed. Harm to the girls, when it occurred, was sometimes (not always) a result of the sex act itself, and sometimes the result of heavy-handedness by police, parents and others in the aftermath. Baurmann has shown conclusively that a child may well become a victim purely because victimisation is expected. More recent police department follow-up studies have confirmed the findings.

Those findings, astounding though they seem at first glance, tally with the experiences of the solicitor whose letter about her experiences of abuse I reproduced earlier in this chapter. They make me question whether the important social issue which both British and American society needs to confront is not abuse itself, but our apparent obsession with it.

Barrie remarks: 'Perhaps most sinister of all, a young woman university graduate working on a doctoral thesis and pursuing the "harm done" aspects of abuse, with help from . . . overseas experts, was denied a grant unless she came up with findings that would help the authorities "detect paedophiles". She found this distortion of her views unacceptable.'

At this point, the truth is so clouded by exaggeration and confusion that one cannot do anything other than speculate about what is really going on. But when celebrities queue up to reveal ever more lurid accounts of their childhood experiences, or publicise abuse helplines, the sickness to which they bear witness may just be the profound suspicion with which Anglo-Saxon society regards sex. That, and the belief that the quickest route to public approval is to label oneself a victim – even if one happens to be a millionaire rock star, or a candidate for the Presidency.

Consider, specifically, the determination with which some women seek to paint a picture of rampant sexual abuse, practised entirely by men. Is this motivated by an altruistic desire to cure a social malaise, or just a fearful hostility towards male sexuality as a whole? Are they simply projecting their own terror onto children? Is there anything to choose between the dysfunction that causes an adult to seek out sex with children, and the dysfunction that persuades a doctor or social worker that she is surrounded, on every side, by a raging sea of sex abuse?

Meanwhile, why won't anyone have the courage and the honesty to confront and deal with abuse carried out by women? Perhaps they assume that it isn't serious. Perhaps the women, trapped with their kids all day long, just inflict minor injuries. Maybe there are single mums who, desperate to get out and earn some money, leave their children unattended, or neglected in an inadequate day-care centre. It's a plausible scenario and it would, after all, ill behoove those of us who live in comfort to criticise the behaviour of women on the breadline. Perhaps the really serious assaults are committed by men.

Fair enough, we'll look at the fatalities. In 1986, the AAPC was only able to collect figures on infanticide from twenty states, representing about 50 per cent of the total US child population. The following statistics are not, therefore, complete, but they come from a sample size sufficient to satisfy the most critical statistician: the margin of error is so minimal as to be negligible. The following, then, are the AAPC's findings:

In the 20 states surveyed there were 556 child fatalities as a result of maltreatment.

The average age of the victims was 2.8 years.

The victim was male in 53.7 per cent of cases.

The perpetrator was a parent in 76.4 per cent of cases.

In 62 per cent of the cases, the cause of death was a physical injury, while neglect was the cause in 44.3 per cent of the cases.

The perpetrator was on average 27.3 years old and was female in 55.7 per cent of the cases.

So, in cases of child fatality, perpetrators are actually more likely to be female than in lesser cases of abuse. And their victims are more likely to be little boys. This is, in other words, exactly the opposite of the line spouted by activists, parroted by the media, and taken as gospel by government legislators.

Figures from the National Committee for the Prevention of Child Abuse and Neglect for 1990 show that there was a nationwide total of 1,211 childhood fatalities in America as a result of maltreatment. Assuming that the male–female proportions have remained constant, that would work out as 654 boys and 557 girls, killed by 678 women and 533 men.

In Britain the situation is less clear-cut. One can say with certainty that rates of child homicide are – like all other forms of killing – far lower on this side of the Atlantic: in 1990 a total of seventy-nine British children under the age of sixteen were victims of homicide. Even allowing for differences in population, that still indicates a homicide rate that is 3.4 times as high in the US as in Britain.

That said, the single most dangerous age that any citizen of Great Britain can be in terms of murder risk is less than one year old. In fact, a baby is nearly four times more likely to be murdered than the average British citizen. Thirty babies were killed in 1990, which represents a rate of forty-four offences per million population within that age range, compared with twelve homicides per million in the population as a whole. Of those babies, exactly half were male and half female. If, however, one looks at all the cases of infanticide in the period 1980–90, the average distribution of victims is 57 per cent male and 43 per cent female.

The relative figures for victims, therefore, are roughly comparable with American findings. One cannot, however, say anything about the perpetrators of these crimes for a surprising, but fascinating, reason. In the years 1980–90, 293 children aged less than one year old were victims of infanticide in Britain. Yet only forty-two suspects were charged with infanticide in the same period. What happened to all the others? After all, allowing for those cases in which the child was attacked by both its parents, one would expect well over 300 people to be charged. There can surely be relatively few cases of unsolved infanticide.

In the years 1989–90, the discrepancy was particularly marked. There were fifty victims and only one suspect brought to court – a clear-up rate of 2 per cent, which, even by the present wretched standards of police competence, could hardly be described as satisfactory.

Could it be that the legal system simply finds it intolerable to contemplate female perpetrators? The notion of a mother who kills her own child is profoundly horrifying. These days we talk about post-natal depression, or baby blues, as a means of explaining acts which are otherwise inconceivable. Yet, purely by virtue of the intimacy of their relationship, the stress imposed on the mother and the amount of time that mother and child spend together, it would not seem unreasonable to suppose that the majority of small babies are killed by their mothers. Unfortunately, as with most of the other social phenomena with which we shall be dealing over the next few chapters, the numbers dry up once men stop being the bad guys.

Patterns of prejudice

What can we conclude, then, about the way in which child abuse, both sexual and non-sexual, is reported? And what should it tell us, particularly those of us who, as men, stand accused of these terrible crimes?

1. The accepted orthodoxy is that all abusers are male. The less accepted, but still widespread view is that all males are potential abusers. (For abusers, read rapists, sexual harassers, violent spouses, etc.) This orthodoxy is offensive, grossly prejudicial, and inaccurate.

2. A denial of reality by political extremists on the one hand, and judicial fogeys on the other, distorts debate, social policy and legal action. Women, it is felt, can only commit a crime if deranged, or misled (by a man), or provoked (by a man), or abused (by a man). I call this the Victorian Fallacy, after the Queen who refused to accept that women could be homosexual, thereby committing gay men to a century of furtive illegality, whilst leaving supposedly non-existent lesbians free to do as they pleased without fear of legal sanction.

3. The male victims of abuse (ditto domestic violence, harassment, etc.) are terrified of coming forward for fear of facing disbelief and contempt in equal proportions. They feel unmanned and humiliated by their experiences. They are not allowed by the prevailing ideology to be victims.

4. Once accurate statistics are made available, it becomes clear that the situation is much more evenly balanced than had previously been

believed. In other words, men and women are equally capable of committing acts of evil.

5. No formal study has yet been carried out on men as victims. No government money or interest is given to men as victims. Nor is there evidence of any official interest in commissioning academic research into their situation.

6. Given men's unwillingness to discuss such subjects in public, combined with the prejudice encountered by those men who do speak out, it often takes action by female journalists and therapists to bring an issue out into the open. Any hope of recognition of men's issues is currently dependent on moderate women overcoming their radical sisters and setting out a more open-minded agenda.

7. Men need a network of support and – with the exception of the gay community, which has been forced to organise in order to survive – they haven't got it. Nothing will change until men are prepared to shed their inhibitions and their fear of female disapproval and get their act together. It is not fair either to blame women or to depend upon them. Not if you want to be a real grown-up.

Now that that's been established, let's go and slaughter a few more sacred cows, starting at the office . . .

Chapter 6

The Rules Of Harassment

In the summer of 1992, two court cases involving British Army personnel made newspaper headlines. In one, a female member of the Ulster Defence Regiment was sentenced to five years' imprisonment for the murder of her lover's wife. She had cut her victim's throat with a knife. In another, a court martial found a colonel in the Territorial Army guilty of sexual harassment after he had entered women's barracks at night, propositioned several officers and fondled two of them. He caused no physical harm to either women. Yet so great was the public pressure to crack down on harassment that he was sentenced to four years in jail.

Meanwhile, on the other side of the Atlantic, the US Navy was having more trouble fighting harassment than it had had fifty years ago fighting the Japanese. The 'Tailhook' scandal had cost the job of the Secretary of the Navy and prompted a 2,000-page report into allegations of misconduct against male Navy pilots at an annual convention. Twenty-six female officers had alleged that they were made to run a gauntlet of molesting men who had also made them drink from a cup shaped like a rhinoceros's penis. In the absence of any confessions on the part of the men involved, 4,500 promotions, retirements and changes of command had been frozen.

To add to the débâcle, a certain Service Agent Laney Spineger, who had been called in to investigate claims of sexual harassment made by one Lt. Paula Coughlin against four Navy pilots, found himself becoming attracted to the complainant. He asked her out. He even called her 'Sweet Cakes'. So offended was Lt. Coughlin that she complained about him, too, and another service agent had to take over the assignment.

One fears for the future of the free world if it is to be protected by naval personnel who take fright at being called Sweet Cakes. Perhaps the US can insist that its future opponents only fight War Lite – a caring, non-sexist version of the previous, high-calorie form of combat. Still, some American women are evidently made of sterner stuff.

On 29 October 1991, as Anita Hill's allegations that Judge Clarence Thomas had sexually harassed her at work rumbled around Capitol Hill, Helen Gurley Brown, creator of the modern *Cosmopolitan*, gave readers of the *Wall Street Journal* the benefit of her opinions on the subject. In a piece entitled, 'At Work, Sexual Electricity Sparks Creativity', the author of *Sex and the Single Girl* and conceiver of that classic slogan, 'If I have only one life, let me live it as a blonde,' recalled her days as a young woman working at Radio KHJ, Los Angeles.

Ms Brown wrote, 'I know about sexual harassment,' before telling the denizens of Wall Street about 'a dandy game called "Scuttle"' which her male co-workers used to play. The game consisted of what English public schoolboys would call de-bagging: in other words, chasing a secretary through the office, catching her, holding her down and removing her knickers. Even the most Neanderthal of workplace chauvinists might be forced to concede that this was just a little bit beyond the line that divides acceptable office behaviour from blatant offensiveness, but Ms Gurley Brown retained a remarkably open mind about it all. She noted that, although they protested about the game, 'the girls wore their prettiest panties to work'. Indeed, her only complaint was that she herself was never scuttled.

So was *Cosmopolitan* magazine, with its bizarre admixture of feminism and flirtation, just Gurley Brown's way of getting back at men for their refusal to scuttle her as a young working girl? Only Ms Gurley Brown and her analyst can say. What is certain is that her tolerant view of sexual shenanigans in the office is not one that would be shared by most career women. Sexual harassment in the workplace is rapidly becoming one of the great *causes célèbres* of the women's movement all over the Western world.

Sacked, or seduced?

Here are two stories, told in the first person, dealing with the subject of office sex. The first, which appeared in the *Daily Mail* of 17 October 1991, is the story of Colin, a thirty-seven-year-old father of three. It appeared under the headline, 'I made a girl's life a misery for a year – what an idiot I was'.

Right from the very first day I liked Maggie . . . she was not only an extremely attractive twenty-five-year-old with long copper-red hair and a lovely figure, but was also very bright. The real trouble was that I never admitted, either to myself or to anyone else, how fascinated by her I was. So instead of behaving naturally with her, I was self-conscious and ill at ease.

One way of dealing with that was to make suggestive remarks. Although as an older married man I was initially quite shy, and found it hard to think of things to say to Maggie, I soon discovered that teasing seemed to have the desired effect of getting her attention and making her notice me more than others. I wish someone had stopped me there and then. Not one of my colleagues ever hinted to me that I might be making a fool of myself. She said later that I had made her life a misery – making it an ordeal even to walk to the office in the mornings. I never realised that, or I would have stopped it straight away. I always believed that Maggie enjoyed my teasing and even fantasised that she found me attractive.

Colin only realised the extent of Maggie's distress when her boyfriend walked into his office and punched him on the jaw. He then resigned from his job on the following morning, after a meeting between Maggie and his boss. When told of what had happened, his wife 'lost respect for me which I can never regain', his teenage sons teased him for being a dirty old man and his daughter said she was disgusted and would never kiss him again.

His reaction? 'That hurt me deeply, but I knew that it was probably less punishment than I deserved . . . there was nothing I could say to defend myself.'

The second story was told by the pseudonymous 'Susan White' in the January 1992 edition of American *New Woman* magazine. She was working at a magazine when 'Tom' joined the staff as a senior editor. When she was introduced to Tom at an editorial conference, 'I felt a rush, a hot river surge through my body. When I heard my name, my face burned, my knees turned to liquid and when I looked up I knew why. Tom was staring dead centre into my eyes.'

Following this somewhat disconcerting introduction, Susan took pains to ignore Tom as best she could.

I tried to fade into the woodwork and part of me wished Tom would also disappear . . . Then my vision became a reality.

I was working late at the office, hunched over my computer, when I heard a knock at my door. Assuming it was my assistant, I didn't even bother turning around as I said, 'Come in.'

But once the door was opened, I knew it was him. When I turned around and looked up, without speaking a word, Tom bent over my desk and pressed his lips on mine. I opened my mouth and encouraged his passion. Our embrace felt like a lifetime of longing had been born, given flight. It seemed an eternity as we . . .

. . . and so on, and on, and on.

Let's just compare these two stories. One is the agonised, guilt-ridden cry of a man who has lost his job, the love of his family and his self-respect. The other is a bodice-ripping true-life drama that might have stepped straight from the pages of a Sidney Sheldon blockbuster. But are the scenarios all that different?

Clearly the men are of a different calibre when it comes to their animal magnetism. Colin, the harasser, comes across as shy, insecure and sexually unsuccessful. We cannot form any opinion as to his physical attractions, but Maggie clearly found them perfectly resistible. Tom, on the other hand, turns out to be a regular office hunk, at least in Susan's eyes: '[He] had startling good looks, thick wavy hair flecked with the same shade of gray as his eyes. He dressed in corduroys and tweeds and had a smile that was at once charming and wry. His humour and intelligence danced across his face.' No one but Harrison Ford or Kevin Costner will do when it comes to playing Tom in the film of this particular story.

Tom is also far cooler when it comes to conducting his pursuit of Susan. Whereas Colin thrashes around in a swamp of misguided dirty remarks, Tom plays it smart. He says nothing at all for a month and then cuts straight to the chase, tongue-wrestling with Susan right there and then on her office desk. You have to admire the man's *élan*.

But what if Susan had said, 'No'? After all, we know that she had done her best to disguise her feelings by going out of her way to avoid Tom. He, being the very paragon of a modern ladies' man, correctly interprets this as a paradoxical form of come-on. But what if he had been wrong? Or, just as possible, what if she had been leading him on, but didn't want to admit it, not even to herself, and so feigned repulsion and horror at the arrival of his tongue in her mouth, even though she was longing for it really?

Under these circumstances, Tom might very well have found himself on the wrong end of a sexual harassment suit. He, too, might have been out on his ear, with the additional penalty of an all-American court action to follow. Granted, the $107 million case reported on in an earlier chapter is a bit steep, even by trans-Atlantic standards, but there are plenty of other precedents. Tiffany, the jewellers, were hit with a $12 million claim when one of their diamond buyers alleged that a manager had tried to rape her. And an Ohio company was forced to pay out $3.1 million when a female employee claimed that her supervisor had demanded she perform oral sex on him, or face dismissal.

That case sounds like straightforward extortion. You don't have to be Gloria Steinem to see that bosses who tell staff, 'Blow my dick or you get the sack,' are asking for more trouble than sex. Similarly, the Geffen record executive who, allegedly, stuck his penis into his secretary's ear, fondled her buttocks and ejaculated onto a magazine that he had placed in front of her was, even by the notoriously lax standards of the record industry, pushing his luck. But when you get down to more mundane levels of interaction between two adults of opposite sexes, the waters become much, much murkier.

In 1991 an American appellate court ruled that the test of harassment was whether a 'reasonable woman' would be concerned by the behaviour under examination. This effectively suggests that harassment is harassment whenever a woman wants it to be so. Thus Susan was not harassed, because she wanted Tom to kiss her, but Maggie was harassed, because she did not want Colin to pester her with juvenile remarks. The problem arises, however, that Tom did not know for sure that Susan was ready for action until he tried his luck that night in her office. And Colin received no indication that his filthy juvenilia were not regarded as a charming antecedent to physical activity until Maggie's boyfriend whopped him in the face.

When you're a man you never know until you've tried. We live in a society in which men are still supposed to initiate sexual or romantic activity. As a result, men become used to playing the percentages. In the same way that Gary Lineker, for example, used to make 100 runs into the opposition penalty area on the assumption that he might get the ball on five of them and, with any luck, score on one, so men try out their arsenal of chat-ups, fondles and tentative kisses in the full knowledge that rejection will outnumber acceptance by a pretty substantial margin. In the cases mentioned above, the only moral difference between Colin and Tom is that Tom timed his run into the penalty area considerably more skilfully than Colin. The consequences of their actions, however, could not have been more different.

Until recently, there have been quite a few successful Toms about. Some 35 per cent of all sexual relationships begin in the workplace – hardly surprisingly, when you reckon that the workplace is where we spend about 35 per cent of our adult lives. But how many men still reckon that the unlikely upside of a sexual encounter is worth the probable downside of an ignominious sacking? The very same behaviour which, in a man whom they find attractive, is seen by women as being acceptable, not to say compulsory, is regarded as harassment coming from a man in whom they have no interest.

The more educated a woman is, according to a *Sunday Times* poll on the subject, the more likely this is to be the case. A successful lawyer is far more likely than a mere shopgirl to perceive a wide range of activities, from physical contact right down to unwanted invitations to dinner, as potentially constituting harassment. The irony that a lawyer is far less likely to face genuine harassment than a young woman at the bottom end of the professional food-chain is neither here nor there. In an age in which the opinions of a 'reasonable woman' are the test, no man can afford to make a mistake. Not when that mistake is considered to be a crime.

The harassed man

Men might be best advised to forget all about sex and live in an atmosphere of monastic paranoia. According to a survey by The Communications Group, published in 1992, 78 per cent of major companies expect their workforce to be affected by the need for politically correct behaviour. In the office of the future, for example, men will neither compliment women on their dress, should they approve of it, nor suggest that it is inappropriate, if they do not. Nor will physical contact, under any circumstances, be appropriate. Sex, of course, is right out of the question.

The trouble is, it isn't. As my grandmother used to say, 'Nothing propinks like propinquity.' Or, to put it another way, if you jam lots of members of opposite sexes into a confined space for a minimum eight hours a day, nature is bound to take its course. And the truth about sex in the workplace is that, just like sex anywhere else, it takes two to tango. Many's the time when the women are dancing just as hard as the men – or so the men, at least, believe. In the words of Michael Bywater, writing in *Punch* magazine, 'The woman who shuffles around at home in a pair of condemned and meaty jeans will dress like a mistress or a $1,000 hooker for the office and exert all the sexual charms to go with it; the batted eyelids, the little gestures, the turning of the wrists, the touching of the sleeve. She will do this to get what she wants.'

Alex Kershaw, writing in the British edition of *GQ*, put it another way when he quoted a friend, Mike, complaining to his fellow bachelors: 'We've got all these babes in little black dresses and high heels at work. You ask them out, you know, ask them if they fancy a drink sometime, and they get really fucking aggressive. When they don't fancy you, they think you're hassling them. If they do fancy you and you don't make a move, they think you're a wimp.'

Many, many women use their sexuality, however well disguised, as part of their professional armoury. In the words of David Bowie, 'It's not really work, it's just the power to charm.' The fact that this is rarely said in public does not make it any less true. Commenting on the record industry, which, as we have seen, is not known for the sensitivity of its male employees, one female publicist told *Entertainment Week* magazine, 'I've seen more women eager to look like bimbos or sexually service someone than I have encountered men who are sexual harassers in this business.'

The same principle applies to the low-level vulgarity that is at the heart of so many harassment cases. We all know about the men who put dirty pictures on the wall or make remarks about women's breasts, but it's by no means one-way traffic.

Take the case of Donna van den Bergh, the legal secretary who won £5,000 in a harassment-related suit for wrongful dismissal. She claimed her boss, Mr Anthony Hammett, had told a risqué story during an office lunch and subsequently fondled her breasts, a charge which he strenuously denied. Prior to this, however, Mr Hammett had been encouraged by various other secretaries to eat a seven-inch chocolate penis covered in cream. This is the sort of scenario that anyone who has ever worked in an office will recognise as all too familiar. Just as the lads can't be trusted once they've downed a couple of pints, so the typing pool invariably descends to previously unimaginable depths of depravity once the rum and blacks have started flowing at the office party.

Mr Hammett, one imagines, did not feel particularly happy about the prospect of sucking on a seven-inch chocolate schlong. He may very well have felt embarrassed by a confectioner's parody of his own genitalia, just as a woman might do when confronted with, for example, a blancmange in the shape of a breast. To add to this, the act of simulated fellatio would be enough to confuse and even upset the most open-minded male heterosexual, touching as it does upon the deepest-seated fears and taboos concerning homosexuality. All in all, a 'reasonable man' might very well conclude that Mr Hammett was being harassed on the occasion of the lunch in question. Indeed, the tribunal itself commented that the secretaries who had bought the penis had been 'crude' and guilty of 'inappropriate conduct'.

That Mr Hammett did not sue was, presumably, due to the ignominy that he would have brought upon himself for so doing. After all, he's a man. And, what's more, he's a boss. The American Navy's lady officers may be traumatised by drinking from a simulated rhino-rod, but he's got no right to get upset just because a bunch of women make him eat a chocolate penis. As with so many other instances in which the man is on the receiving end of an action which is interpreted as reprehensible when done to a woman, any protest is seen as being unmanly.

Female contempt for men who *do* protest appears to be universal. Could it be that women suffer from a failure of the imagination? They simply don't understand that men are just as likely as they are to be hurt by offensive actions. It's as if a man is meant to be invulnerable. Once he has revealed the possibility of weakness, he is somehow less than a man.

Yet 10 per cent of men in an American survey claimed to have been sexually harassed at work (30 per cent of women said the same). And agony aunt Claire Rayner maintains that there is little difference in the effect upon men and women of repeated, oppressive sexual taunting or victimisation. 'The men are as hard put-upon,' she remarks. 'I remember a letter I ran in the paper from a young man who was going through hell because he was the only feller at work, working with women. They de-bagged him. They covered his penis with paint. They stuck feathers over his bottom. They put him through hell and all anyone could do was laugh and fall about. He said, "If I don't laugh I'm a misery and I don't know what to do. I'm getting scared to go to work and I can't get another job. What do I do?"

'It was a terrible situation because he was eighteen, working with women in their thirties, forties and fifties. I was furious. How dare they treat him like that? The other way round there'd be all hell let loose.'

Certainly the courts take a very different line when victims are male. In America, home of the million-dollar harassment suit, a Rhode Island court awarded a man damages of just $1 after he claimed that his boss had coerced him into having sex with his (the boss's) secretary. In another case, a Michigan jury awarded a paltry $100 to a man whose bottom was fondled by female colleagues who also sent him suggestive sex notes. Anyone interested in the relative value of a fondled buttock might care to note that Mike Tyson was hit with a $100 million action by a beauty queen (not Desirée Washington, another one) who claimed that he had laid his heavyweight mitts on her buttocks.

Why, then, do we have such double standards in the way that we judge male and female behaviour in the workplace? The first and most obvious reason is that women still have much less power than men. They can, therefore, reasonably claim a certain licence on the grounds that they are the underdogs. As time goes by, and women rise to the top in ever-increasing numbers, that excuse will start to wear thin.

This could be good news for men, since it will allow them to exploit their sexuality in the same way that women do. Anyone who has worked for a woman will know that even if the relationship between a female boss and her male staff may be less overt than that between a man and a pretty female underling, the capacity to charm is still apt to come in handy. It may only take the form of the mildest, barely noticeable, flirtation, but it's still there and it's potentially very profitable for both parties.

The first cases are already emerging of powerful female bosses making it plain to ambitious young men that their careers will greatly be helped by a spot of corporate sex. According to a survey conducted by Continental Research and reported by *Company* magazine, one man in every thirty has been told by a female superior that his career would benefit if he agreed to have a relationship. Of the men who said 'Yes,' some 50 per cent found that the woman in question was telling the truth.

Inequality, however, is not the only factor that lies behind the hypocrisy of harassment. Burned deep into our minds is the idea that no man should really allow himself to be hurt by a woman. The wife betrayed by her husband, for example, may be humiliated, but she can expect the sympathy of all who hear her story. The man betrayed is merely a cuckold, a laughingstock. For all that women discuss the fragility of the male ego, there seems to lurk in their hearts the idea that men remain fundamentally immune to women's actions. Indeed, female contempt for male fragility could be held to imply an expectation of, and even a need for, male invulnerability.

Watching my small daughters, I have begun to wonder whether this does not have its roots in the relationship between a little girl and her father. At the beginning of her life, a girl learns that daddy is invulnerable. She can jump up and down on him, kick him, punch him, say what she likes, do what she will – it makes no difference. He isn't really hurt and he always loves her.

Similarly, it is absolutely vital for a little girl to be able to flirt with her father, secure in the knowledge that he will respond positively to her, reinforcing her self-confidence, without taking advantage of her in any way at all. It is quite disconcerting, in these days of child abuse and social workers, to discover that your two- and three-year-old daughters will behave in ways that are overtly sexual. But they do.

As they grow up, could it be that women carry with them this memory of their father's immunity? Throughout this book, we will come across the inability of intelligent women to draw parallels between what hurts them and what might hurt a man, whether physically or emotionally. This theme of denial, of the refusal to empathise and of the absolute unwillingness to assume responsibility, will reappear again and again. Many women *need* to be able to blame men for their predicaments. To accept their own responsibility or complicity would be to admit to a series of desires, be they for self-advancement, admiration or, simply, sexual excitement, that they have been conditioned to deny or repress.

This is a process that begins in the playground. As Deborah Tannen has observed, girls' conversations, games and social structures tend to be centred on a search for intimacy, inclusion and popularity. While boys compete for status, girls aim for acceptance within a group. Of course, little girls can be horrid to one another, but studies suggest that that rarely takes the form of face-to-face verbal or physical action. Since, however, girls' fundamental desires may well be as strong as any boy's, they have to learn the ways in which a good girl gets what she wants without actually admitting it. Much is said about the way in which men perceive powerful, assertive women to be bitches. Less often is it admitted that women are just as critical as men when other women step out of line. The demand for self-effacement originates from the moment that little girls learn to play with one another.

A similarly conformist pressure applies to sex. For all the propaganda of the women's magazines, which portray the modern woman as a creature in control of her own sexuality and unabashed about the demands she makes for its satisfaction, there are still strong forces that demand that a woman deny her sexual desires. Just as mummy may have told her that nice girls don't, so a certain puritan strand of the women's movement seeks to persuade her that any sexual encounter – and certainly any encounter that goes wrong – can only be interpreted as a form of male oppression. The politically correct woman is as defenceless in the face of a big, strong, beastly man as any tremulous Victorian maiden.

Just to make matters worse for modern, working women, the signals they send out to the particular man in whom they are interested may be picked up and misinterpreted by a hundred men towards whom they are entirely indifferent. When this happens, a telling combination of upbringing and ideology insists that they must pretend that they weren't sending out any signals at all.

Women are left with a mass of mutually contradictory impulses and instructions. The idea that women can only be considered as passive victims of male abuse has prevented discussion of their own active participation as agents of sexual harassment. Given the relative scarcity of situations in which women both outnumber men in the workplace and control executive power, it is unlikely that there are many examples of the type of overt harassment described by Claire Rayner. But, as with many issues in the sexual debate, the fact that there are not mirror images of misbehaviour between one sex and another, does not mean that there are not traits in women that are equivalent to, if not the same as, those in men.

Dress for excess

The two men quoted earlier, complaining about the way some women dress for work, speak for many of their male counterparts who feel that the overt sexuality of some women's clothes – the 'Executive Tart' look, as it is known in the advertising trade – constitutes a form of what one might term passive harassment. It exploits a man's sexual responses, despite the women's claims to have quite different intentions. Are the men being fair?

Most males in white-collar occupations come to work in clothes that are specifically designed to give away as little information as possible about their bodies. A suit may be smart, but it carries few sexual overtones. Meanwhile their female colleagues can, they believe, parade before them in high heels and even higher skirts, both of which broadcast a clear sexual signal.

Nowadays, as Michael Bywater suggested, garments that were once considered to be the preserve of call girls are turning up on the backs of career girls instead. The power of the erotic was demonstrated by a female friend of mine who applied for the post of editor on a national newspaper. She arrived for her interview with the paper's proprietor wearing the regulation tiny skirt and stiletto heels, both of which showed off her slender physique to its best advantage.

The proprietor suggested that they conduct the interview on his office sofa (the suggestion, it should be said, was that they be placed next to, rather than on top of one another: this was no casting couch). He sat there next to this vision of loveliness, asking her questions and puffing on his cigar. The more that the interviewee preened upon the sofa, the heartier the puffs became. So much so, in fact, that they generated a cloud of cigar-smoke so intense that it set off his fire alarm, whereupon a minion had to be summoned to re-set the building's alarm system, lest the water sprinklers burst into life and drench both the proprietor and his luscious would-be minion.

The gentleman in question may have reacted in a way that is characteristic of his generation as much as his gender. Younger men have become accustomed to the corporate prick-tease. After a while, the chocolate factory principle applies and even the most ardent consumer loses his sweet tooth. The presence of attractively dressed women becomes a delight, but not, with any luck, a distraction.

That, however, does not necessarily diminish the resentment that some men feel. This is motivated, in part, by sheer jealousy of a woman's sexual power, and partly by the fact that, in any discussion of harassment, the very mention of female complicity or encouragement is ruled out on the grounds of political incorrectness. Many women, including the fashion writers and commentators on the women's pages of upmarket newspapers, will strenuously deny any responsibility for the effect that their style of dress may have on their male colleagues. Their appearance, they say, has nothing whatsoever to do with wishing to appeal to men. Are they sure?

This is an area where caution is required. No one wants to give an excuse to any man who mistreats a woman and then claims, 'She was asking for it.' But, at the same time, the belief that it is unacceptable to draw a connection between a grown woman's actions and their possible consequences is fundamentally childish. Yet it repeats itself time and again and will resurface continually throughout this book. Nor is it something that can be allowed to pass without serious comment, since the way in which women are absolved from responsibility directly impinges on another repeated phenomenon, namely the criminalisation of male behaviour.

Men continually carry the buck. In *Backlash*, for example, Susan

Faludi devotes a fascinating but questionable chapter to an account of the way in which the evil moguls of the fashion world attempted to force women into miniskirts and fancy underwear during the 1980s in the hope of reducing their status as independent, intelligent human beings. All American women really wanted to wear, claims Faludi, were sensible knickers and knee-length, size 16 skirts. What she seems unwilling to discuss is the fact that the garments she regards as unacceptable were often the creation of female designers, many of whom wore their feminist credentials with pride.

Katharine Hamnett and Donna Karan, for example, sold their miniskirts as dashing clothes made *by* independent women *for* independent women. The staple sexy garment of the late 1980s – the diminutive black Lycra pelmet – was introduced to the world, not by sexist businessmen intent on the oppression of women, but by Debbie Moore, a former model turned entrepreneur, whose Pineapple label epitomised female enterprise and freedom. To walk down city streets, on either side of the Atlantic, at any time between about 1987 and 1992, was to be confronted with huge numbers of women whose supposed enslavement to the short skirt looked as enthusiastic as it was voluntary. Even when fashion editors were unanimous in proclaiming a new, long look, hemlines remained resolutely high.

But how powerful can an artfully stitched piece of cloth be? Do men have a right to be as bothered by women's clothes as women seem to be by men's jokes, or their pin-ups? Most women do not choose to appear at work as if dressed for the bordello. In the words of Sally Vincent, writing in the *Independent*: 'All women believe themselves to be variously deformed. This is why when they try something on they're not thinking, is this an asking-for-it dress, or does it send out signals I'd be unwilling to deliver on? They're thinking, will it camouflage the enormity of my bum?'

When they go to work, they're also thinking, 'Will this enable me to be taken seriously at this month's sales meeting?' Even so, women know that certain items of clothing are overtly sexual and so do men. You only have to look at the language of the fashion pages to see that clothes are frequently promoted on the basis of their sex appeal.

Cosmopolitan magazine would be the first to echo the line that clothing is unrelated to male response when it comes to sexual harassment. Yet the headlines on the fashion pages of the twentieth anniversary issue of British *Cosmo* tell a very different story. They read, 'Fun-loving ... heartbreaking ... traffic-stopping ...

pleasure-seeking . . . eye-catching . . . show-stopping . . . breathtaking . . . attention-grabbing . . . head turning'.

Underneath these headlines, *Cosmo* girls are enticed with copy like, 'Be flirty and funky with fringes . . . Wear the ultimate in eye-catching cling . . . If you've got it, flaunt it in the ultimate, must-have catsuit . . . Be stunning . . . Be the centre of attention'.

Enough has been written about the pressure imposed on women by the images created by glossy magazines for us all to be aware that beauty is a two-edged sword, the demand for which can be more of a burden than a blessing. But these images are created, not by men, but by women. At the time that its twentieth anniversary issue was published, there were only two men on the editorial staff of British *Cosmopolitan*. One of them was the editor's secretary.

The reason why women 'trap' their sisters by the perpetuation of the so-called Beauty Myth is because the wearing of revealing clothes and seductive make-up is an exercise in female power, albeit one that is considerably more pleasant than some of the power-plays men are likely to make. And as long as men are susceptible to the seductive charms of an attractive woman, this will continue to be the case.

Claire Rayner, for one, has no doubts about the power of sexy dressing. She is, she says, angered by the refusal to connect cause and effect in the sexuality of dress since, in her view, a man is not fully responsible for his reactions once confronted with, for example, a skin-tight miniskirt.

'He can't always help it,' she told me. 'It's what he was born with. He's conditioned to respond to a bottom, to boobs. It's cruel not to keep that in mind as a female. Muslims make a lot of people angry, but they've got a point. If you cover the whole lot up, it does protect women a bit.'

This view is not necessarily one which men would do well to endorse, since it reduces them to little more than helpless victims of their own hormonal urges. I, for one, have managed to work perfectly happily in offices that were full of great-looking women in come-hither clothes. And I have yet to lose control at the sight of an attractively wrapped female behind. But Rayner's underlying point – that women cannot escape some degree of responsibility for the choices that they make – is a reasonable one.

In her recent book, *Women On Top*, Nancy Friday comments upon the struggle between a woman's delight in exhibitionism and her need to deny that delight, or its consequences. She remarks, 'I am not sure whether women's new sense of the power of their beauty extends to a sequential awareness of their responsibility for the erotic wheels they have set in motion by drawing attention to themselves . . . What we have today is a war not just between women but within the woman herself: how consciously should a woman admit to beauty and use it to get what she wants? . . . Perhaps we are . . . close to admitting to women's ancient competition for the eye of the beholder, not as a mindless sport devised by wicked men to set women against one another, but as a powerful force in natural selection, one that is built into the species. What has always made the competition so deadly is women's denial that it exists.'

They may not have the option for very much longer. On 23 January 1992, Jeremy Campbell reported from America for readers of the London *Evening Standard*: 'In New York [this week] a bevy of reputable psychiatrists outraged feminist orthodoxy by blaming sexual harassment on women's willing enslavement to fashion designers and the erotic clothes that are a must for the nineties.

'The psychiatrists poured scorn on the pretensions of designers to promote "female empowerment" with their Madonna-inspired, underwear-out look . . . Business consultants have even started telling female employees: if you want more respect from your male colleagues, put some clothes on.'

Here we have an equal and opposite force from that which demands that men make no compliments towards their female colleagues, lest any inadvertent offence be caused. In order to ensure that no man be charming, no woman will be attractive. Thus will the sensibilities and weaknesses of both sides be protected. The Ayatollah could not have done a better job of making life miserable for us all.

Get a life

There is an alternative. It's called growing up and learning some manners. A man who feels obliged to be offensive to women is not a man who is oppressive: he is quite simply beneath contempt. A man who is not self-controlled enough to temper his hormones at the sight of the first well-turned leg to pass before him across the office carpet is (a) too immature to be trusted with any sort of executive responsibility, and (b) a loser. You'll never compete with women if you fall for them that easily.

Remember, the loser is the person who looks like they're trying too hard. So the correct response to any woman who is attempting to exploit male frailties is simply, keep cool. Enjoy the game. Play along with it if you will. Just don't fall for it. The moment that you are seen to care, the game is over. On the other hand, if handled with a little sensitivity, the sexual chessboard of office politics is one of the greater pleasures of working life – and a mutual pleasure at that.

Equally, any woman who claims to be tough enough to handle a responsible job should also be tough enough to tell a man when to get lost. In the words of Camille Paglia, speaking to Leslie White of the *Sunday Times* in May 1992: 'There is absolutely nothing we can do to desexualise the workplace, so women must be constantly signalling what their intentions are and how they wish to be treated. When a man has crossed that line and said something vulgar, she must stop it immediately. The Clarence Thomas thing was just a crock . . . you're telling me that this guy said he liked her breasts and she went home and cried. Oh, puh-leese, give me a break. The idea that women are victims of men and have to get help from committees is absurd.'

The route to a happy relationship within the workplace lies in a genuine equality of both opportunity and responsibility. The more that each side feels that it is getting a fair deal, the less that it is likely to complain. The American obsession with litigation and political correctness, together with the self-defining nature of their sexual harassment legislation, may point the way towards a hellish vision of a repressed, neo-puritan workplace, but there is an alternative. French law makes harassment (irrespective of the gender of perpetrator or victim) punishable by fines, or even imprisonment, but it is very specific about what constitutes criminal harassment. This is defined as 'a word, gesture, attitude or behaviour by a superior with a view to compelling an employee to respond to a solicitation of a sexual nature'.

In this context, bad manners are not enough. There has to be an element of coercion, blackmail or abuse of power. Faced with the question of a woman who is confronted with dirty pictures, stupid remarks or unwanted passes from colleagues of equal rank, Veronique Neiertz, the French minister for women's rights remarked, 'What is wrong with *un gifle* – a slap round the face? Be clear, it is blackmail to make sexual advances to someone who depends on you for their work . . . In the case of blackmailing harassment the state has something to say. Otherwise, the relations between men and women are merely part of life.'

In other words, the proper response for a Maggie, faced with a sniggering Clive, is simply to tell him to stop. As yet, there is little sign that legislators in Britain will be as adult as their French equivalent. When the BBC, under their harassment supremo Margaret Salmon, brought out a series of guidelines on the subject, Ms Salmon was asked to define what sexual harassment actually was. 'Why do we need to?' she asked.

The answer is that you cannot keep a working population in suspense. You cannot have men wondering whether they are, at any moment, going to be seized by the Thought Police and accused of crimes, the precise nature of which have yet to be defined. Not if their livelihoods are at stake you can't. Nor do we wish to get to the stage some American corporations are said to have reached, in which terrified executives are bugging their own offices to ensure that, should they be accused of committing some terrible misdeed, they have taped evidence of their innocence.

After all, once you have said that harassment – an act which usually leaves no physical evidence of its occurrence – is a crime that can lead to jail for its perpetrators, you have opened the door for an infinite variety of opportunities for blackmail and coercion on the part of pseudo-victims. The mere mention of harassment is enough to ruin a man's reputation, which is why, in October 1991, Dr Alanah Huston was ordered to pay her partner Dr Malcolm Smith £150,000 in damages for slander after she had falsely claimed that he had made sexual advances towards her.

Unproven and untested accusations of sexual impropriety were, by contrast, enough to force American Senator Brooke Adams to abandon his Congressional re-election campaign. Former employees claimed that he had drugged them prior to committing acts of rape. Irrespective of the assumption of innocence to which Senator Adams was, like anyone else, entitled until convicted by a court of law, society passed its sentence without feeling the need for any form of trial. In the present climate, the accusation was enough.

For my part, I think that there is a lot to be said for good, old-fashioned courtesy. No one, irrespective of gender, should force unwanted attentions on another person *once that person has made it clear that the attentions are unwanted.* The obsessive hunting down of real or imaginary sexual misconduct in the workplace will result, like all witch hunts, in far more pain, suffering and damage than the problem itself could ever cause.

As the harassment controversy raged, I was working as the editor of *Punch* magazine. The bulk of our readers and contributors were male, so the tone of voice of the magazine was a masculine one. Yet the workplace itself was even-handed. The numbers of men and women were just about equal and enough women held senior positions, such as advertising manager, features editor and art director, for there to be no sense of disparity in power between the genders.

People who visited the office would remark upon the sexual energy that seemed to be fizzing about the place. I put it down to a Blitz spirit. We never knew when we might not be blown up by some corporate doodlebug – as indeed we eventually were. In the meantime, we took as much pleasure from life as we could. Jokes winged back and forth between the men and women. Flirtation was part of the currency of friendship. There were certain lines, mostly defined by simple good manners and good taste, that were not crossed. The men, for example, did not make remarks about the women's breasts (this despite the provocation created by the women's seeming obsession with the secrets that might be hidden within the men's trousers), nor, in return, did anyone get up on any moral or political high horses.

I do not wish to make a perfectly ordinary office sound like a cross between the garden of earthly delights and Five Go Mad on Fleet Street. My point is that Helen Gurley Brown is right: the presence of men and women can bring spice and creativity to a workplace, but it depends on everyone being in on the deal. If men act like louts, women have every right to get offended. But if women insist on assuming a spurious sense of moral self-righteousness, they should not be surprised if the atmosphere they engender is less than inspiring. The moral is simple: relax. Grow up. Have fun. Get a life.

Chapter 7

Crying Rape And Crying Wolf

According to official government figures, the average British woman in 1991 stood a one in 7,539 chance of being raped during the course of th year. In the twelve months up to October of that year, some 3,900 women were raped. That marked a rise of some 17 per cent on the previous year, a rise ascribed by the Home Office to the increased willingness of women to report the crime to the police.

Those figures would imply that the odds against a typical British woman, who reached the age of consent at sixteen, and died at the age of seventy-six, being raped at some point in her life were 126 to one. This is by no means a happy statistic, but it does not suggest that rape should be amongst the leading causes of female anxiety. A woman's chances of getting breast cancer, for example, are approximately one in thirteen, which, given the potentially fatal nature of the disease, would seem to be an altogether more alarming statistic.

Yet the fear of rape is all-pervasive in our society. Vast numbers of women tell researchers that they feel unsafe on the streets after dark. They are terrified by the prospect of being alone in a railway or tube carriage. Minicabs have long been seen as dangerous and now even black cabs, once regarded as a girl's safest refuge, have been sullied by reports of attacks on female passengers.

These fears are backed up by statistics that purport to tell a very different story about the prevalence of rape. They suggest that those rapes that are reported form a tiny proportion of the total that are committed. A survey of some 2,500 female college students organised by the Cambridge University Students Union claimed that one in nine had been the victim of rape and one in five had suffered some form of attempted rape. In the vast majority of cases, these rapes were carried out by men known to their victims: the phenomenon of date, or acquaintance rape had crossed the Atlantic from America and arrived on British shores.

These figures, if they are true, would imply that within the first few years of their sexual life – and even in these supposedly promiscuous days, most students aged eighteen to twenty have only recently become sexually active – women face a risk of rape that is fourteen times greater than that predicted for their entire lives by government statistics. Extrapolated across the population as a whole, this would in turn mean that the official figures for rape as a whole are out by a factor of thirty, forty, perhaps even fifty times. By this measure, the true number of rapes in Britain might be well over 100,000 every single year – a figure greater than the total number of rapes reported to the police in the entire post-war period.

The very definition of the offence is changing, too. In the autumn of 1991, a decision by the Court of Appeal overturned the traditional view that there was no such thing as rape inside marriage. In future, a man could no longer regard his wife as a chattel, from whom he could demand his 'conjugal rights' when the mood took him. According to some rape crisis centres, this decision came none too soon. They claimed that some 1,370,000 women had been raped by their husbands. Research by Kate Painter, a Cambridge University criminologist, suggests that one woman in seven has been raped by her husband at some time in their marriage.

What is a man to do or think in the face of such statistics? Most of us are afflicted by a mass of different, often contradictory opinions and emotions. In the first place, one feels shame. Then comes a sense of denial. Like revisionist historians disputing the existence of Auschwitz, we tell ourselves that it can't be true. We question the basis on which the research was carried out. What were the questions? How was rape defined? Who replied? We note that in the case of the Cambridge survey, respondents were volunteers and, therefore, self-selecting. They may, we decide, have had an axe to grind. And anyway, we conclude, all these surveys are done by man-haters.

We read Bryan Appleyard in the *Sunday Times* quoting a guidebook from the London Rape Crisis Centre called *Sexual Violence: The Reality For Women*, as follows: 'Rape is all the sexual assaults, verbal and physical, that we all suffer in our daily contact with men. These range from being "touched up" and "chatted up" to being brutally, sexually assaulted with objects. Throughout this book we use rape to describe any kind of sexual assault.'

Appleyard then attacks the view that, 'While men may choose not to commit rape, they are all capable of it.' This he describes as 'sexual fascism'. He admits that 'the objective fact of rape is appallingly common' but wonders whether 'we want the police and courts probing into every contested bedroom scene. Should we drag every movie-crazed, sexually incompetent, adolescent date-rapist through the courts?' Finally he concludes that 'the feminists are right when they say that women have often suffered in silence, but they are stupidly wrong when they use that as a simple, brutal tool of global social analysis or as an indictment of all men'.

Appleyard does not have the space to amplify why the feminists are 'stupidly' wrong, but I do. The first stupidity is an elementary error of logic: all buttercups are yellow flowers, but not all yellow flowers are buttercups. All rapists are men, but that does not mean that all men are rapists. This is part of an attempt to induce guilt by association, the second half of which rests upon a linguistic trick, namely the use of the word 'capable'.

As with man's 'potential' for child abuse, the notion that all men are 'capable' of rape is either, as Appleyard points out, absurdly preju-dicial, or it is meaningless. Given that I, for example, am six feet tall and weigh 175 pounds, I could theoretically overpower most women. So why don't I? Because in the more meaningful sense of the word 'capable' – a meaning that takes account of psychology, conditioning, desire – I am *not* capable of such an act. Nor is the vast majority of men. To brand us with a stereotype that is profoundly negative and carries with it the suggestion of automatic guilt for a series of dreadful crimes is an act that may not be 'fascistic' in the most pedantic sense of the word – there being no authoritarian state involved – but it certainly is unscientific, extremist, obscurantist and antisocial, which should be plenty to be getting on with.

But that doesn't get away from the fact that many women have horror stories to tell. When a man comes to think about these stories and attempts to discuss them, he will come across a further difficulty, which is this: How can a man talk about rape without either accepting the blame that is thrust upon him by the rape crisis centres, or, on the other hand, appearing to condone the actions of the rapist?

I was given an illustration of the problem when asked onto a television debate with Ruth Hall of Women Against Rape. During the course of the broadcast, which took place in the wake of the Mike Tyson trial, we took pains to keep our conversational tone as reasonable and non-aggressive as possible (somewhat, I suspect, to the disappointment of the programme's producers). Afterwards, we had a brief conversation in the studio's green room. I mentioned that I was writing a book about men and would be interested in talking to Ms Hall at greater length to discuss the social or psychological pressures that might be acting on the two people involved in a supposed date-rape, since it seemed to me that seeing the event purely in terms of his assault upon her might be an oversimplification.

Not to Ms Hall it wasn't. Any time that a man had sex with a woman without her express consent, no matter what the circumstances, it could only be seen in one way: he had raped her, and that was the end of it. There could only be one interpretation because there was only one form of oppression, the male oppression of women. There was really no point in discussing it further and, by the way, it might be best not to spend too much time writing about the subject because people might then conclude that you were trying to defend rapists and you wouldn't want that, would you?

I could not have been warned off more effectively if Vito Corleone had left a horse's head in my bed of a Sunday morning. The message was clear: this is our turf and you're not welcome.

It's not that simple.

The traditional rapist

Consider the traditional idea of the rapist, the Ripper-style madman in the dark alley with a knife. One of the few generalisations that can be made about him with any degree of confidence is that, far from being the living embodiment of an oppressive patriarchy, he is likely to be lonely, insecure and inadequate in his relationships with other people. He may very well have been a victim of abuse as a boy. And his grotesquely distorted machismo may be a form of compensation for a childhood spent in overly close contact with an extremely protective mother.

In his book *Body Consciousness*, published in 1973, Seymour Fisher, who was then the Professor of Psychiatry at the University of New York, Syracuse, discussed the idea that violence in young men is a way of re-establishing a long-threatened or repressed sense of masculinity.

Cross-cultural studies ... [have shown that] boys who were relatively close to mothers and distant from their fathers (or often without a father because of his death) and who, therefore, have had a limited opportunity to learn directly about the 'feel' of being masculine, have a strong tendency during adolescence to engage in hostile, predatory behaviour as a way of announcing that they are, indeed, of the male species. It is well known, too, that male delinquency comes with an unusual frequency from broken homes in which there is no visible father and where almost all of the primary socialisation experiences have been with women.

Maternal smothering is not, I should add, the only way in which a boy's masculinity can be distorted to the point at which, as an adult, he feels impelled to rape. The father's sexual abuse or brutality may be equally significant. In the case of Peter Sutcliffe, the notorious Yorkshire Ripper, both patterns were present: he was the child of a violent, hot-tempered father, and was a 'mummy's boy' who came home from school, according to family friends, clinging to his mother's skirts.

That description reminded me of accounts of the childhood of Michael Ryan. His bloody journey through the streets of Hungerford on 19 August 1987 was the single worst act of murder ever committed on English soil, an act triggered off, I believe, by the consequences of a failed attempt to rape a thirty-five-year-old nurse.

When researching Ryan's personal background in 1988, I was told by an old schoolfriend that his mother, who was the playground controller at the local primary school, would hold the hand of her little boy during break, so nervous was he of playing with the other boys. When cornered by police in the John O'Gaunt Comprehensive School, he asked after his mother on thirteen separate occasions. He knew exactly how she was. He had killed her, finishing her off with two bullets fired into her back at point-blank range.

These cases reinforce my contention that extreme acts of violence or sexual perversion are not functions of masculinity *per se*, but of its distortion or suppression. It would be foolish, of course, to suggest that one will ever create a world that is free from psychosis or parental abuse. Nor do I have anything but praise for those American educational reformers who are attempting to wean boys away from violence by showing them the satisfaction that can be derived from behaviour that is non-confrontational or nurturing. Boys who learn to resolve conflicts by negotiation, rather than by force, or who discover that they can look after babies – and enjoy doing so – are learning useful lessons indeed.

Those educationalists, however, who parrot all the currently fashionable clichés about the superiority of feminine principles and who seek to cut down on sex attacks and crimes of assault by attempting to undermine the very idea of masculinity or to feminise young boys, will find that their policies have precisely the opposite effect. Well-balanced men, who are secure and confident in their masculinity, are far less likely to harm women than men who are insecure or resentful. Boys will be boys whatever we do: the question is, what kind of boys do you want them to be? Not, presumably, the kind who rapes the girl he dates. This is Appleyard's 'movie-crazed, sexually incompetent, adolescent "date-rapist" '. What are we to make of him?

Your sexiest sex

To the members of Women Against Rape, there is no controversy here, either. The adolescent is a rapist, just as surely as the maniac. Their crimes are the same. There is no difference of nature or degree. Rape is rape, period.

I would suggest, however, that it is not, and that there is, in fact, as wide a variety in the forms of sexual assault as there is in physical assault as a whole. To take a parallel phenomenon: the law distinguishes between murder, manslaughter and self-defence, even though all those events end in a death. The difference between these various offences is largely concerned with questions of motivation and/or the degree to which the victims' own actions may have contributed to their eventual demise. Much, for example, has been written and broadcast about female victims of domestic violence who finally kill their husbands. Many people feel that these women have been every bit as victimised as the men they murdered.

Why, then, should we refuse to distinguish between various forms of non-consensual sex, even though those events all end in the unwanted penetration of a woman's body by a man's penis? There is surely an enormous gulf between the experience of a wife who has sex with her husband on a night when she would rather not have done so, and the woman who is held at knife-point by a stranger in a leather mask. *En route*, there is an infinite number of permutations of violence or coercion. So why are the very women who insist on the need to examine the possibility of provocation or mitigation in the case of a woman who commits murder, the first to deny such consideration to a man accused of rape?

Once again, I am absolutely not trying to put the blame on women who are raped. In fact, if at all possible, I would like to remove for the time being any consideration of guilt or blame for either party and merely look at the context in which both people find themselves. This is vitally important if there is to be any understanding of date-rape since, as matters stand, the whole phenomenon is overloaded with value judgements.

After all, when a woman makes a claim of date-rape, one of two alternative opinions has to be proved. Either, he wanted sex and so did she, in which case she is blamed, both for the act itself and for bringing the case to court. Or, he wanted sex and she didn't, in which case he is a criminal. Under those circumstances, objectivity soon vanishes and, as was amply demonstrated in the differing fortunes of Messrs Tyson and Kennedy Smith, any court proceedings rapidly become a form of beauty contest in which jurors openly base their judgements upon entirely non-legal criteria suggested by their personal response to plaintiff and defendant.

I would suggest, instead, that the phenomenon of date-rape is an entirely predictable result of the extraordinarily confused state of contemporary sexual morality. Both men and women are being asked to cope with contradictory demands, which can only – as matters stand – end in women enduring the pain and trauma of unwanted sexual experience, while men find themselves treated as criminals.

No one profits from the situation. A woman's relationships with other men may be poisoned for years to come. A man may have his life ruined by a jail sentence for an act regarded as despicable by the whole of society. Meanwhile, debate on this most complex of issues is stifled by the heavy hand of political correctness, whose massive ideological influence is in no way merited by the shoddy, illogical and psychologically inaccurate nature of its arguments.

Taking those points one at a time: it is a cliché to say that we are surrounded more than ever by images of sexuality. Wherever we go, we see advertisements, TV shows, rock videos, newspapers and magazines that flaunt sexual imagery, the vast majority of it based upon the desirability of women.

Something very important has happened, however, over the past decade or so. The woman is no longer the passive sex-object of days gone by. Nowadays she is the active protagonist. She is in control and she is often photographed in advertisements or fashion pages sur- rounded by submissive and adoring men, as if James Bond had been replaced by Jane. Young women, leafing through their glossy magazines, are bombarded with articles and photographs exhorting them to greater sexual activity and achievement.

In 1991, for example, *Cosmopolitan* magazine promoted 102 different features on its cover. Of these, just over half were specifically sexual and included:

How come you're in love after one night of sex?

What men do wrong in bed

Great sex is crazy positions, silly noises and other undignified things

Addicted to sex: is he your hero or your heroin?

Yes, yes, oh yes! Men fake orgasms too

Keep it up! The care and feeding of his erection

When your mind wants sex but your body says no

101 uses of sex

The new sexual fantasies

His ego, his sex drive

The formula clearly works, because *Cosmo*'s circulation soared by more than 48,000 copies a month, taking its audited monthly sales above 450,000 and deservedly winning its editor, Marcelle D'Argy Smith, the title of Magazine Editor of the Year. More to the point, those cover lines represent a philosophy which has long been central to popular feminism. This is that women have every right to be sexual, just as men have always been. There is no reason for a woman to be ashamed of her sexuality, nor need she be shy in setting forward her demands for satisfaction.

I have singled out *Cosmopolitan*, but there is nothing unusual or unique about its preoccupation with sex. Every young woman's magazine in the Western world thinks in exactly the same way. In the words of British *Elle* magazine, introducing its April 1992 sex survey (sponsored by Durex), 'For a growing number of women, the battleground for equality has shifted to between the sheets and they consider it a playground as much as a battle-zone . . . They work hard and play hard (but not hard to get); they know what they like and they make sure they get it . . . "I just won't settle for sleeping with a man who doesn't bring me to orgasm on a regular basis," stated one London woman. "I tell my boyfriends exactly what to do, where to go, which buttons to press and, if they're not getting there, I'll tell them that, too." '

The August 1992 edition of *Company*, a magazine for young British women which is advertised as, 'The magazine for your freedom years', came with a free supplement, whose cover read:

THE BEST SEX YOU'LL EVER HAVE
YOUR SEXIEST SEX GUIDE EVER

(give it to him – it's what you really want)

Revealed – we show you the 12 hottest sex positions

Sexual appetisers – how to fine-tune your foreplay

Oral sex – the pleasures, perils and techniques

Sex toys – we separate the hot from the hype

Raw passion – the glorious abandon of quick sex

16 wonderfully uncensored pages

A similar preoccupation with sex governs the fiction read by women. Writers such as Jackie Collins, Shirley Conran and Celia Brayfield turn out gold-embossed paperback potboilers that compete with one another in the quantity, variety and perversity of the sexual fare on offer. The vagina becomes a receptacle for an extraordinary range of implements, animal, vegetable and mineral. Heroes are masterful and hung like donkeys. Heroines are gorgeous and insatiable.

This manic sex-obsession has no direct parallel in the male universe. The top shelves still groan with tit'n'ass magazines, but these are clearly seen as being smutty and unsuitable for right-on, liberal men. Non-pornographic men's magazines, such as *GQ* and *Esquire*, have just begun to dip their toe into the murky waters of sex and the emotions. But, by and large, they seem much happier with tales of City scandals and sporting heroism. One editor even revealed to me that all his magazine's features on sex had to be written by women: if they ever published anything by a man that was even remotely frank, it was always condemned as offensively sexist by their ever-alert audience.

Men's fictional equivalents to Mesdames Collins, Conran et al. are such hard-boiled thriller writers as Robert Ludlum, Tom Clancy and Frederick Forsyth, for whom women are an incidental diversion from the real issues of power and paranoia. The typical woman's heroine is a beautiful *ingénue* who proceeds to acquire copious quantities of orgasms, money and clothes, not necessarily in that order of importance. The typical man's hero is a solitary outsider faced by a host of enemies, who wins through despite them all. He is expressing men's fears and fantasies, which are all about independence (or the loss of it) and the ability to make one's mark in a hostile world. Sex, as a priority, comes remarkably far down the list.

Perhaps it has always been so. From Medusa through Messalina to Madonna, men have always been fearful of unbridled female sexuality. Ancient myths and modern psychology speak of man's terror of the *vagina dentata* – the wound that has teeth, that leaves a man castrated and diminished. For however erect a man may be when he goes in, by the time he comes out he is flaccid and spent. In a bizarre repudiation of female power, feminism chooses to think of the phallus as the source of all threat, but in the battle between cock and cunt, the cock always comes out the loser.

This was the hidden agenda behind many a social convention. During the 1930s, my grandfather Bernard lived in Buenos Aires. He once had dinner with a friend, whose daughter wanted to go out to the movies with her boyfriend. In order to do this she had to have a chaperone, who, in this case, was her aunt. The aunt was unexpectedly delayed, so the young couple pleaded with the girl's father to let them go out without her. They were in danger of missing the start of the film, they said. They would buy the aunt a ticket and she could join them later. But the father stood firm. Until the chaperone arrived, which she eventually did, he would not let them out of his sight.

Over dinner, my grandfather asked his friend why he had been so strict. 'Don Jose,' he said, 'your daughter's friend is an honourable young man. He comes from a fine, respectable family. I am sure that your daughter would have been quite safe with him.'

The Argentinian laughed. 'But Bernardo,' he replied. 'I have not the slightest doubt that you are right. I am not concerned with what this charming young man might do to my daughter. My only worry is what she might do to him.'

Any modern young man who flicks through his girlfriend's books or magazines could be forgiven for thinking not only that women were – to use a phrase – 'aching for it', but also that he would be falling down on the job of being a man if he didn't give it to them, with orgasmic knobs on. Yet we remain convinced that it is men, not women, who are obsessed with sex. When, for example, Lord Rees-Mogg stated in the annual report of the Broadcasting Standards Council, 1992, that if women ran television there would be less blatant sexuality on screen, he named three particular programmes: *A Time to Dance*, *Clarissa* and *The Men's Room*. The first was, it is true, written and directed by men. But the other two had women producers, directors and writers involved in their production and both were greeted with a frenzy of approbation in the women's pages of Fleet Street.

The Rees-Mogg view, however, does have powerful friends. He's not alone in assuming that delicate, asexual women have to be protected from the insatiable lusts of men. Supposedly radical feminists are only too happy to portray women as eternal victims, helpless in the face of male oppression and sexuality.

There's an American radio talk-show host called Rush Limbaugh who likes to refer to the leaders of the women's movement as 'femi-Nazis'. But they're not. They're femi-wimps. One mention of the male sex and they come over all weak and feeble.

Some radical feminists want to enshrine the victimisation from which they derive their moral justification, even at the risk of undermining female power. The traditionalists want to retain the gentle, submissive, image of women. Either way, the message is clear: 'It's not our fault, it's all those horrible men.'

Clothing is, once again, a point at which society's contradictory impulses collide. There are good reasons for the determination with which some women insist that their provocative clothing can never, under any circumstances, be considered as an inducement to an act of sex. They remember Judge Bertrand Richards, who presided over a 1982 case in which a motorist called John Allen was accused of raping a seventeen-year-old hitch-hiker he had picked up after she had been stranded on her way home from a party. Allen was not jailed and the judge explained that he was only being fined £2,000 because his young victim was herself guilty of 'a great deal of contributory negligence'.

Not surprisingly, this became something of a *cause célèbre* in the fight for justice for women. But has the pendulum swung too far the other way? Here are the thoughts of Nancy Friday on the subject:

For every woman who cringes when the construction workers whistle at her passing, there is another who anticipates the attention halfway up the block and would be crestfallen if heads didn't turn. Yes, it is embarrassing and humiliating to have obscenities yelled, unsettling for anyone, male or female, to be stared at too long. But it can also be a very heady power trip to be able to draw people's eyes and hold their attention, even control their behaviour with your body . . .

I am, of course, against rape, and there are certainly instances of violation that have nothing to do with physical appearance and exhibitionism. But, precisely because the crime is so heinous, isn't it imperative that we try to understand the role exhibitionism can play? ... Women's beauty and exhibitionism play a major role in the mating ritual. It is time we acknowledged the function and importance of beauty in women's lives, not as a male 'plot' but as a pursuit women enter into in their earliest female-to-female competitions. The power of exhibitionism, should we choose to use it, is our responsibility.

Blaming the boy

One can understand why women should fight to defend the innocence of the rape victim. For too long, her suffering was doubled by the attitude that she was as much at fault as her attacker. I do not want to support that view. But are we any better off if we go to the other extreme and see her as being entirely without responsibility, particularly when all the legal consequences descend upon the man?

The degree to which this has become the case was made plain when the American magazine *Details* organised a seminar on date-rape for its October 1991 edition. Four experts were invited to give their answers to a series of questions on the subject. They included Dr Alan Berkowitz, who runs rape prevention clinics for students at Hobart and William Smith, two colleges in upstate New York, and Rikki Klieman, a female attorney who has defended several men accused of date-rape.

Throughout their dialogue, Klieman and Berkowitz took very different views on the issue. Ironically, the latter was far stricter towards men in his interpretations. One wonders whether he was in some way comforted by the idea that the men were fully responsible for what went on: after all, if they bear the full burden of responsibility they must be very much the senior partners. Klieman, on the other hand, saw women as being much more active, much less innocent and, by implication, much more equal.

One of the questions, for example, asked the respondents to imagine a scenario in which a woman invites a man to her apartment. They kiss. They have sex. She never says yes or no. In the morning she claims he raped her. Could she be right?

Berkowitz responded: 'It could be rape, depending on the specifics of what happened. Many men believe that if a woman invites you to her apartment and kisses you, she wants to have intercourse with you and that it's OK to do it because she took the initiative. That's not right.'

Klieman, however, asks, 'How in heaven's name is a man supposed to know that it was against her will unless in some way or other she tells him?' On the other hand, she observes, 'If they are kissing and petting and she says, "No I don't want to do this. I want you to stop," and a man continues to act after that communication, in this day and age he is acting at his peril and would likely be arrested and, I think, probably convicted of rape.'

A similar division occurred over the issue of whether a woman was a rape victim if she had given in to psychological pressure to have sex.

Berkowitz: 'That would still be rape because the perpetrator did not make sure that she was consenting.'

Klieman: 'That's preposterous. Usually these cases tend to fall among young people – late adolescence, early twenties. There's a lot of ambiguity that goes on with young people in those stages. They're not quite sure what is exactly right and what is exactly wrong. It seems to me that to criminalise that conduct by calling the young man a rapist is never what the law intended when it enacted rape laws to protect women.'

What happens if the alleged victim was drunk? Klieman, who is, remember, a woman and so may be expected to have had some experience of the female side of the mating game, remarks, 'I cannot imagine a situation where I have been drinking that I would ever come close to a point of not being able to say no.'

Berkowitz has less faith in a woman's ability to hold her drink, to wit: 'If she was drunk, then he didn't have her consent. How can you consent if you're drunk?'

You will note here the enormous shift that Berkowitz and others are trying to make in the definition of rape. To them, rape does not occur when a woman says 'No', but a man carries on regardless. It occurs whenever a woman has not positively said 'Yes'. One begins to understand how rape activists are able to come up with the figures they like to bandy around. Dr Berkowitz tells the readers of *Details*: 'The research suggests that anywhere from one-third to half of college women will experience an acquaintance rape or some other form of sexual assault.' What he really means is not just that some college girls will be the victims of genuine assaults, but also that lots of co-eds will have bad nights and will then wake up the next morning with a sore head, look at the guy lying next to them and think, 'Oh, shit.' This he wishes to define as rape.

177

So, unless the mores of teenage sexual activity have changed out of all recognition in the past fifteen years, there seems little way in which a boy can avoid being accused of rape. For boys are still expected to take girls out, pour a couple of drinks down them, plead everlasting love and then make a pass. This latter move may or may not be accompanied by a tactic which I seem to remember employing from time to time, namely, going down on my knees and begging. If you don't at least try to seduce them, girls are apt to get offended. And, in my experience, the final decision is invariably theirs, even if – and here is a crucial point – there may never be a moment at which anyone actually asks, 'May I?' or gets the answer 'Yes'.

What if the question is asked, however, and the answer comes back, 'No'? In the words of Rikki Klieman, 'If there are young men around today who think that no means yes, they're in for trouble.' Clearly she's right. Man or boy, one should always work on the assumption that, to quote a slogan, no means no, if only because the consequences of misinterpretation are far too drastic to risk. So it is merely as an aside that I observe that in a 1991 poll, conducted among female students at the University of Texas's psychology department, and reported in the *Sunday Telegraph*, nearly 50 per cent of all students admitted that they said 'No' to sex when what they really meant was 'Yes', or 'Maybe'. Their reasons for so doing ranged from a feeling that it was more feminine to be seen to resist, to a desire to see a man prove his desire by making him work a little bit harder for what he wanted.

Mary Kenny, writing in the same paper a few months later, observed, 'Speaking for myself, it would be a patent act of dishonesty to brandish a No Means No sticker ... I am, indeed, the lady of whom it was originally said, "When she says No, she means, Maybe; when she says Maybe she means Yes; when she says Yes she's no lady." This is not based on sexism so much as human psychology: it doesn't look too good to seem too eager. People only want what they can't get, after all.'

To Kenny, 'What the No Means No campaign really signifies is that young men today have lost the art of wooing, of coaxing, of charming, as young women have mislaid the feminine art of flirtation within controlled limits.'

Have they? Or have they just become the latest innocent victims in a sex war that, according to Barbara Amiel, the Canadian columnist who writes for the *Sunday Times*, 'has moved from the liberal goal of equality between the sexes to the political goal of power for women, and is now well on the road to legislating out of existence the biologically based mating habits of our species . . .'?

'Feminists wish male sexuality to be immaterial in criminal law. Women should be free to engage in any type of behaviour that suits their own sexuality without regard to the consequences. This approach views men as vibrators: women may pick them up, switch them on, play around and then, if the off-switch doesn't work, sue the manufacturer for damages.'

Amiel concluded that the hidden agenda behind the whole date-rape farrago could be found in the fact that the National Organization of Women, America's leading feminist organisation, had just announced that its senior leaders were lesbians. I, however, am not so sure that lesbianism is the key to the whole thing. I suspect that the motivation is fear.

After all, leaving aside the horrifying, but still small, possibility of random assault, why should college girls need to be protected from their peers? We are constantly told that teenage girls are far more mature than boys of the same age. Some might even suggest that teenage girls are incomparably more mature than boys of any age, right up to seventy and beyond. But let that pass. We can agree, I think, that they are certainly not less mature.

We also know that students at university are all of roughly the same age and have approximately the same amount of money, viz., none whatsoever. The male of the species has none of the social or financial advantages which might accrue to him in the outside world. So the notion asserted earlier by Ruth Hall, which saw the man as being in an inherently superior, oppressive position, simply does not hold true among young people.

In which case, if the girl is so mature, and suffers from no obvious disadvantages, why can't she look after herself? Of course, if she has been physically overwhelmed by someone using overpowering force, then she has every right to expect the police and courts to act with utmost vigour on her behalf. The man deserves, and should get, the full weight of their disapproval. I've got no argument with that. But the date-rape panic isn't about real incidents of violence: it's about a fear of sex.

This is demonstrated most obviously as fear of the male. But its roots may lie elsewhere. Could it be that, understandably enough, women are afraid of their own sexuality? Could they feel unprotected, now that the taboos which once limited their activities, but protected their honour, have disappeared? We are, after all, only thirty years into the greatest shift in sexual patterns ever known to humankind: the freedom from pregnancy caused by the arrival of the Pill. We should not be surprised if young women still feel profoundly dislocated, not to say overwhelmed, by the new demands that have been placed upon them. Not everybody wants or is able to be the swinging, demanding, super-confident sex-kitten put forward by the glossy magazines. How much easier to retreat from the fray and blame it all on men.

The assertion that women blame men for problems that are really to do with themselves is increasingly being made by women writers, many of whom have come through the feminist movement themselves. It helps to explain the puzzling way in which such an apparently modern movement so often expresses itself in terms that are so traditional. Now we know why some woman dress their bodies in jeans, but put their minds into crinolines. Faced with the pressures of an entirely new responsibility, a reversion back into the role of the passive, helpless victim must seem deliciously comforting and secure.

The guiding principle behind this book, however, is that men and women should be treated as equals. They deserve equal amounts of compassion and sympathy. And they should accept equal amounts of responsibility.

Lovers' tales

Here are two stories. The first may be apocryphal, although it was told to me as fact by Renate Olins, Director of London Marriage Guidance. She had herself been told it by a female lawyer involved in the case it describes, who was appalled by its outcome. Its veracity hardly matters: what counts is the principle of the thing. The second I know to be true because it happened to me.

Two students went to a ball on a fine English summer's night. They drank champagne. They danced. They laughed and chatted away. One thing led to another and the boy suggested that they go outside, find a secluded spot and see what happened next. The girl was only too willing to agree. So out of the marquee they went, arm in arm, until they came to the sort of quiet, well-camouflaged garden hideaway in which, for centuries too numerous to count, swains and their maids have been getting to know one another just that little bit better.

As bad luck would have it, however, no sooner had they lain down next to one another on the grass than someone else, another courting couple perhaps, happened to pass the same way. So our two lovebirds got up, straightened their clothes and went off to find somewhere else. Finally they found another little nook. It was by now getting late and the ground was dewy. So the boy, being a chivalrous sort of chap, put his jacket down on the ground and invited the girl to lie down on top of it, facing upwards, while he lay down on top of her.

Once again, she consented with alacrity. They kissed, fondled and fumbled. Clothes were removed and elastic twanged. But then, just as he was about to enter her, she suddenly changed her mind and said, 'No.' The young man had not read *Details*. He was not aware that when a girl says 'No,' he had better assume she means it. He thought she was just teasing. So he went ahead and had sex with her. The next day, she reported him to the police for rape.

He was arrested and charged. His lawyers advised him to plead guilty. Their reasoning was that there was no dispute that an act of sex had taken place. If the boy pleaded not guilty and the court found against him, he might face a severe sentence. If, on the other hand, he pleaded guilty but was able to show both mitigating circumstances and a suitably contrite heart, he should get away with little more than a slap on the wrist. He had a completely blameless past, had never been in trouble and, after all, the girl had hardly been seized at knifepoint. So the boy pleaded guilty. He was sent to jail for two years.

Before looking at that case in more detail, here's something that happened to me more than a decade ago.

I had been madly in love with a girl with whom I had been going out for about eighteen months. Our relationship was both physically and emotionally passionate with that all-consuming intensity that is the hallmark of a late adolescent affair. Of course, the other hallmark of such affairs is that they end. Sure enough, she went away to university and began a new relationship with a fellow student. One 'Dear John' letter later, I was heartbroken and, like so many other deluded souls before me, longed for the chance to win her back.

The opportunity came when I threw a party, to which I invited her. This, I knew, was a mistake, since I was bound to get hurt. But then, when you're a young man in the pits of romantic despair, you're liable to do things that are dumb and masochistic in just about equal proportions. Anyway, the girl arrived, looking ravishing. After a while, she suggested we go upstairs to talk. We went off to my bedroom, although, to be strictly accurate, there was no bed. I was sleeping on a mattress on the floor. There we kissed. We took our clothes off. She motioned to me to lie down beside her. My heart was pounding, my dreams were coming true, everything was going to be wonderful again. Then, just as we were about to make love, she said, 'I can't. It wouldn't be fair to Michael.'

Michael, of course, was her new boyfriend, though that's not his real name. I was shattered. I did not force myself upon her. Instead, I simply lay there while she got dressed and left. I didn't cry – that came about three months later in a morning of tears and snot and a heaving chest – I just lay on my back for hours in a state of total emotional collapse. Eventually, I was able to go back downstairs to see what had happened to the party. It turned out that drunks had been spraying obscene graffiti all over the drawing room and hall. It took about a year to wash it all off and apply enough coats of emulsion to hide the stains. And it took about five years, a fair amount of analysis and more love than I deserved to turn me back into an emotionally functioning human being.

Now, whatever one might think of my ex-girlfriend's behaviour, it could never be said to be criminal. I never thought that she had done something evil, even if I did want to wring Michael (not his real name)'s neck. In fact, I interpreted what had happened as a case of genuinely torn emotions (partly, I suspect, because I desperately wanted to believe that she still cared). Female friends, to whom I told the story, were far less forgiving. They saw a classic piece of feminine manipulation. Either way, no one would dream of arresting and imprisoning a young woman because she broke her boyfriend's heart. That's just life. People get hurt. It's all part of growing up – we all know the clichés.

So what, then, was so much worse about the behaviour of the young man in the previous story? Why was it appropriate for him to go to jail? As a convicted rapist, his chances of finding a good job or leading a successful adult life are now practically zero. His whole future has been thrown away because of one impetuous act. But when one examines that act, it is very hard to see any crime that matches so terrible a punishment.

To the best of my knowledge, the young woman suffered no physical injury. She may very well have been traumatised – as much, perhaps, by all the legal proceedings as the act of sex itself – but is the trauma of a one-night stand that goes wrong so totally devastating that it requires the jailing of the other protagonist? And what of his reactions and his emotions? What if he was not the sex-mad beast of feminist myth? What if he was a young man who, if only for that one night, really was in love with the girl he was with? What if he was swept away by his emotions? After all, a woman's supposed helplessness in the face of her emotions is thought to justify her actions. Susan Christie, the female soldier who killed her lover's husband by slashing her throat with a butcher's knife, was originally sentenced to just five years' imprisonment because she was considered to be in the grip of passions beyond her control. In court she said, 'I did it for Duncan. I was so in love with him I would do anything. That love was so strong, it was like a drug that you can't do without.'

Nancy Friday points out that being swept away is the Nice Girl's excuse for sex for which she does not wish to be held responsible. In the American GQ feature on 'What Women Really Want', referred to in an earlier chapter, the six feisty New York women who are being interviewed agree that they want to be 'swept away' by an 'aggressive male sexuality'.

This idea is a staple of romantic fiction, too. After all, when Scarlett O'Hara is picked up by Rhett Butler, carried upstairs and flung on her bed, before (once the bedroom door has closed) being ravished to within an inch of her life, what we have witnessed is an act of marital rape. Her look the next morning, however, suggests that she is the true victor. She has driven her man to act in this passionate way, despite all his attempts to stay cool. And, judging by the success of both book and film over more than half a century, the women of the world agree with her.

A man, however, is under no such freedom to be swept away. No matter how caught up in an event he may be, and no matter how hotly his blood may be running, he must be ready to switch himself off like a light, the very instant his partner commands it.

But what if he does not? Let us return to the sufferings of the woman in question. Now, I do not wish to claim that I was hurt any more than this young woman – no one could possibly determine that one way or the other. But I would say that many, many people, male and female, are devastated by the everyday wounds of love, yet we consider their pain, no matter how deep or long-lasting, far less than that of a woman who happens to have had sex on an occasion when she did not wish to have it.

This places an extraordinary significance on the act of penetration. It implies that nothing that any woman does to a man, short of an act of physical violence, can possibly traumatise him as much as his penetration can traumatise her. And that trauma is so great that its infliction must be considered a criminal act.

This further implies that the female experience of sex is so profoundly different from that of the male that she needs to be protected by a specific series of laws. These are not extended to men who, though increasingly the victims of sexual assault, can never, legally-speaking, be raped. If women are so different in this central area of human experience, then how can they not be different in other areas too? And if they are that different, then how can one justify the raft of equal rights legislation that is predicated on their being exactly the same?

To this, one may reply that the act of insertion is also accompanied by a string of other brutalities. A woman may be menaced with a weapon, beaten, held against her will. These are criminal acts. A penis can, in its own way, be as offensive a weapon as a clenched fist. If one is attacked, it matters little how one's assailant chooses to make his, or her, assault. That assault may very well constitute a criminal offence.

But we do seem to be moving towards a situation now in which the legal definition of rape as 'penetration of the vagina by the penis when the victim is unwilling' can be taken to apply to an occasion whose real dynamic may be one of mutual misunderstanding, or shared complicity in an act that may be grubby and even unpleasant, but is certainly not the criminal exploitation of an innocent victim.

There is, however, no equivalent protection given to men against the manipulation of their feelings or sexuality. I came across an example which illustrates this point when appearing on a Granada Television discussion on date-rape in 1991. A brief studio conversation was followed by a phone-in, during which victims of assault recounted their stories. Most of these victims were, naturally enough, women, some of whom had clearly suffered greatly as a result of their experiences. But one caller was a man.

His story was that he had gone out for a drink after work with three women from his office. They were all good friends and there was no advance suggestion that this was anything other than a pleasant, social occasion. As the evening wore on, however, it became clear to the man that one of the three women was more interested in him than he had supposed. One thing led to another and they ended up at her flat, where they made love. The man left her place in the early hours and went back to his own home with a song in his heart. Not only had he enjoyed the sex, but he felt that this could be the start of a serious relationship. He had always liked the woman. Now they were going to become lovers.

He turned up for work the next morning bearing a bunch of flowers, only to find that the woman to whom he was intending to give them, and with whom he was hoping to start a long-term affair, had accused him of date-rape. He was devastated. Quite apart from the seriousness of the allegation, and the consequences it could have upon his career, not to mention his freedom, the accusation was a bitter blow to his emotions. He felt utterly betrayed and humiliated.

In the end, the accusations were dropped before any legal action could be taken, but the effect upon his feelings towards that woman in particular and his relationships with women in general was far more long-lasting. His pain, however, had no legal significance (it never occurred to him that it might). He had no means of redress. Faced with a psychological assault from a determined and malevolent woman, he was entirely defenceless.

What, though, is the view from the other side of the fence? Not long ago I went out for a drink with an old friend. She's funny, attractive and flirtatious – good company, in other words. And, as friends do over a glass or two, she was telling me about her recent exploits, one of which ended with the hilarious sight of a man leaving her flat in the early hours, simultaneously pulling up his trousers as he tried to hail a cab. It was all good stuff, but the most interesting thing was the reason why the man was leaving.

My friend, you see, had picked him up at a club. 'I just wanted a really good snog,' she said. So, after they had smooched around the dance floor, she invited him back to her place for a snog and a stroke and just about everything else . . . except the actual act of sex itself. As soon as her needs were satisfied, and at the point when he looked as though he might be about to go further than she desired, he was out of the door and onto the pavement, with his trousers in his hands and a sorry expression on his face.

He had, to put it bluntly, been used. She wanted a 'really good snog' and once she'd got it, she had no further use for the snogger. Barbara Amiel would have every reason to use this as an example of women who use men as vibrators, to be picked up, played with and discarded as they see fit, but men can hardly complain. After all, they've been using women as sex aids for centuries. The only difference is, men haven't gone running to the law whenever things went wrong.

Suppose, however, that the man my friend picked up had had a different agenda? Suppose he had not meekly walked out into the night, but had stayed and had sex regardless of her wishes – it would be a crime, but could you say that she was entirely without responsibility for what had occurred? Let me put it another way: say I walked through the streets of the South Bronx carrying a placard which read 'I carry gold Amex and Mastercard.' If I were to be mugged, I would still be traumatised and it would still be a crime. But would anyone have very much sympathy for my predicament?

Responsible adults

This is where we are now: political activists see all acts of sex into which a woman has entered unwillingly as rape. They interpret this as an embodiment of men's oppression of women. Meanwhile, the mass media – often the ones whose content is determined by women for other women – pump out a message of aggressive female sexuality. A continual theme of this message is the inability of men to satisfy the needs or demands of women.

Men are told that their masculinity is, in part, determined by their ability to satisfy these needs, often by being masterful and assertive. However, should these aggressively sexual women have sex on an occasion upon which they did not want it, the man with whom they had sex is a criminal.

The reason we say this is because we place an enormous emphasis on penetration of the woman's body, thus suggesting that male and female experience of sex is profoundly different. Except that we then legislate on the basis that, in every other area of life, there is no difference at all.

My view is that nothing will be solved until responsibility is shared equally. Men should be responsible for their own behaviour, and I do not condone any acts of brutality or unreasonable coercion. But women cannot be raunchy sex kittens on the one hand and delicate virgins on the other. If they want to be as free as men, they may have to accept that they will end up being as unprotected.

One final thought: is this issue really one that turns, not on the maintenance of male power, but on the much more fundamental level of female power? Could it be that what women are really fighting for is the continuation of their monopoly of the ability to control sexual activity through their power of acceptance or veto?

Claire Rayner places date-rape in the following context: 'Women initiate sex, really. It's the woman who's in charge. We make all the choices, we make the decisions, because we invest all the time involved in producing a baby.'

I asked Ms Rayner whether one could, on that basis, define date-rape as an occasion on which a man has made the decisions. 'Yes,' she replied. 'He's misread the signals and he's fed up with her being in charge. So he's decided to be in charge instead.'

That is his first – and criminal – mistake.

Chapter 8

Battered Husbands

On 13 July 1992, Princess Anne, the Princess Royal, gave a press conference in London to launch a report on domestic violence by a charity called Victim Support, of which she is the patron. The report made a number of urgent recommendations to help tackle a problem which, it said, was causing the deaths of 100 women every year in Britain.

It called for a telephone help-line for victims and a new focus for government strategy. In the face of Home Office figures claiming 50,000 calls to the police every year following incidents of domestic violence, crime prevention advice for women should, the authors said, be shifted from stressing violence on the street to emphasising the dangers of violence in the home. Furthermore, if women were to be compelled to give evidence in court against their partners, they should be offered safe accommodation.

The Princess Royal had something to say about men. They should not, she said, be stigmatised. 'We are not going to help women in the long run if the report, or feeling in general, is going to alienate men by making them feel that they are being got at.'

Maybe so, but the report – and, even more so, the coverage it received – perpetuated the notion that domestic violence essentially consists of random, unprovoked attacks by aggressive men upon innocent women. *The Times*, in a sidebar to its coverage of the Victim Support Report, cited the experience of the domestic violence unit at Wood Green police station where, the paper claimed, 97 per cent of the 900 cases a year involved violence against women by men.

The notion of the innocent victim is one upon which the domestic violence lobby has long insisted. Great efforts were made during the 1970s and 1980s to discredit the idea that women in any sense participated in or provoked the violence that was acted out upon them.

Yet, when one starts to discuss violence against men, the very same campaigners and academics who so fervently denied the female victim's complicity immediately insist that the man must in some way have provoked the assault. Furthermore, the people who reject the possibility that women can be violent towards men are also the ones who are fascinated by a hot topic in women's studies – violence in lesbian relationships.

Are women capable of violence or not? Or is it just homosexual women who start acting rough? That seems as unlikely as it is politically incorrect.

Just to get it clear from the start, my personal view of domestic violence, based on conversations with victims, therapists, police officers, counsellors and researchers, is this: people within sexual or family relationships are capable of doing great harm to one another. Some of these people are male, some are female. There is probably little to choose between men and women in the quantity or intensity of the harm they do to other people, although their methods may very well vary.

Within relationships, there may be dysfunctions in which both partners are involved – what Dr Liam Hudson might call perverse acts, taking place in a perverse situation – or there may be unprovoked assaults, possibly induced by factors such as mental disorder, alcohol or drug abuse.

We cannot be sure about the full extent of female-to-male violence because the absolute refusal to investigate or research it on a formal basis means that there is no reliable data on the subject. But since the data on male-to-female violence is also wildly unreliable, that makes matters all-square.

The refusal of feminist academics to take female violence seriously exactly mirrors the refusal of male authorities to take male violence seriously twenty years ago. Even the insults are the same.

This refusal has something to do with the emotional and ideological investment that has been committed to the notion of an abusive and oppressive patriarchy. Anyone who has spent the past twenty years trying to persuade the world that it is organised in one way is hardly going to turn around and admit that it is actually organised in another. But it has a lot more to do with wishing to hang onto research grants and government funding. Because even if academics let go of their principles, they'll never let go of their cash.

Meanwhile, people are suffering. Ordinary, everyday men are

abused twice over, once in their relationships and again by their contact with an indifferent or hostile officialdom. This is just what used to happen to women.

But enough theory. Let's meet an ordinary man. And let's call him Donald, although that is not, for reasons that will soon become apparent, his real name. Over the course of several months, I have come to know Donald quite well and have had his case documented in meticulous, not to say obsessive, detail. This is what he said on the day we first met.

The victim's tale

'This is a story you will have difficulty believing. It will test your credulity beyond belief. But there are plenty of others like it.' Donald was not a particularly prepossessing sight: narrow-faced, with a sallow complexion and thinning hair that was turning grey, scraped back off his forehead across his scalp. He sat hunched up in his chair, pulling on the cigarettes which he chain-smoked as he told his tale.

He was not by any means insubstantial, maybe five foot ten tall and about twelve stone in weight. But he held himself in such a way, hunched up and round-shouldered, as to diminish his physical presence to the point where one would, at first glance, have taken him for a far smaller, weaker man. He was a highly qualified professional. But he was entirely bereft of the middle-class self-confidence that one might have expected. He looked, in short, like a beaten dog. It was entirely appropriate. For Donald had suffered years of physical abuse at the hands of his wife, Mary. It began, he said, right at the very start of their marriage.

'Three days after we got married, we went out for the evening. When we got back to the flat, I went to get something to eat. She suddenly became enraged. She hit me with a flurry of fists. I didn't know what was going on. I was dumbfounded. What she wanted was sex. She was annoyed that I hadn't jumped on top of her the moment we were alone. We had sex. I assure you, if someone is wielding a hammer, or any number of other objects at your head, you will have sex.'

This first explosion of rage was the start of a pattern in which his wife's obsessive jealousy came to rule their entire lives. 'I've been accused of having heterosexual affairs, homosexual affairs, incestuous affairs – anybody and everybody. It's not about sex. It's about control.

There was a time when I could hardly get to work. The front door was barricaded. She'd be up against the door. I could have flung her out of the way, but I didn't want to. I didn't go out for two years, apart from work. My wife would even come to my work to check up on me, so that she'd know where I was.'

If her suspicions were ever aroused, her retribution took the form of violence, both physical and verbal. 'There was one night, she had been hitting me and my chest was covered in bruises. I didn't notice them. In fact, she was the first person to see them, when I had a bath the next day. She said I was covered in love bites. I must have been seeing another woman. So she attacked me again.

'Once when she attacked me with a hammer, I snatched it and held it above her head. She just kept on hitting me with her other hand. When I grabbed that, she went for my testicles. I've played rugby all my life and I've never been scared of a rugby player. But I am terrified of my wife. Trying to restrain her is no good. Even verbal restraint pushes up the level of violence.

'At the end of an attack, the only way that the violence would stop, was that my wife would demand that I get down on the floor and beg forgiveness. Why didn't I retaliate? I didn't want to hit a woman. And if I had retaliated, that would have been the final humiliation.'

There were, however, plenty of other humiliations in store. 'One of the things my wife did was that she would want me to make love to her to prove that I had not been unfaithful. After making love, she had the habit of checking her vagina to see if there was 'enough' semen there. She thought that if there wasn't it would prove I had been with someone else.

'I could always have sex with my wife if I initiated it. It was no problem. She would always accept it. But if she wanted to make overtures to me, she couldn't do it in any way other than jealousy or control. For example, if I did the washing-up wrongly, that would lead to an argument, a tirade, and the final demand would be, "Have sex with me."

'One night we made love, fine, then she gets up. Suddenly, like someone had thrown a switch, she said, "Do it again!" Of course I couldn't. You have to wait a certain time. She started to attack me. She seized my penis and started trying to masturbate it. I had fingernail marks on my penis. She sat on top and tried to have intercourse. Now, okay, my penis was nothing like totally erect, but it was not totally flaccid either. There was still some residual engorgement. By that time I was in tears. I couldn't retaliate.'

The violence was not confined to attacks upon Donald. He alleges that his wife forcibly restrained their daughter, Jane, when she was still a baby; force-fed her to the point of vomiting and then, when she was sick, slapped her so hard around the face that she fell out of her high chair. On other occasions, she hit the child powerfully enough to leave substantial bruising and later, when the little one was two, knocked her off her feet, bursting her eardrum in the process.

Jane was taught, 'You are not to call your father "Daddy". He is not your father. He is a bastard.' So intimidated did she become in the face of her mother's assaults that she would run and hide in a cupboard, rather than face the risk of punishment. Despite this, Donald said, 'I have my suspicions she's training her to say I've hit her. I've only ever smacked her once. I believe you should never use force on a two- or three-year-old little child.'

Why don't you hit her back, sir?

Faced with a story like this, it is hard to know how to respond. Some people might find it irrelevant. The battered husband is so rare, and the battered woman so common, they would say, that it is offensive even to contemplate the male victim in the face of endemic female suffering. Others might find it hard, reading Donald's testimony, not to suppress a laugh at the thought of a man being terrorised by a woman who is, as a matter of fact, pretty, delicate looking, far smaller and, apparently, weaker than he is. For goodness' sake, one might think, pull yourself together; be a man.

Put yourself in the victim's shoes and a very different picture emerges. The vast majority of men who are attacked by their wives or partners never report the fact to anyone. They feel so humiliated and emasculated that they dare not tell anyone what has happened. When they do, they are confronted with a mixture of indifference and disbelief.

The first time that Donald rang up his local police he was told that his wife was probably just asking for it. 'She is just trying to wind you up, sir,' said one woman police officer, an opinion shared by a health visitor, who had been called to examine the physical evidence of his wife's abuse of their little daughter. 'Why don't you hit her back, sir,' opined another PC helpfully. When Donald tried to warn the social services of what was being done to his daughter, the social worker assigned to him walked out of their meeting in mid-sentence. When

Donald's parents voiced their concerns, the same social worker walked out on them, too.

Nor were counsellors able to help. Despite psychiatric reports which diagnosed Mary as having a personality disorder, liable to lead to maladaptive and even psychopathic behaviour, there seemed little that anyone could or was willing to do to remedy the situation. One counsellor advised Donald to get a divorce, forget about his daughter and start again with a new family. 'I wasn't going to take that abuse,' he told me. 'I'd had enough already.'

In any case, divorce is the very last thing that a battered husband can afford, particularly if he is worried about the safety of his children. A battered woman will often be advised to institute divorce proceedings, accompanied by an ouster order, which evicts her partner, and a non-molestation order, which prevents him from attacking, or even seeing her again. A man, however, knows that a divorce will almost certainly lead, not to his wife's eviction, but his own.

No matter how great the degree of abuse meted out by a wife to her husband or child, courts almost never find in the husband's favour. The wife is almost certain to be given custody of the children, and with the children comes the family house. So a battered man who divorces his abusive spouse stands to lose everything he has. First he's attacked by his wife, then he's finished off by the system.

Donald, like all battered men, faced the continual threat that he would be reported to the police at the first sign of retaliation. On one occasion, in March 1992, his wife said she would accuse him of marital rape. 'There she is, with her arm over my windpipe, holding my balls and saying I've got to have sex with her or she'll accuse me of rape. And I remember saying, "If I don't have sex with you, how can you accuse me of rape?" '

Such claims are entirely par for the course. At the height of the attacks against him, Donald was visited at work one day by a representative of Families Need Fathers, a pressure group that campaigns for paternal rights. 'The man came to my office and asked about my personal situation,' he recalls. 'I told him I was thinking of getting a non-molestation order against Mary. Without batting an eyelid he said, "How are you going to cope when your wife makes malicious allegations saying that you've been abusing your child?" That had happened to him. He was a battered man.'

In Donald's case, matters came to a head a few weeks after the 'rape' incident. 'Over the previous month I'd been standing up to my wife and saying, "Mary, you are a bully." That morning we'd had a row and she was in a foul mood by the evening, although there'd been no violence. During the Channel 4 news, Jane went off to the toilet. (The only training that Mary had given her was to hit her when she missed or was sick. I've done everything for my daughter.) My wife noticed that Jane had closed the door, so she went off to see what had happened. I could hear a tirade and Jane being slapped – one, two, three – I thought, "Uh-oh, what's going on?"

'I went to the bathroom and said, "What's going on? Slapping's not the way to deal with it."

'Mary said, "I'll hit my child if I want to."

'Then there was an argument. My wife was getting aggressive. I said, "If you do that again, I'll call the police." She immediately thumped me again. I dialled 999. The operator put me through to the police. I said I wanted to complain about an assault by my wife on my daughter. My wife put the phone down and bundled me out of the way. Well, there are two phones in the flat, so I went to the other one. I couldn't get a line. I didn't think anything of it because the phones were dodgy, but when I went back to the other room, Mary was on the phone, screaming that she was terrified.

'I decided to go to the police, so I grabbed my jacket and went to the nearest police station. I saw the guy on the desk. He said to phone their domestic violence unit in the morning. But I was worried about Jane, what could I do?

'I drove back to the house. When I got there, there was a police Metro parked outside. I knew when I walked up the stairs that I would be arrested. In the living room were my wife, my daughter, a police constable and a WPC. I said, "This is a long-running thing," and named two WPCs that I'd talked to about it in the past, but the copper had me pinned down as the guilty party and he came on very strong. He said he'd seen my daughter in sheer terror of me as I had walked in.

'I was nervous. My wife was still in the room and I was reluctant to give full vent. But then the WPC took my wife and daughter into the bedroom. I leaned forward towards the PC and told him I'd put up with four years of this and that I considered I had been indecently assaulted.

'He was very unhappy about the situation. He said, "I know there'll be further violence tonight and we'll be called back."

'I assured him several times that there would be no violence from me. He tried to say I ought to leave the premises. He said, "If we have to come back here tonight, I will have to arrest somebody for breach of the peace and you know who that will be . . . you." In effect he was saying that no matter how violent my wife was, don't call us, because we'll arrest you.

'However, I could see he was beginning to get perturbed. He said he ought to call on higher authority. So he called up and said, "We've got a battered husband syndrome here." Another car arrived and a gentleman got out and chatted to the policeman for five minutes. The copper came back upstairs and there were all four of us in the living room. My wife said she wanted me out. He said I had a right to live there and he wanted to make a full report. Then she made allegations that I had been sexually abusing her. The police paid no attention to her and left.'

The next day, Donald tried to make a formal statement to the police. Despite a series of phone calls and letters, some to senior officers, no such statement was ever taken. The last time I spoke to him, he had just been served with divorce papers by his wife. The divorce was being sought on the grounds of his cruelty and violence towards her. 'If you think my story's bad,' he said, 'it's not half as bad as some blokes. I've had it comparatively easy.'

The threat of legal action is one faced by all the battered men to whom I spoke. In every case, their divorce had been brought about by their wives' claims that they had been the victims. And in every case, the police, social services, legal advisers and courts had found it impossible to conceive of the idea that the woman might have been the instigator, rather than the victim, of the domestic abuse. Why should they? For years, they have been told that men are the violent sex. To be told that men can be the victims is as shocking as it would be to discover that apples, in fact, fall up.

Sugar and spice

In part, this is a matter of social conditioning. We naturally assume that women – being both smaller and, we imagine, less inclined to violence – cannot possibly do harm to big, strong, aggressive males. When Ron Brown, the Member of Parliament for Leith, damaged the contents of a former lover's flat, he was taken to court. But when Lady Graham-Moon cut up her adulterous husband's suits, covered his BMW with paint and gave away his wine to people in the village, she was hailed by columnists who saw this as typical of the acts of minor defiance to which women must resort in the face of their menfolk's overwhelming physical strength.

One newspaper, *Today*, published an article on 18 March 1992 entitled 'Twenty delicious ways to get even with your man', which included scrawling 'Scum' on his car, destroying his most treasured possessions and kidnapping his new lover.

On the same day, the *Daily Mail* ran another feature headlined, 'Why women will always throw more than abuse'. The writer, Diana Hutchinson, began her piece thus, 'The tension is mounting. He's not listening, beginning to shout. Your hand strays almost of its own accord towards that ugly heavy cut-glass fruit bowl his mother gave you. Crash! Satisfyingly, the shards of glass sprinkle over the TV set. Why is it that when a woman gets mad, really mad, she invariably ends up throwing something?'

Ian Grove-Stephenson, a 'psychologist and counsellor', was quoted in the same article. He saw throwing as 'the straightforward David and Goliath syndrome', the woman, of course, being David. He concluded, 'Throwing things means, "I consider this relationship worth fighting for." '

Would that, I wonder, apply to punching, kicking, stratching or biting? Would it apply if it were the man that was doing the fighting?

Cathy Lever is the administrator of Move (Men Over Violence), a counselling service for violent men in Bolton, Lancashire. The service aims to help batterers come to terms with what they have done, accept full responsibility for their actions and learn not to act in that way again. Ginny Dougary, a journalist who watched a counselling session in action, reported that the men involved, 'talk with raw, smarting candour. They castigate themselves so much it is like a form of masochism.'

I asked Cathy Lever whether any of the men who came to her reported being in relationships in which their violence was just one element in a general dysfunction. She replied, 'When men initially come to us, they invariably won't take responsibility. They say, "She made me," or, "She said this or that." But after a few sessions they take the whole responsibility for their actions.'

Was that entirely fair? Was there no possibility of provocation?

'We say there are always alternatives,' she replied. 'He can always get up and leave the room. He has to take sole responsibility for the violence. There's no excuse.'

I'm not sure about that because I think that it oversimplifies highly complex situations. But I can understand that forcing a man to admit his wrongdoing, whatever the reasons for it, may be a necessary first step along the road to understanding it and preventing further recurrences.

I then asked Lever whether there was any evidence of violence against men by their partners. She said, 'It's a very, very small problem. You've got to consider the power relationship between men and women. When I argue with my fiancé, I've slapped him round the face because I didn't like what he was saying. But I'm five foot five and he's six foot three.'

Oh well, that's all right then. Although well-meaning, Ms Lever seemed to have no idea of the implications of what she was saying. For example, she knew that she could hit her boyfriend without any fear of his retaliating as he would do if struck by a man. His self-restraint, motivated by the taboo against hitting women that is drummed into boys and young men, was being used as a weapon against him. More to the point, I think she had confused intention and effect. Just because a woman isn't very good at hitting a man, that doesn't make her action any more morally justifiable. Either violence is inexcusable, or it isn't.

This is a perfect example of the double standard that we now have for men and women. We are told continually that women have all the drive, energy, intelligence and sheer ambition required to get to the top of any business, army or political party on earth. But as soon as the focus shifts to their relationship with men we consider them . . . well, what do we consider them? What do you call someone who has no self-control, who lashes out, but who expects to be tolerated and forgiven by a big strong man on the grounds that they didn't mean it and couldn't do any real harm anyway? You call them a child.

I don't think that women are children. I think that they are fully grown adult human beings. Which means that they have to take responsibility for their actions. They can't have it both ways, however nice it might be. My preferred solution would not be to turn the clock back to the days when women were treated as children in every aspect of their lives, but to move it forward. Once again, what is needed is more equality, not less.

She's a victim, and that's official

Whenever the matter of domestic violence is discussed, the assumption is always made that women are the primary, perhaps even the sole victims. That assumption is now becoming enshrined in official documents which advise upon and affect the legislation that is brought before Parliament.

On page three of the *Law Commission Report No. 207: Family Law – Domestic Violence and Occupation of the Family Home*, it is stated, 'There can be no doubt of the extent of the problem [of domestic violence]. It has been summarised thus: "All studies that exist indicate that wife abuse is a common and pervasive problem and that men from practically all countries, cultures, classes and income groups indulge in the behaviour" ... Although both men and women can suffer domestic violence, nearly all the studies have shown that in the great majority of cases, men are the perpetrators and women are the victims.'

The report is annotated. Note 5, to which the reader is referred in the last sentence above, remarks, 'Whilst a certain amount of attention has been paid to "battered husbands" e.g. F. Bates, "A Plea for the Battered Husband" (1981) 11 Fam Law 90, other commentators have concluded that whilst some husbands certainly suffer violence at the hands of their wives, this is an individual rather than a social problem. It is uncommon and there is no sound evidence to suggest that any "syndrome" exists comparable to the problem of battered wives. See M. D. Pagelow, "The Battered Husband Syndrome: Social Problem or Much Ado About Little?", in N. Johnson (ed.), *Marital Violence* (1985).'

Mildred Daley Pagelow's paper is a scholarly attempt to examine the subject of violence against husbands. Or rather, it is a scholarly attempt to prove that such violence is insignificant. Its first half consists of a methodological assault on one of the few other reports on the subject, a paper entitled 'The Battered Husband Syndrome' written in 1977 by an American sociologist called Suzanne Steinmetz, who claimed a figure of 250,000 annual cases of husband-battering for the US as a whole.

Having questioned the statistical basis upon which Steinmetz based her conclusions, Pagelow examines evidence from various centres catering for victims of domestic violence and asserts that the true proportion of male victims ranges from 0 to 4 per cent. She then cites other experts in order to determine that violence and even murder on the part of women is not only far less common than that by men, but is almost always an act of self-defence when it occurs.

Pagelow goes on to state that battered men are much freer, given their greater economic power and mobility, to leave the family home than are women. She wonders why an able-bodied man would want or need to remain with a violent wife after being subjected to physical abuse, and is unable to come up with an answer.

She claims, furthermore, that female attacks tend not to be serious and concludes, 'The preponderance of scientific evidence leads to the conclusion that the vast majority of victims of spousal violence are female, whether wives or lovers. *Most importantly, in the years since 1977 when the image of the battered husband syndrome was publicised, there has not been a single report of scientific research on a sample of battered husbands* [her emphasis].

'In sum there undoubtedly are many violent wives and some battered husbands, but the proportion of systematically abused husbands compared to abused wives is relatively small, and certainly the phenomenon does not amount to a "syndrome" as popularised.'

This, remember, is the research upon which official British Government attitudes to male victimisation in domestic violence are based. So one is entitled to question some of Pagelow's blithe assumptions. For example, why should the fact that there has been no research into female marital violence indicate that the phenomenon is unimportant? Might it not indicate instead the priorities of an academic and sociological establishment that has an enormous intellectual investment in the idea of an oppressive patriarchy? Alternatively, might one find that – as with sexual abuse – the notion of female violence is simply unthinkable, and therefore unresearched?

Are we really surprised that the WomenShelter, Long Beach, California, which is cited amongst Pagelow's sources, reports no male victims of domestic violence? If you were a battered man, would you go there? If you did, would they let you in?

Looking through Ms Pagelow's notes one finds references to a plethora of works on the battered wife, often given at such occasions as the Second International Symposium on Victimology and including Pagelow's own paper, 'Social Learning Theory and Sex Roles: Violence Begins in the Home'. She also makes frequent references to the British husband-and-wife team of sociology professors, R. E. and R. P. Dobash, whose cited works include their 1979 book *Violence Against Wives: A Case Against the Patriarchy*, and a *Spare Rib* piece entitled, 'Battered Women, in Defence of Self-Defence'.

Without wishing to call their academic credentials into question, I wonder how interested any of these distinguished authorities would be in any work which succeeded in overturning their preconceptions. In 1991, an English law student called Stephanie Jeavons decided to write an undergraduate thesis on female domestic violence. She soon realised that there was virtually no research on the subject, so she contacted Professor Rebecca Dobash and asked for her advice.

According to Jeavons, Professor Dobash gave her a reading list and then added, 'I had hoped that the British would have more sense than to waste resources pursuing this line,' before remarking that Jeavons was 'politically naive' to be tackling such a subject.

As Jeavons began to research female domestic violence, she began to encounter two sets of responses. The first, from friends and acquaintances, consisted of jokes, unease and then – if those two handicaps could be overcome – serious conversations, often involving personal experience. The second, from feminist academics (in this particular field, there are really no other kind), was one of outright hostility. She came to the conclusion that, 'Domestic violence has been hijacked by hardcore feminists and used as a political weapon. It's treated as a woman's field, whereas actually it involves violence against children, against men, against old people . . . it's whole families.

'We're always standing up for minorities, but men are the last great taboo. Feminists are putting up the same arguments against them as were put up against women when Erin Pizzey started coming forward in the 1970s. The criticism, the hostility, the trivialisation, the humour . . . it's exactly the same.'

I know what she means. At a lunch in March 1992 arranged by British *Elle* magazine, at which my fellow guests included Marilyn French and Susan Faludi, I mentioned that I had just spent several hours interviewing a male victim of domestic violence. I said that I suspected that the phenomenon might be much more widespread than I had previously thought. At this, one of my fellow guests, the Australian author Kathy Lette, turned to me and said, 'You had better get your statistics absolutely right, or we're going to crucify you.' It was the old horse's head tactic once again.

Number crunching: men on the receiving end

Ms Lette might be interested in a book called *Violent Men, Violent Couples*, by Anson Shure, William A. Stacey and Lonnie Hazelwood, Chapter Three of which is entitled 'The Violent Woman'. The chapter covers some of the issues over which Mildred Pagelow passes so blithely. Why, for example, do men not leave their homes? Well, in some cases they are unable to do so: their assailants lock the doors and block their exit.

Shure, Stacey and Hazelwood do not, however, mention a much more powerful argument for a man not leaving, which is: why should he? If he has spent years living in a house, which he may well have paid for and which contains all his most personal possessions, why should he be forced to leave because of someone else's wrongdoing? Pagelow's casual assumption that a man can just walk out the door only makes sense if she believes that men have no feelings, and that they can discard a home as casually as they might a worn-out pair of shoes.

As for attacks not being serious, Shure, Stacey and Hazelwood – whose research data is mostly based on reports from the Texas police and a counselling project in the city of Austin – cite the case of a man on trial for the assault of his former girlfriend. He denied that he had ever been violent, said that he had ended their relationship because of her drinking and aggression, and revealed that he had been hospitalised with a knife wound to the scrotum, inflicted by her while he was sleeping in bed. She had also slashed the tyres of his car. He had never reported any of these or other incidents to the police because he felt that it was wrong to file charges against a woman.

'In one case,' the authors report, 'an Army sergeant could no longer deal with the private humiliation of his wife's violence towards him. Tears streaming down his face as his family said grace together one night before a meal, he quietly pulled a pistol from his belt, put the barrel in his mouth and pulled the trigger. The daily contrast between his macho parade-ground image . . . and the reality of his being the frequent target of his domineering wife's physical abuse (in front of their children) became overwhelming.'

In Texas, 10 per cent of all domestic violence victims listed by the police were male. This figure does not include those men arrested as aggressors who were themselves attacked – a phenomenon of which Shure et al. found considerable evidence. Women seemed far more willing than men to involve the police, often doing so as part of the war they were waging against their partner. One man had his working life ruined by his former wife's habit of filing assault charges for no reason, forcing him to go to court, and then dropping the charges.

There appeared to be little difference in the factors influencing male and female violence: family background, financial pressures, substance abuse and so on. Shure et al. noted that a survey in Austin revealed that two-thirds of all male batterers had had objects thrown at them by their partners, half had been threatened physically, often with being killed, and half had been punched or kicked. As many as three-quarters reported psychological intimidation, including attempts by the woman to limit the man's contact with his family or friends, outbursts of extreme jealousy, and the withdrawal of sex as a punishment. The authors conclude, 'There is undoubtedly distortion at work in these reports but we know from previously documented case reports that women's violence cannot be dismissed as sheer rationalisation.'

They also quote some research done in 1985 amongst American students by a sociologist called Richard Breen. He interviewed 884 students, male and female, married and unmarried, about their experience of violence within a romantic partnership. His findings were surprising: 18 per cent of men and 14 per cent of women reported being the victims of violence within a relationship. Breen then asked the married men a series of questions about their wives. Once again, the results were at odds with received opinion.

20 per cent had wives who threw or broke household objects when angry

23 per cent were punched, kicked or slapped by their wives

30 per cent were pushed or shoved by their wives, either in public or private

9 per cent had wives who had attacked them with objects

9 per cent had received visible welts, cuts or bruises as a result of attacks by their wives

10 per cent had sought medical aid as a result of attacks

14 per cent had wives who had, at least once, threatened either to kill their husband or to commit suicide, and

5 per cent had called the police at least once because they felt that they, their family or their friends were in danger from their wife.

Elsewhere, on 21 April 1992, *The Times* reported 'a 1985 study of 6,000 couples [in the USA] which asked each partner how often they resorted to violence and intimidation. Women were slightly more likely than men to have slapped, kicked, bitten or punched their nearest and dearest.'

In Britain, *Chat* magazine published a survey on domestic violence in January 1992. It revealed that 47 per cent of female respondents admitted to slapping or hitting their partners. One-third of the men said that they had done the same. A similar proportion, one-third, of all women had thrown plates or other objects. Just 16 per cent of the men had thrown anything at their womenfolk.

British *Reader's Digest* published a MORI poll on attitudes and behaviour within the family in their October 1991 edition. The survey consisted of interviews with 2,075 people. Of these, some 1,510 were currently in a relationship. The pollsters asked a number of questions under the heading, 'Which, if any, of the following have you done as a result of an argument between you and your current partner?' Two of the findings were as follows:

Hit your partner	Male 3%	Female 10%	Total 7%
Thrown something at your partner	Male 6%	Female 20%	Total 13%

Now, the figures from these surveys vary quite dramatically. Yet the preponderance of violent women never alters. One might explain it by saying that, as we have already seen, women do not believe that their actions are serious and so admit to them readily, whereas men feel guilty and stay quiet. But even the most gimlet-eyed feminist would have a hard time claiming that 97 per cent of violence was caused by men . . . not, at any rate, based on these four surveys, covering more than 8,000 people in two countries.

Our underestimates of female violence are surely exacerbated by the refusal of male victims to take action against their partners. Of course, women are also slow to press charges against men – much to the frustration of some campaigners – but their inhibitions are as nothing compared to those affecting men, and with good reason. Many British police forces are now, as a matter of policy, dealing with incidents of domestic violence by arresting the man, holding him in a cell overnight and cautioning him that any further incidents will lead to him being charged with assault. When confronted with allegations of female violence, police and social workers often do . . . nothing.

There are, as will soon become clear, exceptions to this rule. But, having met many battered husbands, I have yet to encounter one who received any co-operation at all from any statutory body. In conversation with social workers, it has also been made clear to me that the possibility of female violence never enters their minds. One man, who has been involved in social work for eighteen years, told me that in all his time in the job, he had never been to a single seminar, meeting or training exercise in which the possibility of male victimisation was ever mentioned. For social workers at least, women are eternally oppressed and the patriarchy still rules OK.

Today, violence against men is treated in the way that rape used to be. Victims are considered to be as guilty as their attackers. They are disbelieved, ignored or treated with outright hostility by a dominant culture which refuses to believe in their suffering. And only a tiny minority of attacks is ever reported, still less acted upon.

As a consequence, I suspect that official figures grossly under-report the true extent of female violence. But what of the figures for male violence? Given Ms Lette's concern for accuracy, how sure can we be about them?

Number crunching, part II: men doing it out

In his book *No More Sex War: The Failures of Feminism*, Neil Lyndon, like Mildred Pagelow, examines the methodology behind the statistics used to support claims about domestic violence. In this case, however, his aim is to question the claims of those who maintain that violence against women is an endemic feature of our society.

Lyndon begins by citing a Metropolitan Police spokesman who says that, although the Met has no exact figures, they think that they respond to 'about 25,000' calls a year involving domestic violence. This figure is apparently based on extrapolation from research conducted at two divisional police stations in London – Hounslow and Holloway – by the criminologist Dr Susan Edwards, an academic who, Lyndon points out, believes that, 'It is the precise juncture of bourgeois and male interest which constitutes the corner-stone of women's experience and corresponding oppression.'

Dr Edwards' research is quoted in the *Police Monitoring and Research Group, Briefing Paper No. 1: Police Response to Domestic Violence* (1986), where her work at Hounslow and Holloway is said to indicate a city-wide total of 1,000 calls a week, or 50,000 cases a year. Which of the figures is right – is it 25,000 or 50,000?

Perhaps it is 100,000. That is the number of calls quoted as an authoritative figure by Sandra Horley, Director of the Chiswick Family Refuge, in a letter to the editor of the *Independent*. Lyndon, however, can top that. In her book *The Rites of Man*, Dr Rosalind Miles claims that, 'In the London area alone, more than 100,000 women a year need hospital treatment after violence in the home.'

I tried to find some evidence to support Dr Miles's claims and the first thing I discovered was . . . nobody knows. For one thing: what is 'the London area'? There is no central health authority for the nation's capital. Instead, it is split into a number of regional authorities, which slice up the city and its environs in a pattern that is similar, but not identical, to that of the London boroughs.

So let's look at the hospitals themselves. There are about fifteen major central London hospitals: these being the famous teaching institutions such as Guy's, St Mary's, St Thomas's, University College Hospital and so on. If, however, one defines 'the London area' as including those hospitals served by the London Ambulance Service, that gives a total of forty accident and emergency departments, through which these 100,000 victims of domestic violence would pass. The biggest of these would probably be Whipps Cross, in Epping Forest, which deals with a total of about 100,000 casualty patients of all kinds a year, whereas a smaller department, such as that at the Westminster Hospital, would be looking at closer to 30,000. Most of the major London teaching hospitals see 50,000–75,000 casualty patients every year.

So how many of these patients are admitted as a result of domestic violence? There are simply no official statistics of any sort relating to the subject. With the exception of road traffic accidents, patients' injuries are categorised by their medical nature, rather than their cause. Nevertheless, the doctors and nurses on the ground do, as one would imagine, have a pretty good idea of how, as well as why, their patients come to be seeing them, and they are able to give rough but authoritative estimates of the causes of their injuries.

Mr Hugh Millington is the consultant surgeon in charge of the accident and emergency department at Charing Cross Hospital in Fulham, West London. This receives 65,000 casualty patients every year and covers an area of London that is split fairly evenly between the home-owning, gentrifying, middle classes and working-class council tenants on postwar, high-rise estates. It is, both socially and geographically, a midpoint between the tensions and poverty of the inner city and the leafy contentment of suburbia.

In his ten years as a consultant at Charing Cross, Mr Millington has seen an increase in both the number and the severity of injuries due to domestic violence. He says there is 'a significant number of women presenting with injuries that have come about as a result of domestic violence'.

This sounds like strong support for Dr Miles's position. In fact, when I first put her figure of 100,000 victims per annum to Mr Millington, he said that it 'doesn't sound surprising'. Then we did some sums. If her assertion was accurate, one would expect a large hospital such as Charing Cross to receive at least one fortieth of the London total (given that there are, as we have seen, forty casualty departments in total), or 2,500 patients a year, or roughly seven patients every day. In fact, Mr Millington would put the figure at less than two a day, and some days none at all. He would make 'an intelligent guess' that the total number of victims of domestic violence needing treatment at Charing Cross would be 500–700 per annum: many, many fewer than Dr Miles's figures would suggest.

Now, as he points out, many domestic violence victims would not tell a doctor how they received their injuries. They might very well claim to have walked into the proverbial door. But the point is this: there is no evidence whatever to support the contention that 100,000 women every year are so severely beaten by their husbands or lovers that they require hospital treatment. I could, by extrapolating from Mr Millington's figures, come up with a figure of 20,000. But this, too, would be nothing more than a guess. Once again, the truth is . . . nobody knows.

Let's talk to the police. Chief Inspector Crozier is the Personnel and Training Officer at Leman Street police station in the East End of London. He was responsible for setting up the domestic violence unit that covers the Leman Street and Bethnal Green divisions, two of whose WPCs feature (pseudonymously) in the Metropolitan Police's recruiting advertisements. The unit was created after pressure from women's organisations had alerted the police to the need for a new, more sensitive and better targeted approach to domestic violence.

One might expect that, in an area of extreme social deprivation, with above-average levels of broken homes, alcohol abuse and unemployment, the perfect conditions would exist for high levels of domestic violence. Of course, as campaigners in the field constantly point out, violence is by no means confined to the poor. Nevertheless, it would be surprising if an area that suffered, for example, the second-highest murder rate in Greater London did not also see that pattern extended to other forms of aggressive behaviour.

Yet when the domestic violence unit first opened – covering, it should be noted, not just wife-beating, but also violence between parents and children and even one family and another – the amount of cases with which they dealt was, according to Chief Inspector Crozier 'not enough to justify the officers' employment'. Within eighteen months, after a great deal of time and effort had been devoted to winning the trust and co-operation of other agencies such as the social services and voluntary groups, word of the DVU's existence had spread, referrals were coming in from other organisations and the case-load was up to . . . one call a day.

That's right: in one of the roughest inner-city areas of the most violent city of a country that is supposed to be overwhelmed by a flood of physical abuse of women by men, there were something in the region of 350 reported instances of domestic violence every year. As for criminal prosecutions, Crozier remarks, 'You can count them on the fingers of one hand per month. There are so few mainly because the victims themselves don't wish it. Many just want advice.'

Now, 350 cases is still 350 too many. Extrapolated across the whole Metropolitan Police region, it would suggest somewhere in the region of 15,000 cases per annum. And, just like Mr Millington, Chief Inspector Crozier points out that many cases go unreported, particularly amongst some ethnic groups. 'According to the figures it isn't a problem. But that doesn't mean to say that there isn't actually a problem. It's just that, because of their culture, the women are frightened to report it.'

So there is proof of domestic violence, but not of an epidemic. And there isn't any future in trying to set one set of statistics up against another. Mildred Pagelow can knock down all the estimates made of female-to-male violence. Neil Lyndon and I can put holes in the estimates made about men's attacks on women. In the end, all you can do is talk and, more importantly, listen to the people who are suffering. It doesn't matter whether they are male or female, black or white. It doesn't matter whether there are a thousand of them or a million. What matters is that we should recognise their pain and try to come to some understanding of its root causes.

Let's hear their side of the story.

Love and hate

'James' is in his late thirties. He is the product of a smart public school and he works in the media. But he hardly looks the part. His appearance is dishevelled and untidy. His clothes looked crumpled and unwashed. Unlike Donald, he is not the victim of sustained physical abuse. He is that much-loved figure of fun, the hen-pecked husband: hen-pecked, that is, to breaking point and beyond. The damage that has been done to him is primarily psychological (and, latterly, financial). You cannot see his bruises or his broken bones. But one look in his eyes tells you that he has been torn apart.

He married a woman – let us call her Kate – who looked like every man's dream: slim, blonde, pretty and vivacious. He fell in love with her and, as he noted with a bitter ruefulness, so did his barrister and the court welfare officer appointed to examine his case. Were you or I to meet her at dinner, she would be a charming companion. She is, however, profoundly disturbed, an opinion that James shares with the neurologists and psychiatrists who have examined her behaviour.

Some indication of Kate's hidden personality came a few weeks before their wedding. One evening, she and James went out to dinner. She was, he remembers, 'sweetness and bloody light'. On returning to their flat, however, 'She exploded. It was, "You bastard" this and "You bastard" that. I was gobsmacked. I'd never experienced anger like it. It was like an explosion. I spent all night on the sofa crying my eyes out and thinking, what have I done? The next day she was fine. No remorse. Nothing. I put it down to the curse.'

A few weeks later, James walked in to find Kate with her hands around her sister's neck. When she saw her husband-to-be, Kate took her engagement ring off and flung it on the ground. Once again, when she finally calmed down it was as though nothing had happened.

One might have thought that James would have decided that the wedding was not a good idea. The vicar who was to conduct the service even asked the couple whether they really wanted to be married at all. Kate's own aunt rang James up to warn him that Kate's mother had been unstable, violent and compulsively promiscuous. To prove the point, the mother then made a pass at James. It almost sounds like the plot for a screwball comedy film. Unless, that is, you happen to be one of the leading characters. 'Looking back,' says James, 'I was a lamb to the slaughter.'

Within months of the marriage, Kate was having regular tantrums.

Her rages would be interspersed with constant demands for more material possessions – new furniture, new curtains, new clothes, a new car – and any failure to provide them would be met with withering contempt. 'When you live with a person like that, they get at you. They eat and eat and eat at you. They want you to react. They're very clever. They can twist you like a puppet. Most men in those circumstances drink too much. It's a cushion. Then they use that against you. They tell everyone you're a drunk.'

The psychological warfare was strictly private. 'Before dinner parties, she'd crucify me. I'd be knocked out by abuse and she'd be greeting guests and saying, "Hello darling, how are you?" I'd be lolling in the corner with my head held low. These are exceptionally charming people. To this day some of our friends can't understand why we've broken up.'

One can understand if, at this point, the reader feels like telling James to pull his socks up and get a grip. It seems ridiculous that mere words can do so much harm. I can only say that I have known a couple whose relationship was much like that described by James. He was a man who kept his emotions buried deep within his personality. Though capable of immense charm and kindness, he was also noncomittal and evasive to a degree that could infuriate friends, let alone a lover seeking emotional support. She – with that terrible asymmetry that is common to so many disastrous relationships – was a desperately insecure woman who, above all else, needed total commitment.

Since this was the one thing he could not give, she attempted to provoke him to the point where he would be forced to display some form of emotion, even if it was only anger. She would goad and humiliate him, in public as well as in private. She would greet his witticisms, which were genuinely funny, with withering contempt. Chairs were thrown. Clothes were torn. Affairs were flaunted before his eyes. My friend was a gentle, non-violent man. He would spend all night walking round the streets of London rather than be driven to the point where he might be forced to hit his girlfriend. Had he done so, however, it would have been the logical conclusion of their relationship and, in this instance, she would, quite literally, have been asking for it.

The only woman I know who spent a long time in a violent relationship was, and is, a successful executive. Attractive, talented and stupendously well paid, she is as far removed as one could imagine from the battered, impoverished *Hausfrau* of the popular imagination. To this day, she remains close friends with the man who used to hit her. I once asked her why, given that she was completely independent in financial terms and had a flat of her own in which to live, she had remained in an abusive relationship.

'Well,' she said, 'it was probably just as well that he hit me. If he'd let me keep on talking, the damage I'd have done would have been much, much worse. And in any case, he taught me how to hit him back.'

It turned out that she had been the victim of that most insidious form of child abuse, the wait-till-your-father-gets-back syndrome. Her mother would punish her via her father, who would return from work to be greeted by his wife telling him to hit his children. To the children it seemed clear that what he really wanted to do was hit his wife, if only to shut her up. But since he was prevented from doing so by social taboo, he belted the kids instead. So, from generation unto generation, the pain was passed on.

The reason I tell those stories is twofold: to illustrate the punishing power of words, and to show that domestic violence is rarely quite as simple as it seems at first sight. A man may hit his wife. A woman may wound her man. But the true reasons for that violence and the real, unspoken, unseen targets at which it is aimed, may lie somewhere else altogether. Both characters may be taking part in a drama in which one of them acts out hostility that is felt or in some way needed by them both. In the words of Renate Olins of London Marriage Guidance, 'Relationships are like a marketplace. There's usually a taker for most of the products on offer.'

So, forget the politics. Forget the statistics. Look at the people. Back we go to James and Kate.

Within two years of their marriage, they had their first child, a boy called William. James claims that, from the day he was born, Kate wanted nothing to do with the new baby. 'I can see her now – a face of complete and utter horror. She wouldn't hold the baby. But he was a perfectly lovely, healthy little man. I loved him. I was really pleased.'

Kate, however, refused to feed or even cuddle the child. Once out of hospital, she would find any excuse to be apart from him. James now believes that she was frightened of what she might do to William if left alone with him for too long. 'She once said to me, "How do you think I get over these tantrums? Breaking glass, or strangling William?" When she was thirteen she hit her sister. I think she's terrified she'll do the same to William. I think she *has* done the same to William.

'She once came up with a strange remark. She said, "A friend of mine picked up her baby and threw it across the room, and the doctor told her she wasn't mad." I said, are you talking about yourself? And she said, "No, no, no!" I think it all came down to fear. Kate left home to get away from her mother and then found herself becoming more and more like the woman she loathed. She can't control it and she's terrified.'

As Kate's problems became worse, moving on to occasional low-level physical attacks – scratching at James's face, aiming waste-paper baskets at him while he was holding William, and so on – James sought medical advice. This, incidentally, is typical of men in this situation. Conditioned as they are to seek a rational answer to their problems, they do their utmost to find an objective analysis that will give them a scientific explanation of what is going on.

At first Kate would not have anything to do with any of the doctors to whom he spoke. Eventually she agreed to counselling, but she refused, and still refuses, to accept that she had or has a problem. Over a period of time, however, a picture emerged of a woman who had been mistreated as a child and who had as a consequence become unable to love or relate to other people. One psychiatrist told James, 'Don't have any more children. If you do and it's a girl, that girl will be treated just as Kate was by her mother.'

He himself was advised, 'Don't confront her. Don't say no. Let her do her own thing. Whatever you do, don't let her provoke you. That's what she wants. Don't ever hit her. Walk away.'

And so, James claims, that's what he did. Like my old friend, he spent hours walking around his neighbourhood. 'This would go on night after night,' he remembers. Then things got much, much worse.

One Monday morning Kate announced that she was taking the baby and leaving. Terrified that she would, as she had often threatened, leave the country, James served an injunction, preventing her from going abroad. 'I knew you'd panic,' Kate told him. In court, the following week, she presented an affidavit in which she claimed that James had walked towards her with outstretched arms, as if to strangle her, saying, 'I'd only be had up for manslaughter.'

James's barrister reacted by telling him, 'She's very pretty. I think you ought to leave the flat.' When James told the barrister that he had seen marks on his son's neck where his wife had attempted to throttle him, he was told, 'It's not relevant.'

His solicitor, however, advised him to stay put. Soon afterwards, he returned home from work to find William sitting in the corner of his cot. 'He looked very odd and he was gasping for breath,' James recalls, 'I put him on the changing mat. She came up behind me and grabbed me. I pushed her away. She grabbed me again and I pushed her away again. I said, "You're mad. I suppose you're going to sue me for assault." Two days later the ouster order came. She was doing me for assault. She had bruises on her shoulders from where I'd pushed her away. She showed them off in court.

'My mother swore an affidavit that she had seen bruises on my arms, and my wife admitted to the welfare officer that she had attacked me and that she had tried to strangle William, but it made no difference. The law just will not accept that women can be violent. I lost, so I had to leave her with the child. It was the worst day of my life.'

In the record books, James is down as an aggressor, rather than a victim. Families Need Fathers, more than half of whose members are reckoned to have been on the receiving end of spousal violence, claim that, as both James and Donald discovered, by the time a case comes to court, the roles of aggressor and victim have frequently been reversed.

Women on the front line

Once the domestic violence machinery has swung into gear, it is almost impossible to stop. Almost all the men to whom I have spoken complain that their solicitors seemed all too willing to believe their wives, doing little to fight ouster orders or awards of custody or property rights to the wife. It is simply assumed that, to quote a phrase, further resistance is futile. Once proceedings have been set in train against a man, eviction from his own home is practically a foregone conclusion. Ms Pagelow may think that men can just up and leave without a second thought. But those married men who see their families, their homes and their entire adult life disappearing in smoke tend to take a less casual view. To them it is nothing less than a catastrophe.

Jenni Manners is the organiser of Swindon Women's Aid, where she runs a helpline for the victims of domestic violence. She has been receiving a growing number of calls from men. 'It's a small proportion,' she says, 'but that's because we don't actively publicise the line. Is it the tip of an iceberg? Yes, definitely yes.'

The men report a wide range of abuse, from attacks with bricks, knives and scissors to straightforward punching, scratching and kicking. They never report these attacks to the police. And if they are forced to seek treatment for them, they invariably give a false reason for their injuries. Says Manners: 'Often men can't see a specific reason. When a lot phone, they feel that it's their fault. When you dig further, there's often nothing specific that they've done. The women are just taking out their frustrations on them. I know a man who was beaten because he didn't get a promotion that she was hoping for. She felt he had let her down.'

Many women's groups look on Manners' work with undisguised hostility. 'We've had abuse thrown at us,' she says. 'They say it's just women hitting back in self-defence. They often deny that women are violent. The television programme *Central Weekend* covered the issue. I was on it with Sandra Horley of the Chiswick Women's Refuge. She started asking men what they had done to deserve it and why hadn't they tried to help their wives. I was so angry. If someone had asked that of a battered woman, she would probably explode.'

Another woman who was on the same programme was Detective Inspector Sylvia Aston, of the West Midlands Police domestic violence unit. She remembers the occasion well, and, like Jenni Manners, was incensed that accusations and demands were made of the men that would never have been made of women under similar circumstances. As she says, 'If you want to be treated fairly by men, you have to treat men fairly too.'

DI Aston is a cheerful soul. She talks, in a flat, no-nonsense Brummie voice, at a hundred miles an hour, doling out good humour and common sense in just about equal proportions. She, like Jenni Manners, is unable to put an exact figure, or even an approximate one, on the number of male victims of domestic violence, but she will say, 'It's far more than people think. Women can be very, very violent. The two most violent people I've ever had to deal with were women. I'd much rather fight a man – I'd stand more chance of winning. When women do decide to be violent, they can be lethal. We are not the helpless sex.' In a telling aside, she remarks, 'You could liken men and women fighting to cats and dogs. The dog may be bigger, but if the cat is cornered, it usually wins.'

Aston also agrees that victims of female violence tend to be 'the most decent kind of men', the kind, in other words, that don't hit back. But their victimisation causes problems. 'They feel weak because they think that they should have hit back. They might hear another man say, "If my wife did that to me I'd thump her," so they think they must be doing something wrong. There's a pressure on men to be violent, just like there's a pressure on women to dress sexy. But if a man who is hit by a woman keeps his hands in his pockets and doesn't hit back, he isn't a wimp. He's a real man because he's demonstrating self-control and will-power. That's the mark of a man.'

As far as both Detective Inspector Aston, in particular, and her police force, in general, are concerned, a crime is a crime, irrespective of the perpetrator. 'You don't do anyone any favours by pretending that only one sex is capable of a certain type of behaviour. We'll only move forward when people stop pretending that only men batter women. It doesn't solve anything to say that all men are bad and all women are good. Equality is equality. Women must accept that they're not all victims and that men can be victims too.

'I go to meetings where women say men put women down from birth to death and I say, well, who's putting men down, then? Because I don't see anyone winning.'

She wonders why some of the money that is spent on battered women is not devoted to the men who call her up begging for help to stop them being violent. Would it not be better to prevent them from harming their wives, rather than punishing them once they have done so? Why, she asks, are we obsessed with crimes of violence against women when the overwhelming number of violent crimes are committed against young men? Equally, if we want society to be peaceful, why do we flock to films whose heroes are manically violent? 'If that's all there is to a man, it doesn't say a lot for him,' says Aston of the Rambo/Schwarzenegger mentality.

Aston believes that if women want equality, then they must expect to be treated equally under the law. And if they ask for New Men, they shouldn't complain when they get them. 'If we want men to be more caring, we must be caring to them,' she says. 'They have the right to say that they don't want to be treated badly. It takes courage to say that your dignity has been taken away. If we're asking people not to be violent, that has got to apply to women as much as men.'

Aston also believes – and this is a view she shares with Chief Inspector Crozier back at Leman Street – that domestic violence can be emotional as well as physical. Anyone who has ever seen Mike Leigh's TV play *Abigail's Party*, in which Alison Steadman plays the part of a ferociously and hilariously overbearing housewife who drives her mentally battered husband into an early grave, will know the truth of that statement. But the law takes a different view. Allegations of emotional cruelty may be made in a case of child abuse, but they do not have any place in criminal law as it applies to adults. So, for example, Kate's persecution of James is not amenable to any legal action, other than a claim of unreasonable behaviour in the divorce court. But if she had been able to persuade a court that he had hit her, even once, he would probably have ended up in jail.

There may not even be any recourse in law for a man such as Donald who is forced to have sex with his wife, thanks to a fascinating and blackly humorous bit of case law, namely Willan v. Willan, which was heard in the Appeal Court in 1960 and recounted in that year's All England Law Reports. Mrs Willan was, in the report's words, 'Guilty of persistent assaults on and violence to her husband and in particular demanded sexual intercourse when he did not wish to have it and pulled his hair, caught hold of him by the ears and shook his head violently until he was induced to comply as the only means of getting any rest.'

Mr Willan had applied for a divorce, but had been refused (this was before the 1969 Divorce Reform Act, which made divorce much easier to obtain) on the grounds that 'although cruelty by the wife had been established, it had been condoned by sexual intercourse between the two parties'.

The appeal was heard before Lord Justices Sellers, Willmer and Harman. They unanimously rejected the appeal on the grounds that, to quote an earlier ruling, 'If a man, through whatever blandishment or irritation, decides to have sexual intercourse, that must be a voluntary act,' a point upon which Lord Justice Harman expanded as follows: 'Duress means a degree of fear which operates on the mind to such an extent that a person who is under it is not a free agent. This husband never was in anything like that condition. No doubt he was badgered into having intercourse with his wife: no doubt he submitted to it in the end . . . for all of which one cannot have anything but sympathy. But the rule that an act of intercourse on the part of the husband will operate as a reinstatement of the wife and therefore will be a condonation of her previous misconduct is so well established that we could not possibly go behind it.'

The message to battered husbands is clear: whatever happens, under no circumstances consent to sex with your wife. Because if you do, she won't be the only one who's fucked.

Taking action

At this point, I could not claim to know how extensive the problem of female violence against spouses really is. The only way that we will ever find the answer is to bring the problem out into the open. Dr Malcolm George, a lecturer in neurophysiology at Queen Mary and Westfield College in London, and a member of Families Need Fathers, is currently conducting his own research into the experiences of battered husbands.

By working through organisations like Families Need Fathers and placing advertisements in letters sent out by them and other men's groups, he has contacted a number of male victims of spousal abuse. He, like Stephanie Jeavons, has found that conversations on the subject proceed from nervous laughter to denial and then on to admission. Journalists who have interviewed him, for example, begin by expressing open derision towards the idea of battered men and end by telling stories that begin, 'I knew a bloke once that was attacked by his wife.' They, of course, may well be the bloke in question. 'I can't speak to anyone who doesn't know a case,' says Dr George.

He notes, however, that men are very reluctant to consider themselves to be victims. They will begin stories by saying, 'Of course, I'm not a victim, but . . .' and then go on to describe scenarios in which they have clearly been abused. They never say, 'My wife hits me.' They just say, 'I'm volunteering for your research.'

It is often left to someone else – a new girlfriend, perhaps, or a parent – to come forward on the victim's behalf. 'Women ring up and say that their man is an ex-battered husband,' Dr George says. 'One woman told me, "We go on access visits to see his kids and we have to take the police. They stand there and do nothing while she hurls abuse and assaults him."

'Parents will call up and say, "We know our son is being beaten and we've seen it happen, but he won't talk to us or anyone else about it."

'For every man that comes forward there's another I know has been battered. I saw one at an FNF meeting. He had a black eye and his face was covered in bruises, but he wouldn't say a thing. I know three people whose wives stabbed them. Not one of them has gone to the police.'

He believes that men are extremely reluctant to take advantage of domestic violence legislation. This may be because, if they try to do so, they receive no help at all from police, social workers or even their own solicitors. The last are a vitally important group because violence often occurs towards the end of a relationship as a means of forcing the husband to leave the family home. 'The men are all scrambled up emotionally, but they have to work it all out by themselves. Their solicitor as sure as hell isn't going to help them,' comments Dr George.

Finally, as James's case illustrates, it is often the men who end up on the statistics as the attacker. 'Several battered men admitted to me that they had retaliated. One said, "Yeah, we all hit back in the end," then, bang! He's gone. He's looking at assault charges, non-molestation orders, ouster orders, whatever . . .'

It is vital for male victims to be able to have somewhere to go where they can discuss their problems in a safe setting. The Everyman Centre, which is close to the Oval cricket ground in London, is one of the very few places in the country where men can meet to talk about the issues affecting them. Domestic violence was originally dealt with – as at Move, in Bolton – as an issue on which men were asked to come to terms with the violence instilled in them by their upbringing and their expectations. Increasingly, however, counsellors are coming to realise that the situation is far more complex than they had imagined.

Robert Hart, the centre's Assistant Director, told me, 'It really does appear that violence is the expression of a dynamic in a relationship, and it goes both ways. We had a bus driver here who had battered his wife. He attended our counselling programme and by the time he'd finished he'd changed many of his attitudes and beliefs about sexism and women. We were very pleased.

'He came back a few weeks later very distressed. He was crying. He said he'd been beaten up by his partner. We were very taken aback and we asked why she had attacked him. He said a bloke down the pub had been bothering her, so she asked him to beat the guy up. When he refused, she beat him up instead.

'It makes me wonder who really wants to control the power in relationships. The old idea of the patriarchy is a very unsophisticated idea of how people relate.'

In October 1992, Dr Malcolm George submitted some preliminary findings to the House of Commons Select Committee on Home Affairs, which was considering domestic violence. His sample size – thirty-eight self-selecting volunteers – was tiny and all his statistics possess sizeable margins of error. Nevertheless, they confirm that women need no lessons from men when it comes to violent assaults.

Noting that the typical abusive relationship lasted seven years, with violence occurring within six months of its start, Dr George observed that:

Over 80 per cent of the men reported that violence inflicted upon them involved the use of household objects or the like. Examples of objects used as a weapon included knives, scissors, hammers, bottles, vases, sticks, a baseball bat, an iron bar, a frying pan and various other kitchen implements . . .

The most common injuries were bruising or lacerations and abrasions, but three men reported that they had been stabbed . . . three reported that they had been knocked unconscious and others reported injuries such as broken noses or fingers, being scalded by boiling water and black eyes.

A majority (80 per cent) reported that they had been taunted to hit their partners back and all stated that they experienced a high level of general abusive behaviour [including] verbal abuse and threats, destruction or disposal of their personal possessions, damage to the home, sleep deprivation, being locked out of the matrimonial home, and defamatory remarks to family, friends and even employers. Several men reported that they had lost their job . . . because of their marital situation.

Approximately 50 per cent of men told their GP of the problems of their marital situation, but only 33 per cent sought medical attention for injuries received . . . Over 60 per cent did not seek police involvement . . . In only one case did a man report that any action was taken by the police and in the majority of cases these men considered that the police attitude to them was indifferent.

Less than 20 per cent actually petitioned their wives for divorce. In contrast, 70 per cent of the women petitioned their husbands for divorce, all on the grounds of unreasonable behaviour, with 25 per cent also obtaining non-molestation and/or ouster orders against their husbands. In six cases, these were taken out after husbands had eventually retaliated, but in three cases an order was obtained even though the husband stated categorically and strenuously that he had not used physical restraint or retaliated.

All men with children expressed concern that they might lose their relationship with their children upon separation or divorce. In only two cases was the man granted custody/residence and all the other men reported that there had been . . . frustration or even repeated denial of access visits under a court order. In some cases, violence or abuse by the women occurred in relation to access visits to their children.

To those women who persist in denying that the problem of domestic violence by women even exists, I can only say this: Twenty years ago, you asked for society's understanding of the harm that was being done to women. Now, when it is men whose pain is ignored, is it too much to ask for your tolerance in return?

Chapter 9

Absent Fathers, Violent Sons

What makes a boy turn to crime? That is a question to which the only sensible answer is . . . how long have you got?

Some factors appear to be predetermined. Testosterone does seem to have a significant impact on the general aggressiveness, impatience and predisposition to rough-and-tumble of young children. But that does not mean to say that those characteristics will necessarily be translated into actual violence or antisocial behaviour. Even when the evidence appears straightforward, final judgements are very much a matter of interpretation.

For example, boys who suffer from a metabolic disorder known as Imperato McGinley tend to be born with very low levels of testosterone and small sex organs. Many are even thought to be girls, and are brought up as such until puberty, when their testosterone is, as it were, kick-started and they develop as normal men. At this point, despite their feminine conditioning, they often behave in an aggressively masculine and sometimes criminal manner. From this one might conclude that testosterone will cause bad behaviour, irrespective of conditioning. Or then again, one might decide that these teenagers were merely overreacting against their feminine upbringing and attempting to assert themselves as males.

Other physiological conditions that are more common in males than females, and more common again in criminal than non-criminal males, include hyperactivity, learning disorders, mild forms of autism and mental retardation. These conditions, however, are not evenly distributed throughout society, but are skewed towards the poor. This is because poor mothers are much more likely to suffer from bad diet, alcoholism or drug addiction than their middle-class sisters and, as a consequence, the babies that they produce are less healthy.

Then there are the pervasive influences of the general culture in which children grow up, and the pressure of the peer groups within which they move. The vast majority of all crime, particularly small-scale car thefts, burglaries and muggings, are carried out by youngsters in their teens (or even pre-teens) and early twenties. This is an age at which young males are desperate to prove their masculinity, an age at which they define masculinity in terms of being tough, or hard, and an age at which they are profoundly influenced by the opinions of their peers. As a consequence, young men *en masse* will often behave in ways which few of them would consider if they were alone.

Even then, however, there are reasons for violence which seem impossible to pin down. During the 1992 European Football Championships, English soccer fans once again ran riot, causing havoc in peaceful Swedish towns and shaming their nation. Yet Scottish fans, who come from a country which is ruled by the same laws, speaks the same language and has roughly similar levels of general violence and criminality, were so good-humoured and charming that their hosts presented their representatives with a special award. What was the difference?

It might have been the performances of their respective teams. England's supporters only became seriously violent after their team had revealed itself to be sterile, gutless and incompetent. Scotland, on the other hand, played with flair and courage. They lost, but they did so with dignity, so their fans were able to hold their heads high and felt no need to work out their frustrations on innocent Swedes. Or was it that the English are more xenophobic than the Scots? Certainly, there is a streak of narrow-minded nationalism in some English fans that is unequalled anywhere else in Europe.

Whatever the reason was, it is not enough to blame it on maleness, pure and simple: there always has to be something else. Traditionalists use phrases like 'lack of moral fibre' or 'loss of discipline', which suggest that the problem can be solved by the reintroduction of standards which they believe were maintained in days gone by – a belief which looks decidedly questionable if one considers rates of crime and violence in Victorian cities.

For most liberal commentators, however, looking at social disorder, that 'something else' is poverty. We have already seen how the wealth and well-being of the mother can affect her children's predisposition to crime. Then there are the simple facts of deprivation, both financial and cultural, that bear down upon the members of the so-called 'underclass'. Dependent on welfare, deprived of traditional social networks by supposedly progressive housing schemes, and torn apart by drugs and violence, the people of the inner cities are – like their Victorian slum-dwelling predecessors – society's guilty secret.

But poverty cannot be the only factor. After all, many football hooligans have good jobs: they need them in order to have the money to follow their club or national side all over the world. And then again, many people who are poor are not in any way delinquent. Perhaps the most important common denominator lies elsewhere.

Increasingly, researchers are coming forward who place the blame for antisocial behaviour on criteria that go beyond the simple effects of financial deprivation. In the United States, current rates of divorce and illegitimacy suggest that 51 per cent of all children will grow up without a father living permanently under the same roof. David Blankenhorn, president of the Institute for American Values in New York, told *The Times* that, 'Fatherlessness is the engine that drives many of our worst social problems. The most important predictor of juvenile delinquency is not race or income, it is the absence of a father. For teenage pregnancy it is the same story. Young fatherless women are twice as likely to get pregnant outside of marriage. The explosion of juvenile crime and teenage pregnancy tracks the increase in fatherless homes with eerie precision.'

In Britain, some 60 per cent of all boys from highly disadvantaged backgrounds will end up with a criminal record. So what stops the other 40 per cent? Since 1947, the Newcastle Thousand Family Survey has been examining cycles of disadvantage in the same family groups. Reporting on the survey's findings for the *Guardian*, writer Liz Hodgkinson revealed that, 'The overwhelming risk factors for young delinquent behaviour are a poor work record and alcoholism in the father. Parental criminality before the child's tenth birthday is also a major background factor . . . 40 per cent of sons of recidivist fathers are also persistent offenders . . . the ratio was the same with adoptive or stepfathers.'

Other factors such as the number of children (first- and second-born children of small families were significantly less likely to be criminal), complications at birth and childhood accidents (which might imply slipshod parenting) were also significant, as was the general ability of the mother to cope with her family. 'The presence or absence of toys was not significant either way, but firm management and the ability to reason with children were protective. Mental resilience is far more important than social disadvantage.'

In fact, 'Social anarchy is directly related to the breakdown of family structure, personal responsibility and social order.'

Except that no one from the Newcastle Thousand Family Survey, still less Liz Hodgkinson of the *Guardian*, said those last words, which are actually taken from a speech made by the then Vice-President Dan Quayle, shortly after the Los Angeles riots of 1992. Quayle went on, a couple of days later, to criticise the makers of *Murphy Brown*, the top-rated American TV sitcom, for an episode in which the show's unmarried heroine, played by Candice Bergen, gave birth to a baby boy. 'It doesn't help matters when prime-time TV has Murphy Brown mocking the importance of fathers by bearing a child and calling it just another lifestyle choice,' said Quayle.

Coming from the man who once addressed the United Negro College Fund (motto: 'A mind is a terrible thing to waste') with the words, 'What a waste it is to lose one's mind – or not to have a mind. How true that is', who announced, 'I didn't live in this century', and who could not spell potato, this seemed to be yet one more tragic example of congenital foot-in-mouth disease. Pundits on both sides of the Atlantic united in condemning Quayle, both for his repellent opinions and his political insensitivity. As it happened, however, Quayle's public approval ratings rose somewhat after his remarks. But that wasn't the most amazing thing about the whole incident. The most amazing thing was, Dan Quayle was right.

Why Daddy matters

The relationship between fathers and sons is one of the great unspoken issues in men's lives. So much is left unsaid and so many misunderstandings created, purely for want of the ability to communicate with one another.

I remember sitting in a London cinema watching a movie called *Field of Dreams*, in which Kevin Costner stars as a man who is convinced that he has to build a baseball field in his own back yard. One of the central themes of the film is the way in which men so rarely tell their fathers how much they love them, so that the father's death leaves all the tensions in their relationship unresolved. I am not ashamed to say that I blubbed almost continuously through the second half of the film. And, judging by the sniffs and snuffles emanating from the men (but not, interestingly enough, the women) around me, I was by no means the only one. By targeting the pain caused by all that is left unsaid in the struggle between fathers and sons, the makers of *Field of Dreams* had created the first male weepie.

As I researched this book and talked to men about their lives, their feelings about their own fathers would often emerge. Fathers set an example, to be emulated or, in many cases, to be challenged and denied. On one occasion I was talking to two workers in the American men's movement. I asked them what had moved them to become interested in men's issues. One replied that he had been so inspired by his father's love that he became determined to ensure that as many of his fellow men as possible were made aware of the redemptive power of positive, unrepressed emotions. The other said that he had been abused. He just wanted to do everything he could to prevent the same fate befalling anyone else.

So fathers were the markers against which we measured ourselves. But the particular significance of the father as a determinant of antisocial behaviour was not something which I had remotely anticipated, however obvious it seems to me now. When it came to male perversity and violence, I merely had a general view that it would be in everyone's interests – male and female – to try to find out why so many men, particularly young men, behave in the way they do. To put it crudely: if there were fewer fucked-up men, there might also be fewer beaten-up women.

Wherever I went, experts from a wide range of fields kept making the similar points about the importance of paternity as a formative influence. Think back to all those rituals by which men acquire masculinity; think of the Male Wound and the importance of the father's presence to the successful development of the child; think of Seymour Fisher on the effect of an over-feminised upbringing on later misbehaviour in adolescent boys.

A well-balanced man – just like a well-balanced woman – has to be taught how to channel his energies, many of which are potentially destructive, along constructive paths. Only another man can do this and that man should, if at all possible, be his father. To return once again to the *Star Wars* trilogy, Luke Skywalker is guided by elderly men to choose the light Force, rather than the dark. Luke depends on Obi-Wan Kenobe and Yoda for his lessons. His problems arise because he has been deserted by his father, who turns out to be Darth Vader, the ultimate abusive parent.

What has *Star Wars* got to do with life on earth? Well, in *Boys Will Be Boys*, Myriam Medzian asserts that, 'Major nurturant paternal involvement in child-rearing would play an important role in reducing male violence. It would signal the end to adherence to the masculine mystique and would lead to significant improvements in mothers' behaviour towards their sons.'

Not only that, women have a strong self-interest in promoting successful fatherhood. Good fathers, producing healthy sons, are women's best hope of diminishing the dangers they face from abusive or violent men. As the British criminologist Patricia Morgan puts it in a 1983 paper for the Social Affairs Unit entitled 'Feminist Attempts to Sack Father – A Case of Unfair Dismissal', 'There is something pathetic and perverse about demands for rape crisis centres, security bolts and self-defence classes from those doing their best to promote the very social conditions which necessitate such services.'

A number of immediate objections arise. Men, one might say, do not have the natural child-rearing instinct that is innate in women. This, however, is an argument into which one should proceed with extreme caution. Suppose, for example, that it were true. Would it not imply, then, that women should stay at home and exercise their instincts as exclusive, full-time carers? After all, with so much of their minds taken up with maternal affairs, there could not be much left over for professional matters.

For what it is worth, however, I do not think that the evidence suggests that the parenting instinct is exclusive to women. It would be surprising if there was not a natural tendency for mothers to have extremely strong feelings towards the children to whom they have given birth, and there is – as we have seen – evidence to suggest that women's brains are designed to assist them to raise children, but that does not mean that men cannot feel deeply about their offspring too.

What is certain is that, in this case as in so many others, any differences that are present naturally are greatly enhanced by the way we rear our children. Little girls are observably more interested in fantasising about babies, marriage and home-making than little boys. But much of this is due to the efforts that are made to turn boys away from forms of play that could be thought of as cissy. Both sexes play with dolls, but girls play house with Barbie while boys play war with Action Man. One of the reasons that boys ask for Action Man is that they want to play with dolls, but are terrified of seeming cissy: a doll that acts out acceptably macho fantasies of war is an allowable substitute.

There is a biological parallel for male nurturing. In his book *A*

Question of Sex, Dr John Nicholson reports on experiments carried out with rhesus monkeys. The male monkey is usually indifferent to his young and may even attack and kill them. But researchers gradually exposed male monkeys to the presence of motherless baby monkeys, with the following results:

The baby monkey . . . approached the adult and tried to cling to him. At first, he was repulsed angrily, but after a while the adult began to groom him – an important ice-breaker in the social life of rhesus monkeys – and from then on the two became steadily more attached to one another. In fact, they became closer than most rhesus mothers and their children, and remained so long after the time when young monkeys usually break with their mothers and start to lead an independent life. Their relationship was not the same as that of the typical rhesus mother and child – they went in for more rough-and-tumble play than female monkeys will tolerate – but the younger monkey developed into a perfectly normal adult male and remained on excellent terms with his foster-father.

Research on humans suggests that men, like monkeys, tend to give their children more active stimulation and play with them in a more physical way than do mothers. But there is nothing to suggest that males are any less capable of caring for children should the need or desire arise.

At the Germantown Friends School, a Quaker institution in Philadelphia, a programme called Education for Parenting has been running since 1979 (it has since been taken up by a further nine schools in ghetto areas of the city). From their first year, pupils spent time with babies brought into school by their parents, charting their progress and discussing it in class. They will even take responsibility for a particular baby and act as its caretaker for a few hours a week. Children learn about the demands and pleasures of parenthood and also discover their own capacity for emotional involvement and the pleasure that brings. There is little difference between the aptitudes of boy and girl pupils.

Maybe not, but surely, our sceptic might say, men who are allowed too close to children may very well abuse them. There is some force to this argument. A tiny minority of male teachers, like some female childminders, may be drawn to their profession by the opportunities it offers for sexual activity, but among fathers there is evidence to suggest that active parents are actually less likely to abuse their children.

Myriam Medzian cites research conducted at the University of Utah by Hilda and Seymour Parker. 'The Parkers did a comparative study of fifty-six men who were known to have sexually abused their minor daughters and fifty-four men with no known child sexual abuse in their backgrounds. They found a very significant correlation between lack of involvement in child care and nurturance, and child abuse.'

The Parker study reinforced previous findings which suggested that, in general, stepfathers were much more likely to abuse children than natural fathers. But those stepfathers who had been actively involved in nurturing their stepdaughters were no more likely than blood relatives to abuse them subsequently. The Parkers conclude that, 'If primary child care were shared more equally by men and women, one basis for . . . the sexual exploitation of females might be eliminated.'

There is, I should have thought, a fairly straightforward rationale for the behaviour the Parkers uncovered. Abuse is often a substitute for a more natural relationship, either with the mother or the child. But a man who has spent time with his child, who has loved it and cared for it, is far less likely to want or need to betray that relationship. Not only has he invested too much of himself and his time, but he will also have received the emotional satisfaction that seems so clearly to be lacking from the lives of abusive parents.

Even if we accept this, one final objection arises. Surely any boy who is raised by his father will be all the more deeply inculcated in the evils of machismo and the patriarchy. Isn't he likely to behave in a way that is even more harmful to women?

This might well be an opinion put forward by the more extremist, separatist elements of the feminist movement. And there are plenty of educators and political theorists who might, I suspect, be seduced by the prospect of converting young men towards a more ideologically sound, feminine mode of behaviour.

This point of view is fatally misguided and the reason for that is very simple. By definition, any man who nurtures his child is bound to be a man whose masculinity is not compromised by gestures of overt sensitivity or gentleness. A man who cares for his baby may do so in a way that is more physically robust than a woman might employ, but he will still be overwhelmed by love for his child. If that child is a boy, he will look to his father for information about how a man should be. If the father is absent, the boy may create an exaggerated, over-aggressive masculinity of his own. If the father is distant or abusive, the boy will learn from that, too. But if the father is loving, the boy will learn that masculinity and tenderness are not mutually exclusive and will carry that knowledge forward into his own adult life.

226

I do not need research to tell me this. I learned it from my own father. Looking around at my friends, I see it in them, too. I know few men of my generation who do not regard fatherhood as the most magical part of their lives. Lord knows it can be tiring, not to mention expensive, and there are times when the burden of responsibility weighs heavily on one's shoulders. But the thrill of rediscovering through one's children feelings of unfettered love that have lain repressed in one's soul since childhood far outweighs any possible cost.

It would, in every way, be a benefit to us all if fatherhood were looked upon as something to be treasured. In a perfect world, boys would be raised from birth with the expectation that being a parent would be one of the central experiences of their lives. When they become fathers they would find that it was a state that was honoured, both by custom and by law. The result would be happier children, adults at peace with themselves and a marked reduction in violence and malice, on the part of women as well as men.

So why, then, does society act in such a way as to ensure that none of these good things can ever occur?

The patriarchal conspiracy

The image of the adoring, attentive father is rapidly becoming a media cliché. Glossy magazines are full to the brim with movie star dads and their celebrity babies. Jack's got one, Warren's got one, Arnie's got one, and so have both the Bruces – Willis and Springsteen. Mel's got half a dozen. Forget cars and girls, the hottest accessory a chap can have these days is a soiled set of nappies.

Advertising has also caught the baby bug. If you want your gas-guzzling, fume-belching, road-hogging luxury saloon to be smothered in positive values, just show it being driven by a man with a baby-seat in the back. Car advertising, in fact, has seen a complete gender turnaround in the last five years. Sporty hatchbacks are all sold with images of sexy young female execs, while station-wagons are packed with dads. Of course, if you check who's doing the school run, it still turns out to be mums, but who said commerce and reality ever had to mix?

The fact is that men who become fathers receive wildly mixed and confusing signals about the validity of their role. On the one hand they are exhorted to help out as much as they can with every stage of the process, from pre-birth breathing classes, via attendance at labour, through to the final dirty nappy. On the other, they are assaulted by scare stories about their 'potential' abusiveness, generated by social services and social sciences that have accepted as gospel truth the idea that patriarchy – the institution of fatherhood – is the root of all evil.

The modern father is ranked somewhere between a surrogate mother and a scullion. His job is to change nappies, wash dishes and mind kids. Parenting is presented as a genderless exercise in which Dad just tags along wherever Mum may lead. Because, however trendy being a dad may be, the idea of fatherhood *per se* is now politically incorrect.

Writers such as Kate Millet and Beatrix Campbell have consistently sought to portray the family as an institution created and imposed by men as a means of controlling female reproduction and colonising them as individuals. This runs quite contrary to those cultural traditions – one thinks immediately of both Catholic and Jewish life – in which the mother is the heart of the family and its dominant force. Nor does it tally with men's psychological fear of entrapment and engulfment by their female partner. Nevertheless, a determined assault has been made upon the father's role by a range of writers and academics.

This is often seen as an irrelevance to everyday life. 'Why do you worry about these people?' one is often asked. As my sister, herself a former postgraduate anthropologist, remarked to me, 'No one cares about the patriarchy any more.'

Except that they do. Or, more to the point, the few people that care, care very much. And they are in a position to ensure that their cares are hugely influential. There is a relatively small number of institutions in Britain that cover the gender-based aspects of social research. The academic community is very tightly knit and, rather like the literary community, closely interwoven. In such an atmosphere, it may be hard for researchers to be aware of the implications of their own research, let alone anyone else's.

Consider, for example, 'Developmental Status and School Achievement of Minority and Non-Minority Children From Birth to Eighteen Years in a British Midland Town', a 1983 study in the *British Journal of Developmental Psychology*, by Sandra Scarr, Barabara K. Caparulo et al. The study clearly shows that there is a massive difference between the academic performance of West Indian and Asian children. The former do far worse than the latter. Why?

Both groups are poor and live in sub-standard housing. It cannot be a matter of linguistic handicap, since Caribbean immigrants speak English, whereas many Asians do not. It would be distasteful to suggest some form of racial inferiority, and, in any case, West Indian children score as well as Asians in IQ tests at the age of five. The authors are thus left with a long and in-depth study which fails to come to any definite conclusions.

But even if they can't see it, the answer is staring them in the face. As the paper's own evidence demonstrates, Asian families are close-knit and extremely stable. Parents are married and live together. Afro-Caribbean families suffer high rates of marital breakdown, illegitimacy and domestic conflict. The world of single parenthood in which children grow up is observed to be both materially and emotionally sparse. Absent fathers are the difference between West Indian and Asian society.

In 1984, the same journal published a Canadian study of the effects of father absence on children's self-esteem and motivation. The authors found that 'the adverse effects associated with father absence are evident fairly early in the development of children and are cumulative over time.' Boys, in particular, suffer 'lack of confidence and personal adequacy . . . and a continuing sense of social alienation and self-centeredness'.

Such findings would not surprise most ordinary people, but they would surprise our legislators. The Children's Bill notes the correlation between single parenthood and poor academic achievement, but goes into extreme contortions to ascribe this to economic and social factors, even leaving half of all variants unexplained, rather than commit the heresy of accepting that the absence of the father as an emotional as well as economic unit may be of influence.

My personal belief is that one should look on feminist notions of the patriarchy not as scientific explanations of genuine phenomena, but as forms of conspiracy theory. In other words, the patriarchy can be made to stand for whatever you want it to. If you're looking for an enemy, or if you suffer from the delusion that everything in the world is rotten and you want a reason why, then the patriarchy is the perfect solution. Why bother with blaming society's problems on Free-masons, or the Elders of Zion, or the Communist plot to take over the world, when you can blame it on the patriarchy?

Of course, you can't see the patriarchy. You can't touch the patriarchy. But it's there. In fact, it can only be a matter of time before some lecturer in Women's Studies staggers out of a backwoods university, clutching a copy of the Zapruder film and claiming she can see the patriarchy standing on the Grassy Knoll.

One might note, in passing, the profound irony underlying the feminist obsession with the supposed powers of patriarchy, which is that two of its most celebrated priestesses, Gloria Steinem and Germaine Greer, were childhood victims, not of the oppressive nature of fatherhood, but of its absence. Dr Greer wrote a book, *Daddy We Hardly Knew You*, as her attempt to uncover the truth about her father, while Ms Steinem was left to tend for her sick and mentally unbalanced mother alone after her father deserted the family when she was ten years old.

Might their joint obsession with patriarchy's alleged wrongdoing arise from their childhood devastation? Certainly the evidence of Dr Robin Skynner's forty years of family therapy, presented in a later chapter, would tend to suggest that the absent or ineffectual father is the one that is most deeply resented by daughters. Put it another way: might they really be calling for more patriarchy, not less?

While we're on the subject of these two fascinating women, who have between them done as much to shape this century as any male politician, one further observation: both are famously single and neither has ever had children. Great female thinkers seem to have as much trouble as their male counterparts when faced with the normalities of relationships and reproduction.

There are, of course, other ways of looking at the organisation of the family. In a 1983 paper published by the Royal Anthropological Institute entitled 'Rules and the Emergence of Human Society', the anthropologist Meyer Fortes puts forward a very different view of family organisation. In his view, the family is the basic unit of social order since it introduces the concept of non-biological rules and of commitment between individuals. Within this unit, the father's role is not oppressive, but altruistic. He is asked to look after children whom he does not know for certain to be his own. Fatherhood is a suspension of his own self-interest for the greater good.

In conversation with me, Patricia Morgan asked the question, 'If you destroy the family, you go back . . . to what?' She further pointed out the human need for affiliation. We need to know who we are and to whom we are linked both vertically from one generation to another, and horizontally across the same generation. Take away the father and you take away half the affiliative possibilities: half the uncles, aunts, grandparents and cousins. 'That negates the notion of human society,' she concludes.

My Daddy, the gook

However benevolent the family may be, one can state with a fair degree of certainty that the notion of the evil father is embedded deep within the social practice and legislation of the state. At every stage in the process of fatherhood, a man's rights are consistently undermined, whilst his obligations are reinforced.

In America, both parties in the 1992 election put forward policies designed to ensure that men took financial responsibility for their children. In Britain, the recent Child Support Act imposes upon men the obligation to give financial support to any child whom they can be shown to have fathered. It is, however, a classic case of taxation without representation, since it confers no decision-making power upon the man.

As matters stand, a woman can have an abortion irrespective of the views of her partner. The reason for this is that we accept the idea that abortion, which some might feel involves three parties – the mother, the father and the foetus – in fact concerns only one: it is a matter of the woman's reproductive rights. Yet the moment that the baby is born, the man, who was considered so irrelevant just a few short weeks ago, is now thought to be so important that he should bear a sixteen-year commitment to the child's financial well-being.

Suppose, however, that the father is one of the 28 per cent of all British parents who is not married at the time of the birth. If his partner should decide to end the relationship, or move to Australia, or raise the child within the teachings of a religious sect of which he disapproves, he will rapidly discover that, while his financial commitments remain, he has no automatic rights whatever to make or even share in any decisions concerning the child. The Children's Act of 1989, which came into force in October 1991, recognises the right of unmarried fathers to joint parenthood, but it is not a right that is administered automatically. The father has to apply for recognition as the child's parent.

No sensible man would write out a five-figure cheque for a car that he had not ordered and which he would not be allowed either to drive or to keep. Yet every year, tens of thousands of men father children, whose upbringing will cost them at least as much as a brand-new Porsche, over whom they will have no automatic control.

In a much-publicised article for *Options* magazine on the reasons why women should not marry, the radio presenter Jenni Murray said that marriage meant that 'he' might be able to get control of 'your' children. As long as a woman remained single, then she could prevent any man getting his hands on her kids. For this she was much applauded. No one pointed out that children belong to both parents. No one tapped Jenni metaphorically on the shoulder and said, 'By the way, men have rights, too.'

Or, at least, they ought to have rights. Once again, however, men stand around like helpless sheep, unable even to protest. There are more than 600 male MPs. And not one of them had the guts or the sense to suggest that fathers should get something back in return for all the money they've been forced to shell out. A little earlier in this book, I referred to 'femi-wimps'. I did those women an injustice. Sometimes they're not half so feeble as the male wimps on the other side of the great sexual divide.

When one enters the realm of the new biotechnology, in which fertilised ova can be kept, deep-frozen, for an indefinite period, the question of paternal rights becomes even more confused. At the time of writing, the US Supreme Court has yet to reach its decision in the case of Mary Sue and Junior Davis, a divorced couple who are fighting over the custody of their frozen embryos. But Carol Sarler, writing in the *Sunday Times*, had little doubt about where the rights and wrongs of the issue lay.

Where we run into trouble is when men start to show a proprietorial interest in – well, in sperm . . . The issue is not one of parenthood . . . No, what this is about is power and control. The syndrome of 'You take the kettle, I'll take the embryo' is the syndrome of reducing everything to the status of possession and ownership, a status traditionally better understood and exploited by men than by women. To exercise control in this way is part of a frightened backlash against the increasing control women have over their bodies and their reproduction. They have leapt light years in three or four decades. It has been the work of a single generation, a remarkable achievement, a true cause of celebration and, beyond doubt, the most crucial factor in women's emancipation.

I think that this is a classic piece of doublethink. But I'll start by agreeing. Yes, effective contraception and women's liberation are, without any question at all, indissolubly linked. Would I want to rid the world of either of those two phenomena? Absolutely not.

One might ask, however, what the difference might be between male 'power and control' and female? Why is it such a 'frightened backlash' for men to have the temerity to be interested in the fate of their own sperm? Why is women's power and control an end to be celebrated, whereas men's is to be despised?

Note, if you will, the 'poor little me' implied in the suggestion that men understand property better than women. Are we seriously to believe that there has ever been a period in history in which women did not possess or comprehend a proprietorial attitude towards their own offspring?

Note, too, the suggestion that there is something more noble in the woman's motivation than the man's. Once again we encounter that implacable conviction that the man's feelings are somehow inferior and need not count. You wouldn't dare say that about black people, or Jewish people, or handicapped people. But you can say what the hell you like about male people.

During the Vietnam War, American commanders justified using napalm on defenceless Vietnamese villagers on the grounds that they – the gooks, the slants, the zips – didn't feel the same way about their children as honest, God-fearing Americans. If a few baby gooks went up in flames, well, Mom and Pop Gook just made a bunch more. That, fundamentally, is the belief that Carol Sarler is expressing about men's attitudes towards paternity. They don't love their kids, she says, they just want to own them. They're not like us. They're just gooks.

But what if the father of those frozen embryos felt that there were moral issues involved that went far beyond the mere division of spoils? What if he had the temerity to feel that he was just as much of a parent as their mother? After all, she has not, at this stage, endured the burdens of labour or childbirth. Her investment is no greater than his. Her ovum, his sperm: why is her position so much more sacred than his?

Surely the truth is the very opposite of what Ms Sarler pretends to be the case. Women have not been released from the chains of their fertility by female activists, but by the efforts of predominantly male research scientists, gynaecologists and obstetricians. Besides, motherhood may have greatly handicapped women over the years, but it has also been the source of female mystery and power. Men who proclaim the rights of fatherhood are starting to encroach on female territory in a manner parallel to women's encroachment into the male powerbase. And women don't like having their power eroded any more than men do.

In this issue, as in so many others, we have to decide what we want to believe. If the role of the father is considered to be central, then the father's obligations must be reinforced by rights. I am not asking for men to have a veto on abortion decisions, nor do I wish to make any judgement at all about the rights and wrongs of abortion *per se*. All I am saying is that men are either involved, or they are not. Reproduction cannot be a shared endeavour at one moment and purely an issue of women's bodies at another. Personally, I would hope that, wherever possible (and clearly there will be many occasions in which it is not), a man's involvement should at least be acknowledged. If he is going to foot the bill, he should at least be allowed to look at the menu.

In the meantime, it should be observed that Carol Sarler's inability or unwillingness to recognise the genuine significance of paternity represents a very potent force in some women's views about men. It's no different from the notion that a woman can hit a man because he's bigger and it doesn't really hurt (those gooks, they're simply not as sensitive as we are). Or that a man can leave his house if he's being attacked by his partner (those gooks, they can soon build a new straw hut). Or that men can't be embarrassed in the workplace (gooks eat chocolate penises all the time, it's a well-known fact).

The irony, however, is that the end result of all this prejudice – mixed-up, resentful, violent men – should be so harmful to women. But not, one might add, before one final, monstrous harm has been done to men.

So long, farewell, *auf wiedersehen*, goodbye

While writing this chapter I have been conducting a crude and simplistic opinion poll among people I happen to meet. 'Suppose,' I say, 'that someone you vaguely know were to come up to you and tell you that unless you consented to have sex with him, he would take away your children and you would never see them again. What would you do?' Naturally enough, everyone to whom I have spoken, whether male or female, says that they would consent to the sex.

My point, of course, is to demonstrate that on the scale of life's tragedies, coercive sex with an acquaintance, or date-rape as it is now known, is less traumatic than the loss of one's children. Yet, whereas the former is regarded as a crime, the latter is merely something that happens to hundreds of thousands of men without any form of legal recourse or retribution.

In Britain, the numbers are conveniently parallel. According to a

1991 report by the Family Policy Studies Centre, more than 750,000 British children never see their fathers. Let us assume that there are two children for every father. I would be surprised if there were – I suspect the figure would average out at rather less than that – but let's be generous and say that there are approximately 375,000 fathers who never see their children. Then let's divide that by eighteen, since all children are, by definition, less than eighteen, and thereby arrive at an annual figure of rather more than 20,000 fathers per year who lose contact with their kids.

Now, the 1992 rape figures show an 18 per cent rise from 1991, to about 4,000 reported cases. As we know, these are reckoned to represent about 20 per cent of all actual cases, so we multiply by five and the answer is . . . 20,000 cases a year.

Now, one might argue that there are many fathers who don't actually want to see their children. In the words of Andrew Gerry, who is a partner at Withers, one of London's smartest firms of solicitors, and the Secretary of the Solicitors Family Law Association, 'Not every father goes along there, racing to have the children every day. Some of them can't stand the little buggers.'

True, but the Family Policy Studies Centre report suggests that the majority of fathers who lose touch with their children do so either because they are denied access or because the conditions under which they are allowed to see their children are so difficult or emotionally painful that they cannot bear to continue the relationship. After a while, a couple of hours spent walking round a park, or sitting morosely in a McDonalds can become more distressing than a clean-cut parting.

If the numbers involved in rape and familial separation are roughly comparable, the consequences to the perpetrator are not. Any man who assaults a woman runs the risk of severe punishment under the criminal law. Any woman who denies a man access to his own children runs . . . no risk whatsoever. Somehow, the all-powerful patriarchy appears to have had a bit of an oversight when it comes to the protection of patriarchy itself. As the law currently stands, a woman can leave her husband, sue him for divorce, kick him out of his house, take his children and, best of all, make him foot the bill for everything. Now where, I wonder, had the patriarchy popped off to when that little lot got passed?

That sounds paranoid, but look at the numbers. Most heterosexual men can expect to become fathers at some point in their lives. Of these,

28 per cent at current rates will have babies out of wedlock. As we have already seen, they have no automatic rights over their children. Of those who marry, some 40 per cent can expect to be divorced at least once. The vast majority of those divorces will be instigated by wives and when you look at the fine print of the marriage contract you can see why: women aren't dumb and they know a bargain when they see it.

After non-contested divorces, roughly 90 per cent of all children live with their mother – usually in the family house which the father may very well have paid for, but been forced to vacate. After contested divorces, the figure rises to 95 per cent. Roughly half of all the children of divorced parents lose contact with their natural fathers within two years of the divorce.

In other words, at least half of all fathers (i.e. most of those who are either unmarried or divorced) can expect either to be denied joint control of their children by virtue of their extramarital status, or to lose it as a result of divorce. And an absolute minimum of 20 per cent of all fathers (and probably a great many more, since I have not included any extramarital parents in this calculation) will, at some stage in their children's early lives, be permanently separated from their own flesh and blood. Consider the odds, gentlemen. Whichever way you roll the dice, the game of parenthood is more viciously loaded against men than the meanest crap shoot in Vegas.

So please, let's not have any more of this patriarchy nonsense. Once again, let's cut the politics and speak to the people.

Desperate dads

Trevor Berry is the Chairman of Families Need Fathers, a group that looks after the interests of men who have been separated from their children. A slim, grey-haired suburban man in late middle age, Berry is not your typical activist. Yet to hear some people speak, he and his organisation are little short of fanatical. Andrew Gerry, the solicitor, told me that, 'I have had a certain amount of correspondence with Families Need Fathers and Dads After Divorce, which are pretty active groups, both of which, in my view, from the correspondence that I have seen, adopt rather a polarised attitude. They use language of a supremely emotive nature and it is very difficult to correspond with them because their starting point, if you like their terms of reference, is that husbands are victims.'

Mr Gerry is a charming, kindly man. But he might be less certain about his attitudes towards groups like FNF if he went along to one of their weekly open nights, and saw men in tears of rage and despair at their situation; men giving support and friendship to others in distress; men desperate for someone who will even believe their stories, let alone help them to cope. He might think differently if he met men like the champion amateur boxer who visited an FNF meeting in London in the summer of 1992. His wife had been attacking him. He dared not retaliate for fear of doing her damage, so he left the house. When he tried to go back to see his young child, he was set upon by the woman's new boyfriend and her mother. The police were refusing to take action. He was desperately worried about his child. He told his story with tears streaming down his face, a hard, proud man, reduced to nothing. What was he to do?

These lonely fathers are the fallout from the explosion of the nuclear family. Their lives have been torn apart and now they are at the mercy of their former partners if they want to see their children again. Says Trevor Berry, 'It depends entirely on the attitude of the mother. Even when joint custody is awarded, unless the woman is prepared to be rational and co-operate, there is nothing you can do. It's an old story: possession is nine-tenths of the law.

'Fathers are increasingly unwilling to accept being marginalised when the couple separates. There is an increasing number of cases now in which parents split the children's time 50–50 or 60–40, so both parents can have a significant impact on upbringing, but those are still the minority.'

Berry feels that attitudes to divorce have lost touch with the real needs of children, and, for that matter, parents. 'Research suggests that parents don't communicate with children during divorce. The children are often unaware that their parents are not getting on and would very much prefer them to stay together. Other surveys suggest that significant numbers of people wished that they had never got divorced. It's roughly half of all men and a third of all women.' We are, in other words, generating vast amounts of unhappiness to little positive purpose.

When one speaks to members of FNF, the same points are raised again and again. To these men, solicitors, social workers, welfare officers and judges all work within a system which assumes that the benefit of any doubt should always lie with the mother. Furthermore, they say, whereas strong measures are taken against any father who steps out of line, courts are extremely unwilling to take any serious action to enforce judgements against mothers who break contact or residence agreements. In theory, the new Children's Act, which talks of shared responsibilities for both parents, should have enshrined a father's parental rights. In practice, they say, it has made no difference at all.

Sometimes fathers are driven to such desperate straits that they take the law into their own hands. 'Mark' forcibly abducted his child from his ex-wife's house. 'I had not seen my children for about six months, despite a court order allowing me to see them every other weekend. I had no assistance at all from the police or the court system in enforcing the order. They had no enthusiasm at all. They'd say, "It's a waste of time." Eventually I ran out of patience. I went along at the correct time one weekend with a witness and enforced the access order myself.

'I used minimum force, but I had to break down the door to collect my children. She had said they weren't in the house, but I knew they were there. I could hear them. I went off, had a nice weekend with them and returned them very politely at the end of the weekend. I was promptly arrested and thrown in jail.'

Mark claims that while he was on remand, the police offered him bail on condition that he agree never to see his children again. 'I felt that was wrong, so I refused,' he says. 'If I had agreed to that, I would have lost access for ever.'

In the end, although Mark was charged with kidnapping, the judge found in his favour and even ordered his wife to obey the original access order on pain of imprisonment. Yet he remains angry about his treatment. 'I'm fairly certain that if I hadn't made a fuss I would never have seen my kids again. I was forced into the position of breaking the law because of lack of support from the system.

'The advice I give to people now is that the legal system is so bad that it's not wise to get married in Britain now. With one in three marriages ending in divorce, the risk – financially and emotionally – is simply too great.'

For other fathers, the consequences of abducting their children are entirely negative. In May 1989, 'Chris' tired of a routine that allowed him to see his son for six hours every three weeks. One weekend, he did not return the boy, but took him for a fortnight's holiday in the Mediterranean. On his return he was arrested at the airport. The police took him and his son into a small room, where they told Chris that his ex-wife and her new partner were waiting to take the boy away. 'He was holding onto me and screaming, "Daddy, daddy," ' says Chris. Since then he has seen his son for a total of four hours. Their last meeting was in October 1989.

Chris has paid a heavy price for that fortnight abroad. The police have arrested him on several occasions, believing that he may be about to kidnap his son again or take violent action against his ex-wife, both of which charges he strongly denies. He finds it impossible to create new relationships with women; none of them, he says, can stand the strain imposed by the struggle for his son.

Chris claims, 'I have been described by the courts as obsessive. But if you want to win these cases you have to be. Most fathers lose contact. It's the sheer strain. I am fighting for the right of my child to a proper relationship with a father who loves him and I don't let anything get in the way. People like me are not going to be treated like child abusers. We have done nothing wrong.'

His paternal feelings are clearly sincere. But there's no denying that they are inextricably bound up with the conflict between him and his former wife. He claims she has turned his boy against him, even tearing up pictures he has sent to remind the child of his father. For his part, he admits, 'My attitude towards my ex-wife won't change. My hatred is even stronger than it was five years ago. I'm damned if I'm going to let her off the hook.'

When asked why he kidnapped his child, he replies, 'Thinking of another man playing Happy Families with my child really got to me. I wanted my ex-wife to know what it was like to be away from your child for that length of time.'

Lucy Jaffe works for Reunite, a charity that helps the parents of the 1,200 children abducted from Britain every year. She believes that the traditional tabloid description of 'tug-of-love' cases misses the point: 'Tug-of-love is an absolute misnomer. It's tug-of-hate. Mainly what comes across to us is that these are relationships that have gone wrong and people are trying to hurt each other through their children.'

Anne-Marie Hutchinson, a solicitor who specialises in family law and who sits on a Parliamentary working party on abducted children, remarks that, 'There is a school of thought that says abduction is a form of abuse. If you love a child, one of the worst things you can do is to remove it in circumstances the child doesn't understand.'

Ironically, the child may end up blaming the wrong parent for what has happened, as Lucy Jaffe explains: 'The little psychological evidence that has been produced suggests that the child feels abandoned by the non-abducting parent and feels very angry. We've had reports of children coming back home and hitting the parent they're coming back to.'

The fact remains, however, that many divorced or separated parents are driven to a point where they consider abducting their own children. 'Every one of us entertains the notion at some stage,' Bruce Liddington has remarked. 'The vast majority pull back from the brink.' But why should they be driven into that position in the first place? Are the campaigners right when they say that it is the legal system itself that causes unhappiness on a massive scale and provokes a few people into actually committing criminal acts?

The fathers seem united in their contempt and bitterness. They live in a world of affidavits and *ex parte* judgements, of rumours and allegations that can deny a man all access to his child, no matter what evidence he presents. They talk of solicitors who seem more interested in causing conflict than reaching an amicable solution; of judges whose opinions are those of a bygone age; of social workers whose political inclinations are fatally biased against what they would call the patriarchy, and of court welfare officers who dash off careless and inaccurate reports upon which a child's whole future may depend. And all unite in attacking the enormous sums of money that can be wasted as cases drag on across the years.

Anne-Marie Hutchinson admits that there is some basis to these complaints. 'I've got cases at the moment where the client feels, and I agree with him, that the welfare officer spent far more time with the mother of the child, rather than seeing him with the child. I think that is a danger, but the problem is that welfare officers are overworked, especially in London, and they just haven't got the time.'

Andrew Gerry remains convinced that legislation such as the Children's Act, by emphasising the responsibilities of both parents and the benefits of conciliation, has helped to reduce the pain of divorce. But, as he admits, 'It's very easy, if you have the day-to-day management of children as their mother and you feel like the woman scorned, to become very bitter. And what you do – despite what the law tells you, and despite the advice of your solicitor that what you are doing is hurting and is meant to hurt – is that you poison minds. You make it difficult: the child is ill; the child is going out; the child is unavailable. And therefore the contact with the father is damaged.'

The hope, of course, is that conciliation between the two parents can take some of the bitterness out of their dispute. Marian Roberts, who also sits on the parliamentary working party on abduction, is the Training Co-ordinator of the National Family Conciliation Council. This has fifty-six offices throughout the country, offering mediation services to couples involved in child-related disputes. Her work is part of a general trend within family law, to try to move away from the adversarial atmosphere of the traditional English courtroom, in favour of a less aggressive or legalistic approach.

The aim is to involve both parties, so that they solve their own dispute without recourse to the law. Often, in fact, the law may be part of their problem. 'Extraordinary as it may seem,' Marian Roberts remarks, 'when people sit down and communicate, they often find that they do not have a fundamental dispute, even though they have been in conflict when they've been communicating via their solicitors. At a time of marital conflict, communications often break down and misunderstandings are created.'

Participants are encouraged to try to shift their focus away from each other and their past, towards the child and the future. 'People come to accept that a child needs both parents. Women have admitted that they were going to deny access. Until they came to mediation and sat down and looked at the consequences of their actions, they hadn't realised what they were really doing.'

Even so, Marian Roberts is under no illusions about the process. Mediation is not, as she puts it, about becoming 'palsy-walsy'. Instead, her clients learn to negotiate with one another, on an almost business-like footing, about an issue of mutual importance – their child. The process has, she claims, a success-rate of around 70 per cent. But the trouble is that the remaining 30 per cent, let alone those couples who never experience any conciliation at all, still form an enormous number of people.

Anne-Marie Hutchinson observes that, 'In some ways it's very patronising to say, "You must get on with each other for the sake of the children." I sit there and think, the judge can say that till the cows come home, but it's not going to change her hate of him and his hate of her. In some situations, no matter how many conciliators you appoint, it won't make any difference.'

Yet the collapse of the family is a curse that can hurt both former partners equally badly, as Lucy Jaffe points out: 'Families are a refuge and the fragmentation is terrible. A man can end up living in a bedsit on his own and the isolation of that is appalling. Meanwhile the woman is under immense pressure being a single parent alone with the kids, perhaps on a low income, trying to get out to work – maybe the maintenance didn't get through. It's a quagmire. We are just not prepared, structurally, for the number of divorces that are happening.'

Meanwhile, the malice continues. Ron Brake works as a volunteer for Families Need Fathers in the West Country. His files are filled with cases of men who have been left bankrupt and homeless as a result of their fight for more contact with their children. 'The judges just laugh at you,' he says. In one case with which he is familiar, a father had succeeded in getting the care and control of his daughter, who was eleven. One weekend, he left her with her mother for a routine visit. When he returned to pick her up and take her home, he was met by a team of police and social workers, who arrested him and charged him with sexually abusing the child.

Medical examination and interviews established that there was no truth to the allegations, which had been made by the mother, and the case was dropped. By then, however, the child had been placed in care. In a subsequent court case, the judge ruled that the girl should live with her mother. When she said that she did not wish to do so, but wanted to return to her father, the judge insisted that she be put back into care, where she remains. 'The judge's mind was made up before the court case,' claims Brake. 'He believed that a child should be with its mother and that was it.'

As long as judges continue to hold those opinions, no matter what the law may say, fathers will continue to feel resentful. And some of them may just end up deciding that, if the law can't help them, they'll find another method that can – whatever the cost of that may be.

Chapter 10

The Skynner Interview

The research for this book took me from Hollywood to the Australian bush. I sat around half-naked in a men's commune and I walked through the streets of Manchester in drag. My study shelves are groaning with the files of newspaper and magazine cuttings, the books, the videos, the interview tapes and the notebooks that mark the process that led, for better or for worse, to the words you are reading now. But of all the people I met, or read about, or to whom I spoke, two in particular stand out in my mind. One of them was an Australian called Henry Tunks. A former alcoholic and prison warden, he had become a stalwart of the men's movement down under and he appears in the next chapter.

The other was Dr Robin Skynner. He will be familiar to anyone who has read the best-seller *Families, And How to Survive Them*, as the psychiatrist who guides John Cleese through a series of Socratic dialogues towards a better understanding of the dynamics of human behaviour. To academics, he is also known as the author of the textbook *One Flesh, Separate Persons: Principles of Family and Marital Psychotherapy*. Now seventy, he has retired from his work as a family therapist, but he still writes and talks about the inner workings of the human mind with warmth, understanding and, I believe, great wisdom.

What the plain text does not tell you about the conversation that follows, is the tone in which it was spoken. Skynner's most shocking remarks – shocking, that is, to people whose ideology would prevent them considering the possible truth of what he says – were made with a smile and often a chuckle. If he seems on occasion to contravene the rules about what may or may not be said in politically correct society, then that is simply because the decades he has spent observing the way people actually are may contradict some theories about the way they ought to be. Given the choice between Skynner's kindly, tolerant and open-minded humanity and the bitter dogmatism of the politically correct, I know where my sympathies lie.

I print our conversation at length because it seems to me to sum up much of what has been discussed up to now in this book and to point the way towards a more positive consideration of what can be done to re-evaluate and redefine the position of men in society. I must apologise to Messrs Skynner and Cleese for aping the pattern of their work and for being such a clumsy interlocutor. I hope they will forgive my impertinence.

The interview took place one morning in December 1991 at Dr Skynner's north London flat. I began by asking Skynner about the differences between men and women. To what extent were they inherent, as opposed to being conditioned?

SKYNNER: It's a most difficult area in that the more you try to find differences and to pursue them to some clear kind of conclusion, the more everything slips through your fingers and you're left with almost nothing very definite. And yet at the same time we know that there is an enormous difference that is somehow so difficult to pin down.

There are a number of things to say about it. The first thing is that because biological influence is very important and isn't black or white, and because social conditioning is not only variable but often reversed, so boys are brought up to be girls and vice versa, you get this huge overlap, whereby anything you can say about men that is true in the average sense is not true about some men and it is true about some women.

The second thing is that it's hard to disentangle basic biological influence and social conditioning, so that no one quite knows how much is which. And finally, you can't trust anybody and we can't trust ourselves. It's not that people are deliberately deceitful – although some are, many are – but that people get committed to a particular position about gender, as they do about politics, and everything has to be fitted into it.

So we don't know what to make of evidence. We have to distrust even apparently basic physical studies, where they claim to have measured things and found statistical differences. For example, in the textbook I wrote, I had a whole chapter on gender differences. One crucial bit of evidence was that John Money at Johns Hopkins Hospital in Baltimore had studied twin boys where both had been circumcised early on and due to some accident the penis of one had been destroyed . . .

[Author's note. In the case referred to, the child was operated on and given a sex change. 'She' was then brought up as a girl and appeared, according to all the evidence, to be happy and completely normal, behaving exactly as a typical girl would be expected to do. This case was referred to repeatedly by writers attempting to put forward the nurture rather than nature argument.]

I couldn't get around that. I thought, that's the clincher if it's true. I couldn't really believe it. On the other hand I had to believe it, this was a prestigious institution. But the BBC heard about it and made a programme called *Open Secret* and they saw Money and what had happened was that this family had moved to the Midwest and had come into contact – because of problems with their 'daughter' – with a local child psychiatric team. The BBC interviewed the team about this child and showed drawings that the child had made and the opinion of these people was that the child was very disturbed. Now that's typical of different views that are genuinely held.

That leads us on to what genetic differences are [here Dr Skynner quoted from *One Flesh, Separate Persons*]:

[Girls who received abnormal doses of male hormones before birth,] but who had all been brought up as female with early correction of any anatomical abnormalities, displayed many statistically significant differences from matched female controls. They tended to be tomboys; were highly active physically; showed a lack of satisfaction with female roles, choosing male rather than female playmates, wearing slacks rather than skirts and rejecting preening, perfume and hairstyling. They played with toy cars and guns rather than dolls, and demonstrated a lack of interest in looking after babies and an absence of fantasies about marriage, pregnancy and motherhood, being more interested in a career instead.

The exact counterparts to these syndromes do not exist. Although male hormones produce a masculine pattern, the female pattern does not need the presence of female hormones but occurs in the absence of male influence. However, genetic males [deprived of male hormones] show many physical and psychological features more usual in a female. Besides physical feminisation, they are likely to show a preference for marriage and homecraft instead of a career, as well as fantasies about raising a family, playing with dolls and other toys usually associated with girls; strong interest in infant care and contentment with the female role, preferring female clothing.

It's very hard to get away from the fact that there's some physical thing operating there. You've got to go to stuff like that where as far as you know the social conditioning was the same and the only difference is physical.

THOMAS: One of the things that bothers me is the degree to which we limit male behaviour. It starts very young, with the way that boys are taught about what is and is not manly. But perhaps we have to do that, because masculinity is so tenuous that it has to be clearly defined.

SKYNNER: The boy has extra things to do and more things can go wrong.

THOMAS: Like violence, for example.

SKYNNER: If you look at the physical differences, you end up with one indisputable fact that everyone agrees about, and that is the enormous difference due to different levels of the male sex hormone. Men are naturally and normally and properly, biologically designed to be more aggressive and more competitive and all the other things which follow from that. Therefore, they are more violent when they are *uncontrollably* aggressive. So if some people are going to go around hitting other people or inflicting pain and injury it's more likely to be men, simply because of that.

THOMAS: There are plenty of women who batter men.

SKYNNER: Yes, but what I'm saying is that there's more of that particular energy in men. Other things being equal men are going to show more instances and more magnitude of aggression than women do, simply because of that natural difference. Now, whether it takes a violent form in either sex is something else.

THOMAS: If men have more aggressive energy in a negative sense, are they more likely to have it in a positive sense too?

SKYNNER: Sure, yes, yes. What I'm saying is that the aggression is normal. It's supposed to be there. It's necessary and it can't be got rid of. It shouldn't be got rid of. But the important question is, why is it harnessed in a constructive version in some instances where it serves the community and serves the family and protects the women, and why in other cases is it directed at society? It's an enormously important difference. A lot of the feminists talk as if aggression itself was a bad thing, which is absolute nonsense. It's a good thing.

THOMAS: How do you educate or condition boys so that you get the good side of their aggression without getting the bad side?

SKYNNER: To say that you want the good things, but you don't want the bad things may not be possible or even desirable. Maybe one has to have the bad things before one gets the good things. If the bad things are uncontrolled, unharnessed aggression and the good things are socially channelled aggression, then obviously you have to have one before you can have the other. You might have to go through a wild stage in which you behave badly and go around screwing girls and not caring about it and misbehaving, before you come to a point where that begins to be influenced by, and guided and contained by other emotions, like meeting girls you're really crazy about and having babies and so on.

THOMAS: So Shakespeare was right: you have to be the wild Prince Hal before you can be Henry V?

SKYNNER: Absolutely. So I'm not sure it's even a desirable way to approach the subject to think of having good things without having bad things. They may both be necessary.

THOMAS: That sounds as if all those Victorian ideas about making chaps play football to work off their surplus energy and aggression may well be true after all.

SKYNNER: That's right. If you've got a lot of wild young Turks who insist on smashing everything up, then being in the Army and driving tanks may be just right for them. Or, when that doesn't exist, then other things may be needed like adventure courses or things which challenge them. That's necessary for men.

THOMAS: Most boys are now being educated in a system that sets out to be non-competitive, non-sporting. All the things that are natural to those boys are now thought to be macho and therefore a bad thing. So perhaps, instead of working things out on the rugby pitch, they go joyriding in stolen cars and smashing up football stadiums instead.

SKYNNER: I think that kind of approach, which tries to stop these male, bad impulses, is almost bound to make them worse. They're just going to take more and more socially deviant and uncontrollable forms.

THOMAS: The other thing about the male upbringing is that boys learn not to get too close to anyone else. That surely leads to isolation and pain.

SKYNNER: It's a very bad beginning.

THOMAS: Exactly. So how do you keep the things about being male that are valuable, while getting rid of that terrible emotional deprivation?

SKYNNER: I went through all that. It's what I'm interested in and it's very central to me. It's all about the missing father, including my father, and trying to find answers to that . . . Can I tell you about the first men's group I attended, because the key to it must be in something like that? The summer before last, John Cleese and I were invited to speak at the American Family Therapy Association, which is a gathering of teachers in that field.

About 300 people were there and Robert Bly was also to speak. It was no accident that John and I and Bly were invited together. It all happened because women had got in charge of the event, so they invited men to come and speak in a way that the men had previously felt that women wouldn't like. That was interesting in itself, the idea that the men were so frightened of the women's disapproval that the *women* had to be in control before men's issues were addressed. So . . . we listened to Bly, got to know him a bit and had dinner with him.

At the end of the conference there was a men's group. It was the first time that they had ever arranged one. The women have had a very powerful, strong group for ten to fifteen years and it shows. They're an amazingly talented, lively bunch and they had the men on the ropes for a long time – the men didn't know what was happening to them. Finally a lot of young people convened this men's group. There was no leader, just these three or four younger men who arranged the room and suggested that we should go round the room and talk about ourselves.

We spent the morning doing that – I went along and there were quite a few men there, I suppose about 20 per cent of the men attending the conference. (This year, when they had the group for a second time, I gather about 40 per cent of the men turned up to it.) First of all, I didn't know what kind of men would be there. But in fact there were a lot of people I knew about and respected – leading American figures. We spent the morning going round the room and each person would spend about five minutes saying why he was there. And the feeling in the room was incredible, so powerful.

What puzzled me was why it was happening now and why I hadn't been able to do this sixty years or so earlier. What was the difference? Of course Bly had been giving the talk earlier, so that message was in the air and he had been talking about it . . . but the depth of feeling and the openness and frankness with which the men spoke was staggering, and many of them were weeping. And in all this, the main thing was the lack of relationship with their father.

I was about three-quarters of the way around the room and was listening to what was being said and feeling that when this gets to me I'm not going to be able to avoid weeping. And then just before it got to me, about two places before, someone mentioned the word 'joy'. I don't know how it came into this conversation, but that kind of opened up my feelings in a different way. I realised that what I wanted to weep about was not sorrow, or the lack of my father, but joy that it was possible to have this kind of experience.

It doesn't matter what our fathers were like. What's getting in the way is something to do with the fact that you felt you could only get that kind of affirmation from your father when you were a little boy. And if you didn't get it then, you would never get it at all because you would never have that kind of relationship again. And it was quite clear that you could have it at any time. It was a totally transforming experience.

THOMAS: Do you think you need some kind of mentor?

SKYNNER: Bly says this and it also happened in the couples groups that my wife and I ran together before she died about four years ago. We ran them for about fifteen years. And in those groups, the men change in the same way. It was something to do with me being there and giving permission. It was as if a spell was broken. That's the only way I can put it.

THOMAS: It's funny you should talk about joy. I've done lots of market research on various publications and one of the things that has most struck me, when you watch and listen to groups of men talking, is that there's a point in a man's life when the joy leaves it. Up until their mid-twenties, guys are up for anything. They're full of confidence. They'll take risks and they'll experiment with things that are new. But at some point the shutters come down. The concept of fun leaves them. It's as if once a man has a marriage and a mortgage he doesn't dare let the concept of fun enter into his life for fear that it will tell him there's a better way of living. That doesn't seem to happen to women in quite the same way.

SKYNNER: Women have children and they get enormous fun and enjoyment out of their kids. Also women get together and have a lot of fun there too. For men, certainly my experience was that you feel you're getting older and older and you're at your oldest when you're about forty-five. After that you start getting younger again, if that's any comfort! I've been getting younger and younger since about that age, when the mortgage and the school fees . . .

THOMAS: There has to be a better way of doing it. The sense of obligation can be so crushing.

SKYNNER: The question is, would men feel like that if they had better relations with other men? I don't know the answer, but it must lie in this experience I've had. Later on, I went to a Bly weekend here in England. It was very interesting and even entertaining, but I'd got all I wanted from the first one. It was as if I had been touched by a magic wand. Someone had said, 'You're not in a glass box, even though you thought you were all your life.' Now, if the whole bloody thing can be dispelled at the age of nearly seventy by sitting in a room for one morning with thirty men and no one telling you what to do, then surely there must be some way of not setting up that thing in the first place. That's what I'm interested in.

THOMAS: Speaking of Robert Bly, what was your view of *Iron John*?

SKYNNER: I had very mixed feelings about it. I think Bly's got it absolutely right, but when he talks about it, the kind of language he uses and the kind of psychologising he does makes me feel very unhappy. He's understood things from his own experience and his group work and if he just said that, then you couldn't fault it. But when he tries to justify everything in terms of anthropology and myth and his kind of psychological explanations I think he runs the risk of people saying that a lot of this is very dubious.

THOMAS: In other words, his intuition is more accurate than his science.

SKYNNER: Well it's a very valuable book, but it's unfortunate in the way that it's been written.

THOMAS: Why was the reception in this country so hostile to *Iron*

John? I could understand the anger from the women critics – that's just a knee-jerk reaction. But the men were just as bad. I mean, sure, the book has many faults, but the response was out of all proportion: they seemed so desperate not to admit any sense of need.

SKYNNER: The impression I had was that there was a tremendous fear of homosexuality, much more than I had realised, and they were reacting with that. Homophobia is very prevalent amongst British men . . . One thing that I remember that might be interesting in relation to that . . . Many years ago, when they were developing various forms of training in the USA to help doctors and psychologists to be more at ease with people who had sexual problems, my wife and I arranged for a day's training modelled on the way American medical schools were doing it. This was to show a whole lot of very explicit films with normal intercourse, homosexual intercourse, lesbian intercourse and so on, on several screens at the same time, a kind of flooding experience, and then have a group discussion afterwards.

One thing which came out was a lot of talk among men about homosexuality and their awkwardness about homosexuality. What became clear as the discussion went on was that the reason non-homosexual men are frightened of homosexuality is that they're frightened that women will be jealous of them getting together. That, I think, makes sense in terms of boys being fearful of joining their fathers and really forming good relationships with them and pushing their mothers aside, provoking their mother's jealousy because she won't let them go. I think it's about that. And it makes absolute sense therefore that the more fear there is of that particular issue, of mother's jealousy, the more men are going to react to the idea of men's groups or the men's movement in a similar way.

THOMAS: Jealousy explains something that has puzzled me, which is why when women get together it's an act of consciousness-raising and sisterhood, but when men get together it's an act of sexism and exclusion. One of the other things that has baffled me is the sort of self-defined, willed victimisation you get among some women, who aren't victims at all, but who want to be seen as victims of someone else's oppression – male oppression – and blame all their problems on that.

SKYNNER: The women's movement's been basically positive. But the fact is that when people do that they are showing a very great deal of immaturity. The way you deal with that, I think, is to see that it is a normal way for people who are emotionally immature and less healthy to operate. If you see that, you see it for what it is.

THOMAS: Are you saying that the archetypal militant feminist woman is emotionally delinquent?

SKYNNER: Yes, I am, in the sense that they are using very immature psychological mechanisms . . . 'It's all your fault. It's Daddy's fault. It's not my fault' . . . That's distorting reality and not taking responsibility. It is blaming others rather than accepting your own limitations and faults. It is immaturity. And that needs to be said steadily, repeatedly and without any quarter.

THOMAS: But the idea that men, as a whole, oppress women, as a whole, is very widespread. Just look at the argument that's going on over date-rape. People are trying to define almost any act of sex which takes place without the woman's explicit consent as rape. If the woman gets drunk and he sleeps with her that's rape. If he says he loves her, but he doesn't really, that's rape.

SKYNNER: You sound as though you're taking it seriously.

THOMAS: Well, it is serious.

SKYNNER: It's serious in the fact that it's being taken seriously by a wide body of opinion in society, including a lot of men. It's become the fashion. People are actually taken in by this. But it is not something that should be taken seriously. It is absurd.

THOMAS: You're not disputing that a violent and forcible act of sex is a crime.

SKYNNER: Absolutely not. No, I'm all for proper safeguards and provisions which will encourage and arouse feelings of healthy respect for the law in people who are thinking of abusing confidence and trust. I'm all for that. But the actual way in which the problem is being presented is absolutely terrible.

THOMAS: From conversations I've had, I think a lot of women feel angry about that, too.

SKYNNER: So they should. It's stupid, childish, it belittles and degrades women.

THOMAS: Well, it defines them as helpless children.

SKYNNER: I don't think it should be taken seriously. One has to make one's voice heard. More men need to say this is rubbish.

THOMAS: People under forty have no experience of anything other than feminism. It's a bit like growing up in Czechoslovakia, or somewhere, when people had no experience of anything other than Communism. How do you set about reacquiring masculine self-confidence when men are being made to feel guilty by association with a wave of criminal activity?

SKYNNER: When you talk about it you obviously do take it seriously because you've grown up with it, but it's so ridiculous I can't give it room in my brain. It's absurd. Once you start arguing about whether you're persecuting people, when it's absolute nonsense, you're lost.

THOMAS: Whenever I talk or write about this sort of subject, there's often some flak in the papers, but I always get incredibly positive mail. One of the things that is clear from it all is that the New Man, whoever he may be, doesn't seem to be working out well for anybody.

SKYNNER: Can I tell you why this is? I'd like to tell you something about the main experience that my understanding is coming from because it's more useful than just coming to conclusions. My views were formed through having been one of the first people in this country to start working with families seen together. And what immediately struck me when I began doing that was the importance of the father. In case after case, more than half the cases, the problem seemed to be one not so much of children who were inhibited or fearful, but children who were uncontrolled. They were all over the place, not getting on with their work and generally not structured or organised, with no self-discipline.

In all those families the father was not playing a full part. The mother had usually taken over his role as well as her own. It was impossible to say whether the mother had pushed him out or he had opted out. It was a double thing, they were both responsible. But if you got the father to come back in and take a more active role, the problem would often be solved in a week or two. Whereas dealing with the mother and child alone could take two years with not much change. We saw these miraculous results from reintroducing the father and usually getting him to take a more authoritative role, creating structure and ordering limits.

You may say, what was the justification for that? The justification for that was that the children asked for it and the wives asked for it. We'd talk about the problem and then in the end I'd say, well what do you think we should do about it? What do you think Daddy's contribution is? And they'd say, he's too soft, he lets us get away with it.

So I'd go on to him and he would say that when he tried to do anything, she'd say he'd been too hard on them. And the children would always say, well you should do it anyway. The mother would usually agree that, even though she would appear to want to protect her role and stop him being the heavy father, nevertheless, she really wanted him not to let her stop him. So the message both from the children and the mother was that he should be a man.

THOMAS: How did you establish that this was what was really going on?

SKYNNER: I worked with my wife and we'd have forty couples a week come and see us, so we'd see a lot of people. Now, the pattern we saw was almost standard, over and over again with hardly any deviations, some variations, but no major differences.

To start with, it was clear that the man had a problem because she was more powerful and her power came from the fact that he was seeking mothering from her. He wanted her to be a mother to him as well as a wife. Although she resented this, at the same time she didn't want to give up the power this gave her. It kept him under control, both by the fact that she was giving him dog biscuits, as it were, by nurturing him, and also by the fact that by not challenging him on his dependence she could keep him feeling inadequate without knowing quite why. He had the feeling she knew something about him that she could tell the world about. She knew about the little boy inside him that he was keeping hidden.

THOMAS: 'Men are such little boys' . . . you hear that all the time.

SKYNNER: That's how they would start. The woman would usually come when she had had a baby. She was no longer willing to have two babies and the man resented the fact that he wasn't getting attention. So he had gone off and had an affair or was tuned out sexually, or whatever. That was often the crisis, it could be other things. So they had come into a negative relationship. The woman was angry with the man for not supporting her as she felt he should be doing, since she had to support the child, and the man was angry that she didn't love him any more and often the sexual relationship went wrong.

Now, what could we do about it? What we found we had to do was to encourage the woman to be much stronger in her attacks. In other words, she was pulling her punches, because although she was angry and dissatisfied, at the same time to challenge him that he wasn't behaving like a man might make him rise to the occasion and become one, in which case, we later saw, she would have to change and would lose her power.

Anyway, what would happen is that my wife became particularly attuned to egging women on and I would pick the poor chap up, dust him down and send him back in with some fatherly encouragement. The strength of the arguments would intensify with great shouting matches until at a certain point the worm would turn and he would be driven to a point where he couldn't bear it any longer and he would fight back. There would often be a brief episode of violence. He would hit her or she would hit him or throw plates. And at that point they would then suddenly become equal. Their sex would improve because it became exciting at that point and he would be a match for her. And that was the pattern we saw all the way through.

THOMAS: I've known of cases in which the woman would needle the man, almost daring him to hit her.

SKYNNER: Often it's not sustained. She then backs off and she keeps the advantage. This business of going silent or being hurt, that's a process of manipulation, which has to be disregarded. It always puzzled me why women were so fearful of going for the man's balls, really saying, look you're not a man, I despise you. And if you asked them they'd say well that would be like castrating him, like taking his manhood away. But [that attitude] in itself takes his manhood away, because if you treat someone as if he hasn't got any balls he starts wondering what it is he hasn't got, whereas if she goes for his balls he has to fight for them.

THOMAS: He rediscovers them.

SKYNNER: That's right. The inhibition in women about doing that is enormous. I came to think in the end that the reason for it was that if they really challenge the man totally and he responds, he then becomes free. He then can fight back and she then may lose him, she hasn't got him under her control. And also he can then challenge her and she has to really become a woman once he becomes a man.

THOMAS: I can see that that might be frightening, but at the same time, it's what we're all trying to achieve. It's liberating, too.

SKYNNER: Yes. I asked my wife once, I said, why is it you want us to go after you so hard and really pin you against the wall? And she said, 'Well, can't you see?' – very impatiently – 'can't you see? It's obvious. When you do that we come into our own. We don't have to worry. We can use our energy and aggression and be what we really are and not worry about whether you can take it or not. We become totally free.'

THOMAS: I suppose that's what my friend really meant when she said that men were so feeble that they wouldn't even tell her to shut up. She needed someone who was strong enough to handle anything she could throw at him.

SKYNNER: Now one other thing is if you expand that up to the social level, one has to question whether that's the point we are at. You see, maybe we need to have these immature, rather paranoid extreme feminists pushing the rules to such an extreme degree that the men finally say, this is just too much, and then come back and become real men.

THOMAS: It's funny how the same women's magazines that are always going on about sexual harassment and women in the workplace and goodness knows what else are also the first to run stories about how there are no real men any more. Perhaps the answer lies in being more masculine, rather than less.

SKYNNER: Real women are never threatened by that. They love it if their men become more male.

With that, our conversation ended. But I left thinking of what Skynner had said about his experiences at his first men's group. There had been a lot of material in the British media about the so-called wild man weekends that were going on in America. People were banging drums and getting into sweat pits. They were chanting and crying, shouting at the ghosts of their absent fathers and looking for the warrior within. To the cynical eyes of English journalists, it was utterly ludicrous. And yet, the funny thing was that all the writers or TV reporters who actually went to these events, instead of just sneering from afar, came away feeling much more moved than they had expected. I knew how they felt. Exactly the same experience had happened to me. Except it wasn't in Texas or Minnesota. It was down under, on a hillside near Sydney.

Chapter 11

Camomile Dundee

It sounded like a really good joke. A bunch of Australian men were getting together for a week-long festival of male liberation. 'Yeah, they're learning how to cope with their Sheilas,' chortled one Aussie journalist I knew. This was too good to be true: had the Australian male, the legendary Ocker, become so hen-pecked and pussy-whipped that he could no longer cope with his life of sunshine, sport and beer? To any Englishman, brought up by Monty Python to believe that Rule One of Australian life is, 'No poofters,' the prospect of all these Camomile Dundees getting sensitive around their billabongs was just too good to be true.

I should have realised that there was going to be a bit more to it than mere laughter when it was revealed that the only way to discover where the festival was being held was to call the telephone number of the Sydney Men's Network and establish genuine *bona fides*. The reason for the network's secrecy was simple: the previous year's festival had been raided by gangs of local hooligans intent on beating up the queers and freaks whom they expected to find there.

At this point I might have asked myself why anyone would be so threatened by the presence of men who were questioning the rules and regulations of traditional masculinity. But I didn't. Instead, I just asked for and was given the festival's clandestine location: it was in the bush beyond Minto, which was a dreary, low-rent suburb, part of the endless sprawl that stretches for mile upon mile through the Sydney hinterlands. So, on 4 November 1991, I got on a train and headed out.

On the way I read an article from the Sydney *Sun–Herald*, which began to make me wonder whether I ought not revise my thinking. It was a double-page spread headlined 'Men In Crisis'. In a box, with the sub-head, 'How the facts stack up against men', the paper listed some of the statistical evidence about the lives of men in Australia and

New South Wales, the state of which Sydney is the capital. For example:

82% of all suicides in NSW are men, one-third of whom are aged under thirty

72% of all Australians under sixty-five who die of heart attacks are male

95% of all patients admitted to government alcohol treatment programmes in NSW are men

95% of people arrested by NSW police for drunkenness are men

90% of those arrested for drink-driving are men

Men in jail in NSW number 5,700; women number 320

After divorce, men take 60% more sick leave from work than married men and have a death rate two to three times higher than that for married men

Life expectancy for Australian men is 72.8 years. For women it is 79.1 years. Yet, while there is a $17 million annual budget for women's health programmes (1991 figures), there is no allocation whatsoever for specialised men's healthcare.

These statistics were local, but they were all remarkably similar to comparable figures for men in Britain and the United States. Some of them could be taken to imply the inherent evils of men, who were obviously drunken, criminal and dangerous on the roads. But those problems, particularly the ones relating to alcohol, were bound up with the particular culture of masculinity down under.

In fact, the contradictions inherent in Australian masculinity could almost be taken as a textbook case of the ways in which society manages to screw up its male members. The crux of the matter lies in the fact that Australian society cherishes above all else the concept of 'mateship' – the friendship between true-blue, fair dinkum, red-blooded blokes – but is, at the same time, rampantly homophobic. This is, perhaps, the natural consequence of a country founded upon the sufferings of prisoners, most of them male, who were transported to a land that was harsh and unforgiving. In order for the men to survive, they had to stick together and yet, as in many modern all-male societies, the fact that homosexuality was the main – possibly the only

– dish on the sexual menu only added to the taboos and tensions surrounding it.

The consequence today is a society in which men are encouraged to become friends, without being allowed to display any form of closeness or affection which might indicate or imply the possibility of sexual interest. All manifestations of effeminacy have traditionally been regarded with total disapproval. These manifestations have included such namby-pamby concepts as emotion, art, sensitivity or the displaying of personal weakness. In the words of Dr Michael MacAvoy, head of the Drugs and Alcohol Directorate in the NSW Department of Health, 'It's okay for women to say they can't cope, but it's not okay for men.'

Some of these limitations are becoming less strict. Culture, for example, is no longer regarded as a subject fit only for 'poofters'. It will, however, come as no surprise to readers of the preceding chapters, in which perversity is ascribed not to masculinity itself, but to the ways in which it is distorted, to discover that Sydney, Australia is not only a city famous for its prowess in the game of rugby league – a super-tough sport that makes both rugby union and American football look decidedly namby-pamby – but is also the transvestite and transsexual capital of the southern hemisphere.

The majority of Aussie men, who do not work out their frustrations through dressing up, have one other socially sanctioned emotional outlet available to them, which is going out and getting smashed. If young men are emotionally abused and alcoholically befuddled, we should not be surprised to find them turning to crime as another outlet for their pent-up anger and pain. It may be illegal, but it's also seen as an authentically male activity and therefore reinforces, rather than diminishes their precious, and desperately vulnerable, masculinity.

Of course, since men are human beings, neither the rugby, nor the Toohey's beer, nor the crime, nor anything else can truly deal with their real problems. Which is why a survey by Sydney City Mission, reported by the *Sun–Herald*, revealed that:

More men (35%) than women (28%) said they felt a need to overcome loneliness or fear.

More men (56%) than women (47%) felt the need to cope better with the stresses of life.

And more men (31%) than women (27%) felt the need for a greater faith in God.

Ken Harrison, a spokesman for the Mission, said that the men who went there for help were often desperate for affection. Many were widowed or divorced and, cut off from the world around them, they were suffering from a medically documented condition known as touch deprivation – a form of physical and emotional starvation that can become as acute as the need for food or water.

According to Paul Whyte, the organiser of the Sydney Men's Festival, there were no class barriers to male distress. 'Most middle-class men talk about competition and isolation. Most working-class men talk about fighting and abuse and isolation,' he said.

Yet it was clearly impossible to place men's issues on the Australian political agenda. One man who had tried to do so was Graeme MacLennan of the Australian Democrats, who had hoped to complement his party's women's policy with an agenda on men's issues, such as male health, child custody and discrimination. The attempt was abandoned because, as he told the *Sun–Herald*, 'I couldn't go on with it. The bad publicity would have been political dynamite and we were better off without it.'

Into the bush

The train pulled into Minto station on the sort of day that would have British weathermen proclaiming a heat wave, but which, in New South Wales, was just a mild dose of spring. There I was met by Peter Shalles, a middle-aged, bespectacled, bearded Abe Lincoln lookalike, although Abe probably never wore shorts and floppy sandals or drove a VW camper van. He was on his way to the local supermarket to pick up a bunch of guys who were stocking up on food. The festival proper had not begun. Today was the day of preparation and mood adjustment: getting out of the swing of everyday life and into the swing of the bush.

He'd been coming to these events since he read about the first one, back in 1985. 'I read an article that said there had been 168 men in a paddock for three days, talking and laughing with no fights or squabbles. I thought, if blokes can get together like that, I don't care if they're 100 per cent gay, I want to be part of it.'

Now he was a stalwart of the men's movement. Previously both widowed and divorced, he was now living with a new partner. 'She's delighted that men are taking responsibility for their own feelings,' he said, before telling a story about a woman he'd met behind the supermarket's checkout counter when he was buying food for the previous year's festival. 'She asked if I was part of the men's movement, out in the bush, talking about men's issues and feelings and so on. I said yes. She said, "My husband could do with that. I'd send him along, but I've got no hope of getting him out there." '

'Out there' turned out to be the old summer camp of the Australian Communist Party, a group of tin shacks on a scrubby, wooded hillside, surrounded by a motley collection of beat-up cars and bikes. Next door was a second camp, which had belonged to another organisation that was equally intent on changing the world for the better – the Salvation Army. I was powerfully reminded of a commune in Topanga Canyon, outside Los Angeles, where I'd spent a few months fifteen years before. No matter where you go in the world, the alternative bunch always look the same: tanned and tatty and tucking into lentils.

Some of the early arrivals at the festival were the wispy, angst-ridden, middle-class types one might have expected. But by no means all. Peter Shalles – who was, by trade, a telephone technician – introduced me to his mate, Henry Tunks. Thickset and balding, the fifty-seven-year-old Tunks came straight out of the Norman Mailer book of grizzled old tough guys. He had been an Assistant Super-intendent in the Department of Corrective Services: a senior prison warden.

'He was a screw,' said Shalles, amiably. 'He was dishing out shit to the people dishing out porridge.'

'I wasn't a screw,' replied Tunks. 'I was a screwdriver.'

Not only that, he was a working-class, Irish Catholic alcoholic. He was as far removed from the muesli belt as it was possible to get. What on earth was he doing in the men's movement?

It turned out he'd been having trouble at home a few years back. His marriage had broken up and his daughter, who was in her mid-twenties, suggested that if he wanted to find out why his own life, and the lives of all the people around him, was so messed up, he should read a book called *Men Who Hate Women and the Women Who Love Them*. He tried, but he couldn't get into it, so someone put him in touch with a group called Men Opposing Patriarchy. From there he moved on to the festivals.

'It was a bit of a change to leave jail on a Saturday night and turn up here on Sunday morning. People I'd known for ten or twelve years thought that if I was coming out here and we weren't getting drunk, we must be a bunch of poofters. But after the first week I went back to Sydney and I was on a high. Most of the release was from understanding I could be in contact with other men and that it would not be threatening to me in any way.'

His daughter had not been impressed by the changes in her father. The two had not spoken since Christmas, some eleven months beforehand. 'My family don't know how to deal with me now,' said Tunks. 'They don't believe the change is genuine.'

Shalles, however, had no doubts about the differences wrought on his mate by the men's movement. Last year, he said, someone had turned off the TV set while Tunks and some other festival visitors were watching the cricket. The point was, Tunks hadn't hit him, but had peacefully requested that he turn the set back on. 'That bloke doesn't know how close he came to having his neck broken,' Shalles reminisced. 'He pressed all Henry's buttons, but the reaction wasn't there any more.'

Tunks seemed genuine enough to me. Men, he felt, were as imprisoned as the convicts he had supervised. 'The poor bastards can't rattle their chains, because they don't even know that they've got them.

'If you look at the monolithic block that's patriarchy,' said Tunks, 'the gays have split off, the women have split off, the ethnic groups have split off and all that's left is a great heap of shit and that's us. The job of the middle-aged Ocker in Australia is to be responsible for everything that ever went wrong for everyone. But it really hurts when you get blamed for something that's nothing to do with you.'

He mentioned a poster campaigning against child abuse. 'The implication was that it was a bloke doing the harm. People assume a woman couldn't do it, but who does the screaming and shouting and hitting at kids? Women use men as a threat – "Wait till your father gets home" – that's psychological abuse.'

This related directly to his own childhood. 'Our mother did a number on us when our Dad was serving in New Guinea during the war. She used the leverage of all the goodies Dad would give us when he got back home to make us behave. She had this book where she used to write down all the things we'd done wrong and the punishments we were going to get. The ultimate threat was – and I can still remember the exact words to this day – "Forgo all outings with Dad." She was a smart old bitch. She'd stuffed all the blame on him and he wasn't even aware of it. The poor bastard was 6,000 miles away, up to his neck in mud, and he was still being used as a threat.

'It's not fair. Little boys cop a lot of that. They get restrained, confused and frustrated and a lot of anger comes out. If a little boy is four or five, he's told he's not supposed to cry. He's not allowed to play with girls, because if he does, he's a cissy. He can't hug boys, because if he does, he's a poof. He can't hang around with Mum, because then he'd be a mother's boy, and he can't hang around with Dad, because he's not there. So from then until the age of eighteen he's officially dissociated from the human race. And the only way he can reconnect with the human race is through his dick, which is terrible.

'You get a lot of trouble when families split up because you're dealing with someone who's got an adult body, but who's a six year old emotionally. He's shit scared of being thrown out into the cold again. And he's being told that he's failed as a father and failed as a lover.

'A guy spends his life working, down the pub, chasing a football, beating up his wife. *He's* the one who needs help.'

In the middle of this peroration, a bloke walked by complaining about the food. Tunks looked up and in the kind of ice-cold voice that quells prison riots remarked, 'You could always cook it yourself instead of bitching.' And then, a few minutes later, this prototypical tough bastard talked about the wounds his life had left upon him. 'My Dad was thirty and my Mum was eighteen when they had me. They married because she was pregnant and when her mother found out she wouldn't speak to her. I always felt I was known as "Oh no, not that." I could have been done without. I've still got that.'

By now, half the guys in the camp were walking around without any clothes on. One of them, Luke, came by and joined in our conversation. Luke was gay, a fact which bothered Henry not at all. This in itself was a mark of the distance he had travelled. For most men of his age and background, the idea of sitting next to a naked homosexual would have been as threatening as sitting next to the Devil himself. But the more understanding Tunks had become about himself, and the more relaxed he was about his own masculinity, the more tolerant he became towards other people's differences. 'If you fix men, you'll fix the world,' he said. 'They're basically caring, loving people, not thugs and dictators.'

The key thing was to understand the way in which the positive qualities in men became negative. Reliability could become autocracy. Logic became obsession. Strength became thuggery, and so on. You had to deal with the bad properties without getting rid of the good ones. And you had to know where you wanted to end up: 'It's no good going on a journey just because you want to leave some place. You've got to want to end up somewhere else.'

From time to time, the essentially competitive nature of men would intrude. Peter Shalles wandered by holding a plate of food. He was stark naked, which revealed the fact that he was astoundingly well-endowed. 'Yours'll be along in a minute,' he said, referring to the food.

'As long as you don't dangle your dick in it,' replied Tunks. 'Jeez, you'll give us all an inferiority complex. It's like my old man's looked like when I was four – a monstrous fucking donger.' Shalles beamed contentedly.

The conversation meandered through the afternoon, touching on relationships between fathers and sons – how neither would say that they loved the other, even though both wanted to say and hear the words. We talked about the women's movement and the anger that was still such a potent factor within it: anger that illustrated the way that oppression could be eased, but also that nothing was solved unless you dealt with the distress that was left behind after it had gone. Just look at the rage left behind in Eastern Europe after the Communists had pulled out, we agreed. Same thing.

Tunks explained the rules of a game he had invented called 'foo-ball'. The idea was, two sides lined up, five metres apart, and shouted 'foo!' at one another. They weren't allowed to stop and they weren't allowed to shout anything else. At first they'd feel embarrassed, then they'd get angry at the stupidity of it all. Then, since they would not be allowed to relieve that anger by taking it out in the form of violence against the opposition, they'd get frustrated, which would in turn lead them to the feelings they'd had when they were first hurt and angry as children. At this point, special counsellors, or 'foo-fathers', would step in and reassure them that they had not deserved the treatment they had received as kids, whereupon they could begin to start working things out and getting rid of all the residual pain.

Well, I don't know . . . lots of it was bullshit. But that wasn't the point. Because, as the afternoon wore on, I began to feel exactly the same sort of elation as Tunks and Shalles had done when they had gone to their first festivals, or as Robin Skynner had done when he went to that men's group in the American Family Therapists' convention. The point being, it wasn't so much that what was said was particularly significant or novel, although some of it, to my ears, certainly was. It was more the discovery that you could chew the fat with other guys, but instead of talking about work or football, you could share some of the worries, hopes, insecurities or emotions which were normally kept bottled up inside.

It was wonderful to be in a world without fear. Women live their lives oppressed by the fear of what might be done to them as they walk down a city street at night, or even stroll through a park in broad daylight, but men are burdened by a different fear: the terror of seeming weak or unmasculine. It is fear which prevents ghetto school kids from playing with babies until they are reassured by the presence of their entire class. It is fear that prevented Cambridge undergraduates from going to a party in drag until they knew that their mates would be too. It is fear that stops men who have been beaten by their wives from reporting them to the police.

But when you are sitting around, talking with guys like Shalles and Tunks, you soon realise that you don't have to be afraid. You can say whatever the hell you like and they won't think you any less of a man. The weight of masculinity is lifted from a man's shoulders and he is free to be the person he wants to be, rather than the person that society has imposed upon him. And one thing's for sure: if you want to feel better about yourself fast, it beats the hell out of psychotherapy.

Walk like a man

Slowly, we are emerging from the dark ages of male self-repression. Just think of the aspects of everyday life that used to be considered unmasculine. Not so long ago, only 'poofs' wore pink shirts, or put on aftershave, or read men's magazines that weren't filled with naked tits, or cared about food, or noticed the furniture in their living rooms, or went to the gym, or did half the other things that extend a man's life beyond birds and booze. Heterosexual men owe a substantial debt of gratitude to the homosexual community for the liberating effect it has had on all our lives.

I was thinking not long ago about the men who could be considered to be modern heroes. The British have reason to be proud of Stephen Hawking, for imagining the whole universe from the confines of a wheelchair; of Sean Connery, for getting older and balder without in any way diminishing his cool; of Gary Lineker, for being as good a father as he was a goal-scorer and for proving that you can go in where it hurts and still remain a gentleman. Those three, I suspect, would be on a lot of people's lists, but I would name one more: Quentin Crisp. Here is a limp-wristed, mauve-dyed, rouged and mascara'd, effeminate homosexual . . . and yet he has lived the life he wanted to live. He has stuck to his path with a courage and independence that would do a marine sergeant major proud. He's been a man.

Those of us who are not gay should learn from the way in which, faced with first prejudice and then AIDS, homosexuals have organised, campaigned and fought for the things that matter to them. Because that is what heterosexual men have to do next.

This is a far cry from the original demands that were placed upon the men's movement. It arose, after all, as a splinter from the plank of feminism and its early members accepted without question the Marxist-feminist notion of the oppressive patriarchy. Their aim, therefore, was to atone for the sins of the past by trying to do better in the future. And, by and large, the way in which they would do better was by becoming more female.

Since then, the Robert Bly school of hairy New Machismo has talked about putting men in touch with the repressed selves that lie within. Read a few of the books of Bly's ilk and you'll discover that there's a regular cast of thousands nestled away inside your soul. There's the child within, the warrior, the priest, the wizard, the hairy man . . . they should get together and form a football team.

There's a lot of good stuff mixed up with all that mumbo-jumbo, and I know many men who have been helped by the teachings of Bly and men like him. But I don't believe that there's a warrior in me, or a wizard, or anyone else. Inside me, all you'll find is . . . me. I may be mixed up and we all may be mixed up. But men are no more mixed up than women, any more than the reverse is true. We're all human. We all live with the knowledge of our own fallibility and our own mortality. In the wee small hours of the morning we all feel alone and afraid. There really are no exceptions.

Some people say that the reason why women are still in pain is not because they have had too much feminism, but because they haven't had enough. To me, that sounds a bit like saying the trouble with Russia was that it wasn't Communist enough. Truth is, Communism doesn't work, feminism doesn't work, and no ism you can think of works, because the world and the people in it are much too complicated to be reduced to a set of simple formulae.

It is, however, true to say that we've only gone halfway down the road to sexual equality. And now it's men that need to be liberated. As matters stand, we have removed all the legal prejudices against women, without touching the ones against men. Or, to put it another way, we have said that women are the same as men when it suits them to be so, but different when it does not. At work, men and women are – in law, at any rate – equal. At home they are not. When a woman is an executive, she is exactly the same as a man. When she is a mother, she is not. When a woman wants an abortion, reproduction is entirely her own affair. When she wants child support, it suddenly becomes the man's responsibility.

I do not blame women for this state of affairs, even if I think that some feminist campaigners have added to the human pain that it has caused. Men's rights are men's responsibility. Men passed the laws that got them into this sorry state of affairs. Men should damn well change them.

The first thing that they can do to help themselves is to stop apologising. There seems to be no middle way at the moment between the bastard and the wimp. For every man that attacks and degrades women, there's another one who's down on his knees saying sorry. A plague on both their houses.

British people, of both sexes, who go to live and work in America often comment upon the incredible anger of American women. There are a number of causes of this. The sex war has always been much more intense in the States than in Europe: the struggle between the bullying man and the ball-busting woman has always been as violent as every other American conflict. Then there's the traditional American belief in human perfectibility and, more than that, the sense that people have a right to be happy. Women are not happy, so they look for a reason why, and the obvious one is men. It does not seem to occur to anyone that happiness is not the lot of the average human being, whatever their gender, nor that a person's happiness is by and large their own responsibility.

But there's another major factor that lies behind women's rage . . . men's weakness. So cowed by feminism have decent American men become that they no longer dare argue back at their female assailants. Ever since my conversation with Dr Robin Skynner, I have been asking women I know for their opinions on the need for men to stand up for themselves. One woman with a six-figure salary said to me, 'I could never fall in love with a man who could not beat me in an argument.' Another, less well paid but equally intelligent and asser- tive, said, 'There's nothing sexier than a man who disagrees with me.'

These remarks did not mean that the women wanted to be subservient to their men, by any means. But they did want to feel that they were dealing with an equal whom they could respect. If everything they said was met with meek acquiescence, respect would be impossible. Besides, disagreement – if expressed in terms that are not overly aggressive or offensive – is a sign of attention. Someone who has taken the trouble to form an opinion about something which you have just said, even if it is a contrary one, has clearly been listening. And most women, like most men, like what they say to be heard.

Nothing is more infuriating than having an argument with someone who won't argue back, particularly if you know that they are going to go off and mutter insults behind your back. That is what is happening to the two sexes now. Women argue against men. The men either say nothing, or give in to ensure a quiet life, but then they mutter misogynist jokes to their male friends in locker rooms or bars. MPs and congressmen pass laws designed to appease women, and then go back to their clubs to complain. If I was a woman, and that was the treatment I was getting, I'd be angry too.

I genuinely believe, and this book is a testament to that belief, that one of the best things that men can do to help their relationships with women is to stand up for the things in which they believe. This does not imply any need for hostility. On the contrary, I think that if men spoke out, they might get rid of some of the frustration and anger that cause the hatred that so many of them so obviously feel towards the other sex. First, of course, they've got to work out what those things that they believe in might be.

One of the most striking things about the men I have met while researching issues such as domestic violence and child custody is how many of the victims are middle-class professionals. All their lives they have operated on the assumption that the world was run by chaps like them, for chaps like them. Suddenly they discover that they are only half right. Chaps like them do indeed sit in government or on court benches but, in some respects at least, it doesn't make a damn bit of difference. So they sit there like clowns who've just had a custard pie slapped right in the kisser. They're dumbfounded. 'There's nothing we can do,' they say.

Yes there is. They can do what women did, and continue to do – they can get out onto the streets and march. The report from the Sydney *Sun-Herald* with which I began this chapter was illustrated with a photograph of Australian men campaigning for their rights.

There was Paul Whyte in the vanguard, and next to him Peter Shalles. They looked like a sorry old bunch. But at least they were giving it a go.

If those men from Families Need Fathers want a campaign, here's one with which to start. It should be an offence for a parent – any parent, regardless of sex – deliberately to deny their children contact with another parent or close relative who has a right to such contact. If, as I have suggested, it is true that the psychological harm done by a vicious former spouse can be as great as that done by an acquaintance rapist, then is it unreasonable to expect there to be a similar legal sanction against the act?

If the men's movement still felt energetic once that had been achieved, it might turn its attention to the representation of men in the media. On television, as in newspapers and magazines, negative generalisations about men are put forward by people who would rather die than make a sexist remark about women. When, for example, Channel 4 broadcast a series called *Men Talk*, it showed up the male sex in the worst possible light, and was followed by a session in which a panel of women discussed male failings. The show's presenter, Richard Jobson, made the standard media *mea culpa* in all the best papers, flagellating himself for his sex's shortcomings. What a wimp. No woman would have done that, because no woman would have set out to badmouth her sex in the first place.

Advertisements compete to show men in the most foolish or unpleasant light: the stupid dad who has to have the simplest domestic task explained by his wife; the cretinous boyfriend who cannot match up to his partner's understanding of the benefits of a building society account; the chauvinist pig who tries to compete with the snazzy female driver in her new, bright red sports car . . . and fails. These are, the makers of the ads assure us, light-hearted images that are intended to amuse. That's just what they used to say about all those silly housewives and feather-brained secretaries that women complained so much about, and it wasn't true then, either.

The truly depressing point is that most of these programmes and advertisements are created by men. Instead of indulging in this orgy of self-criticism – which is as phoney as it is demeaning – why don't men tell the self-appointed representatives of womanhood, if you want to share in the benefits of masculinity, you can share in some of the crap that comes with it, too? If you're enough of a grown-up to run the country, you're also enough of a grown-up to live with the consequences of your own actions.

If you hit us, we feel it. If you kick us out of our houses, we feel that too. And if you take away our kids, we are destroyed. Those things are wrong. They are as wrong as the terrible things that men do to women. So we should treat them in the same way.

Men and women should accept and appreciate their differences without having to fight like children over who is the best or the worst. If there was more equality, then we wouldn't do quite as much harm to one another in the first place.

Children who grow up with a loving father are happier, do better at school, get better jobs, have fewer teenage pregnancies and are less of a burden on the state. Women who are supported by a loving partner are less tired, feel less resentment and can spare more of themselves for themselves, and for everyone else. People who don't drive themselves crazy working for dollars and pounds which they are then going to waste on nannies, school fees and consumer toys they don't really need can lead lives which have room for a little peace of mind.

When I was eleven or twelve, my mother taught me that men and women were equal. Take away the conditioning, and we would, in fact, turn out to be exactly the same. Looking at my two younger sisters, I'm not sure that I ever quite believed that bit then, any more than I do today. But I had no doubt that women were as capable and intelligent as men, and that men could be as loving and caring as women. As far as I could see, my Mum was seriously clever, my Dad was really kind. I had no trouble at all with the notion of equality, then or now.

The way I learned it, we were all trying to create a world in which the liberation of both sexes would act to everyone's benefit. A new world order would arise in which men and women would be equal partners as workmates, friends and lovers. The sun would shine, children would be happy and glorious formations of flying pigs would wave benevolently at the fairies frolicking at the bottom of the garden.

We all know now that it didn't work. The pigs are as earthbound as ever. The conflict between men and women has become a sexual civil war. But it was still a nice idea. We could at least try to get a little of the way towards it. And the contribution that men can make towards that ideal is to stop being bullies on the one hand, or feeble, guilt-ridden apologists on the other.

Meanwhile, those campaigners who accuse us of being bad by

definition, those propagandists who maintain that all men are violent and all violence is male, and even those well-meaning young women who assume – as who would not after the sexual politics of the past twenty-five years? – that right is on their side, must come to terms with the fact that life is not that simple. Neither sex has the monopoly on virtue or vice. Men do not wear the black hats nor women the white. We are all of us fallible souls decked out in shades of grey. As a man I stand accused of violence, aggression, oppression and destructiveness. Members of the jury, I plead . . . not guilty.